BENJAMIN GRAHAM

GRAHAM

BUILDING A PROFESSION

CLASSIC WRITINGS OF THE
FATHER OF SECURITY ANALYSIS

JASON ZWEIG
RODNEY N. SULLIVAN, CFA

Editors

Mc
Graw
Hill

New York   Chicago   San Francisco   Lisbon   London
Madrid   Mexico City   Milan   New Delhi   San Juan   Seoul
Singapore   Sydney   Toronto

ISBN 978-0-07-163326-0
MHID 0-07-163326-X

This publication is designed to provide accurate and authoritative information in regard to the subject matter covered. It is sold with the understanding that neither the author nor the publisher is engaged in rendering legal, accounting, futures/securities trading, or other professional service. If legal advice or other expert assistance is required, the services of a competent professional person should be sought.
—*From a Declaration of Principles jointly adopted by a Committee of the American Bar Association and a Committee of Publishers*

McGraw-Hill books are available at special quantity discounts to use as premiums and sales promotions, or for use in corporate training programs. To contact a representative, please e-mail us at bulksales@mcgraw-hill.com.

CONTENTS

Part 3
Broadening the Profession

Part 4
The Voice of the Profession

PREFACE

The purpose of this book is to collect, for the first time in a single volume, Graham's classic shorter writings on financial analysis. The book also serves as a companion reader to the commemorative sixth edition of Graham and Dodd's *Security Analysis*, published in 2009.

Through the development of Graham's thinking from 1932 through 1976, we can trace the evolution of financial analysis from a cottage industry to a full-fledged profession. Graham was a voice in the wilderness crying out for shareholders' rights. He was a prophet who warned of the hazards of bull markets and proclaimed the opportunities created by bear markets. He was a pragmatic tinkerer seeking new methods of valuation. He was a profound thinker determined to place security analysis on the sound foundation of the scientific method. And he was, in his business life, a model of honesty and integrity, consistently placing the interests of his clients ahead of his own.

These essays, then, are not merely the story of how Graham founded the profession of security analysis. They also show what he felt the field should take as its central priorities.

Every decade or so, critics have fired their peashooters at Graham, carping that he is out of touch, obsolete, irrelevant. What the nitpickers always fail to see is that the passage of time has the same effect on Graham as it has on Shakespeare or Galileo or Lincoln: The unfolding years provide ever more evidence of his importance. No one else, before or since, has surpassed Graham's intellectual firepower and common sense, his literary mastery, his psychological insights, and his dedication to the dignity of security analysis as a profession. He matters more today than ever before. Can anyone possibly doubt that the Internet bubble and the credit crisis would have been less devastating if more investors had taken Graham to heart?

There are few things we can be certain of in the world of financial analysis. This is one: A generation from now, and in all the decades to come, Benjamin Graham will be regarded as an even more indispensable guide than he is today.

Read on, and see why.

—Jason Zweig

INTRODUCTION

More than thirty years after his death and nearly sixty-five years after he put forth the radical proposition that financial analysis ought to be both a science and a profession, Benjamin Graham still stands with the sun at his back. He is a towering example of Ralph Waldo Emerson's pronouncement that "an institution is the lengthened shadow of one man." The nearly 90,000 holders of the Chartered Financial Analyst designation in more than 135 countries and territories and more than 200,000 students seeking formal membership in the profession are living testimony to the power of Graham's ideas and the colossal length of his shadow.

Emerson understood that great institutions are created by lone crusaders—those with the brilliance to see the same old world in a radically new light, with the vision to build castles in the air, and with the stubbornness to build a foundation under those castles, brick by brick.

If Benjamin Graham had not founded the profession of financial analysis, someone else might have done so. But we should not be too sure. At the outset, Lucien Hooper, one of the most influential analysts in the United States, protested that Graham's proposal was "unnecessary formalism" that would do nothing to make analysts more ethical, intellectually honest, or competent.[1] The first Chartered Financial Analyst designation was not awarded until 1963—more than two decades after Graham had proposed a formal standard. Think of seeing your newborn child all the way through to graduation from college, and you will have some idea of how long and patiently Graham nurtured the idea that financial analysis should be formalized as a profession.

Throughout those intervening decades, Graham pushed his colleagues to recognize that analyzing and evaluating securities should be regarded as a structured process patterned after the scientific method. He also stood stubbornly for the principle that financial analysis must always conform to the highest standards of ethical conduct.

When Benjamin Graham came to Wall Street in 1914, he had no experience, no money, and no conventional qualifications. Graham had never even completed a class in economics. He did, however, have assets: prodigious energy, a rigorous education in mathematics and classical philosophy, extraordinary gifts as a writer, a passionate belief that business should be conducted fairly and honestly, and one of the most subtle and powerful minds the investing world has ever seen.

Graham later described his way of thinking as "searching, reflective, and critical." He also had "a good instinct for what was important in a problem . . . the ability to avoid wasting time on inessentials . . . a drive towards the practical, towards getting things done, towards finding solutions, and especially towards devising new approaches and techniques."[2] His most famous student, Warren Buffett, sums up Graham's mind in two words: "terribly rational."[3]

Graham arrived on Wall Street at the age of twenty. He had not passed through college; he had burned through it. Graham entered Columbia at age sixteen and completed all his coursework in three and a half years, skipping a full semester to conduct operations research for a shipping company. The month before Graham graduated as salutatorian of his class, he was offered faculty positions in three departments: mathematics, philosophy, and English.[4]

Graham declined, prodded by his college dean into joining the firm of Newburger, Henderson & Loeb as a back-office boy for $12 a week. Graham promptly memorized the relevant details on more than 100 prominent bond issues and was soon poring over the financial statements of leading railroad and industrial companies. In no time, he had risen to become a "statistician," as a security analyst was then called.

Wall Street in 1914 was chaotic and lawless—a netherworld where rules were unwritten, ethics were loose, and information had to be pulled out of companies like splinters from lions' paws. The U.S. Federal Reserve was barely a year old. The first "blue-sky" law, enacted in Kansas to mandate basic disclosure of a security's risks before any public offering, had come only in 1911. There was no Securities and Exchange Commission. Companies published rudimentary financial statements at sporadic intervals; often, investors could view an annual report only by going to the library of the New York Stock Exchange. To stymie the prying eyes of outsiders, family-controlled firms hid assets and earnings through accounting chicanery and deliberate disregard.

In such an environment, "statisticians" had grown accustomed to thinking of their craft as much more art than science. Most of them stuck to bonds, where rigorous evaluation of long-term trends seemed to matter more; those who ventured into stocks rarely took a company's financial statements as the foundation for their labors. "The figures were not ignored," Graham recalled, "but they were studied superficially and with little interest." Instead, who was buying and selling was of paramount importance. Advance notice of takeovers and mergers, in an age before trading on inside information had been banned, could make traders a quick killing. Early word of cattle disease in the Chicago stockyards, or a blight in the wheat fields of the Ukraine, could put a speculator out in front of soaring stock or option prices in New York. As Graham recalled, "To old Wall Street hands it seemed silly to pore over dry statistics when the determiners of price change were thought to be an entirely different set of factors—all of them very human."[5]

For all these reasons, analysts in Graham's day regarded themselves as diagnosticians, using their contacts and their own intuitions to size up the "feel" of the market. They applied what the great psychologist Paul Meehl would later call "clinical judgment," evaluating each security in the heat of the moment, emphasizing the subjective factors they regarded as unique, and estimating its future price movements in relation to the market trends swirling around it.[6]

Analysts prided themselves on the belief that this sort of judgment required great sensitivity, diligence, and skill. And so it did. But their belief in the *quality* of their judgments was an illusion. Most statisticians' "intelligence had been corrupted by their experience," Graham said.[7] Whenever they made a correct call, they took it as validation of their methods. On all other occasions, they blamed forces beyond their control: the capriciousness of the market, the tides of global politics, the power of market giants like the Morgans, Rockefellers, or Vanderbilts.

What analysts did not do was verify whether their qualitative judgments had any quantitative validity: Could the subjective analysis of securities reliably distinguish, over time, those that were cheap from those that were dear?

From his earliest days, Graham sensed that the answer was a resounding *No*. He set about putting financial analysis on sounder footing. Instead of forecasting the price of a security by taking the psychological temperature of the market or by getting wind of news before anyone else could, Graham dug into assets and liabilities, earnings and dividends. An astronomer in a world of astrologists, he placed the burden of proof squarely on the quantitative data.

Graham broke ranks with tradition in another, more basic way. Wall Street had long drawn a distinction between "investment" and "speculation."[8] An *investor* cared primarily about obtaining a stable and constant stream of income—which could be provided only by bonds whose strict covenants and solid assets ensured that the principal value of the investment would not be impaired. A *speculator*, on the other hand, was interested in cashing in on big movements in market price—which, in those days of relatively steady interest rates, could be found only in stocks. For the investor, what mattered was protecting principal from fluctuations in value; for the speculator, what mattered was exposing it to fluctuations in price.

Thus, as a general rule, bonds were the proper domain of investors, and stocks were the natural habitat of speculators. When Edgar Lawrence Smith published his 1924 book *Common Stocks as Long-Term Investments*, he intended the title to be a provocative slap in the face: No respectable person believed that stocks should be regarded as investments at all. (Thus went the popular sayings: "Gentlemen prefer bonds" and "Bonds for income, stocks for profit.") In 1931, after the Great Crash had seemingly made mincemeat of Smith's arguments, Lawrence Chamberlain's best-selling *Investment and Speculation* declared that only bonds could be considered investments; stocks were inherently speculative.

After starting as a bond analyst and then gradually switching most of his attention to stocks, Graham realized that the prevailing view was a lazy oversimplification. He was exasperated by the popular notion that bonds were only for investors and stocks only for speculators. "The bond of a business without assets or earning power would be every whit as valueless as the stock of such an enterprise," thundered Graham in 1934. "Yet because of the traditional association of the bond form with superior safety, the investor has often been persuaded that by the mere act of limiting his return he obtained an assurance against loss."[9]

Graham understood that the intrinsic value of stocks need not be ignored merely because they constituted a junior claim on a company's assets. Nor should the market price of bonds be regarded as irrelevant just because they promised return of principal.

What should separate investors from speculators, Graham argued, was not what they chose to buy but *how* they chose it. At one price, any security could be a speculation; at another (lower) price, it became an investment. And in the hands of different people, the same security—even at the same price—could be either a speculation or an investment, depending on how well they understood it and how honestly they assessed their own limitations. Most shockingly of all to readers traumatized by the Crash of 1929, Graham insisted that even a margined trade on a merger arbitrage need not be speculative. Analyzed properly from the right point of view, it turned into an investment.[10] The task of the financial analyst, Graham proposed, was to think like an investor regardless of the form of the security being analyzed.[11]

In immortal words that should be inscribed upon the doorposts of every fiduciary, Graham wrote: "An investment operation is one which, upon thorough analysis, promises safety of principal and an adequate return. Operations not meeting these requirements are speculative."[12]

With inexorable logic, Graham defined each of his terms. There was nothing "either/or" about his definition. The analysis must be thorough, safety must be assured, *and* the return must be adequate. By thorough analysis, Graham meant "the study of the facts in the light of established standards of safety and value." Safety signified "protection against loss under all normal or reasonably likely conditions or variations." A satisfactory return was "any rate or amount of return, however low, which the investor is willing to accept, provided he acts with reasonable intelligence."[13]

In one mighty blow, Graham had shattered the false dichotomy between bonds as investments and stocks as speculations. Bonds could be speculative, and stocks most assuredly could be investments. The job of the analyst was to determine which was which—based not upon the form of the security but rather upon its quality and its price relative to value.

And its quality must be determined quantitatively. Graham was the ideal person to solve the problem of evaluating securities by the rigorous discipline imposed by the scientific method. His love of Euclidean geometry and calculus—Graham had published a paper on the teaching of integrals in the *American Mathematical Monthly* at the age of twenty-three—supplemented his mastery of logic and classical philosophy.[14]

The time was also right. In 1927, Alfred Cowles had begun compiling the massive database of stock returns and market forecasts that became the raw material for the Center for Research in Security Prices at the University of Chicago. Meanwhile, Frederick Macaulay was beavering away on the mathematics of bond duration. In late 1934, only a few months after Graham and David Dodd published *Security Analysis,* the philosopher Karl R. Popper published the first edition of his influential book *The Logic of Scientific Discovery.*[15] The renowned mathematician-philosophers Alfred North Whitehead and Bertrand Russell were preaching, like a new gospel, the virtues of applying the scientific method to all walks of life.[16]

"In arriving at a scientific law there are three main stages," wrote Russell in 1931. "The first consists in observing the significant facts; the second in arriving at a hypothesis, which, if it is true, would account for these facts; the third in deducing from this hypothesis consequences which can be tested by observation." Added Russell: "The most essential characteristic of scientific technique is that it proceeds from experiment, not tradition."[17]

In the stock market, of course, Graham had at his disposal the world's largest and most active experimental laboratory. And he knew it. In the second sentence in Chapter 1 of *Security Analysis*, Graham made the radical declaration that the process of determining the value of stocks and bonds "is part of the scientific method."

When Graham, armored with the techniques of science, hit the stock market head-on, tradition died instantly in the collision: The old belief that analysis is more art than science was done for.

In short, Benjamin Graham had found his calling. And he shaped it for all those who have come after him.

—Jason Zweig

NOTES

1. Lucien O. Hooper, "Should Security Analysts Have a Professional Rating? The Negative Case," *The Analysts Journal* (January 1945), p. 41.
2. Benjamin Graham, *The Memoirs of the Dean of Wall Street* (New York: McGraw-Hill, 1996), pp. 141–142.
3. Jason Zweig interview with Warren Buffett, Oct. 8, 2009.
4. Graham, who first applied for admission at age fifteen, would have graduated from Columbia at nineteen, but the college misplaced his application, delaying his matriculation for a year.
5. Graham, *The Memoirs of the Dean of Wall Street*, p. 142.
6. Paul E. Meehl, *Clinical versus Statistical Prediction: A Theoretical Analysis and a Review of the Evidence* (Minneapolis: University of Minnesota Press, 1954).
7. Graham, *The Memoirs of the Dean of Wall Street*, p. 143.
8. Dennis Butler, "Benjamin Graham in Perspective," *Financial History*, no. 86 (Summer 2006), pp. 24–28.
9. Benjamin Graham and David Dodd, *Security Analysis* (New York: McGraw-Hill, 1934), p. 58.
10. Ibid., p. 56.
11. Graham's warnings about the distinctions between investing and speculating were particularly timely in the 1930s. In the wake of the Great Crash, most individuals had deserted the

stock market, and many of those who were left no longer invested according to Wall Street's traditional definition of the term. John Maynard Keynes noted, in Chapter 12 of *The General Theory of Employment, Interest, and Money* (London: Macmillan and Co., 1936), "It is rare, one is told, for an American to invest, as many Englishmen still do, 'for income'; and he will not readily purchase an investment except in the hope of capital appreciation."

12. Graham and Dodd, *Security Analysis*, p. 54.

13. Ibid., pp. 55–56.

14. Benjamin Graham, "Some Calculus Suggestions by a Student," *American Mathematical Monthly*, vol. 24, no. 6 (June 1917), pp. 265–271.

15. Published in Vienna as *Logik der Forschung*, the book was first translated into English in 1959 but widely read long before by scientists and philosophers. Popper has had a revival in recent years thanks to the trader and scholar Nassim Nicholas Taleb, who adapted Popper's metaphor of "the black swan," in which only a single exception is needed to falsify the statement "All swans are white." However, Popper's views on falsification remain controversial.

16. As early as 1928, Dwight Rose had published his book, *A Scientific Approach to Investment Management* (New York and London: Harper and Brothers).

17. Bertrand Russell, *The Scientific Outlook* (Abingdon, UK: Routledge Classics, 2009; first published London: George Allen & Unwin, 1931), pp. 37, 105.

PART 1

The Foundations of the Profession

If you navigate a maze backward—placing your pencil on the exit and tracing the path back, turn by turn, to the starting point—it will seem trivial to solve. On the other hand, as any child knows, starting at the entrance and trying to wend your way to the final goal without any wrong turns is far more difficult.

Likewise, it is all too easy to take today's world for granted. The Chartered Financial Analyst designation is the gold standard of intellectual rigor and ethical conduct in security analysis. Getting a CFA charter is such hard work that it seldom occurs to the people who have one that the designation might have been even more difficult to create than it is to obtain. Only by taking a closer look at how the CFA designation came about can you fully grasp how difficult the struggle was.

But there is an even more important reason to understand how the CFA designation developed: To know what it means to be a security analyst today, you should know what it meant to Benjamin Graham.

From the outset, when he first proposed what he called the QSA (qualified security analyst) designation in "Should Security Analysts Have a Professional Rating? The Affirmative Case," Graham insisted on professional standards that were both broad and deep.

Graham was bitterly opposed to the traditional view that analysts (or "statisticians") should rely on art rather than science. As he summed up the customary view: "Skill in this field rests largely on judgment rather than on specific knowledge or technique." Graham thought this was nonsense: "While judgment plays an important role in security analysis, it requires the aid of well-established methods and of specialized knowledge and experience."

The qualified analyst, he wrote, would:

- Possess "good character"
- "Observe rules of ethical conduct"
- Pass an exam to demonstrate "knowledge of his field"
- Obtain required experience to show "professional competence"
- Be devoted to "advancing the standards of his calling"

It is striking how Graham emphasizes the element of "good character." In the introduction to the 1945 essay that kicks off Part 1 of this volume, he places it first, ahead of even "education and experience." In his final sentence, he returns to it, placing it before "sound competence."

What exactly did Graham mean by good character? In his own private life, he flouted conventional standards of morality. Graham certainly would have agreed with the pungent observation of H. L. Mencken in 1919 that great achievers do not "come from the ranks of the hermetically repressed."[1]

But in the conduct of his business, Graham was beyond ethical reproach. Unlike many of his peers, he never traded on, or even sought, inside information. There is no record, from his roughly forty years of managing other people's money, of a serious grievance from a client who felt Graham had acted unfairly.

At age twenty-two, Graham was already running an arbitrage account. The client agreed to split the profits evenly with Graham. Once the account showed considerable gains, Graham withdrew a portion of his profits, lending the proceeds to his brother to start a small business. His brother's venture soon failed—just as the account fell in value and was hit by a margin call. Like clockwork, once a month for the next two years, Graham deposited $60 into his client's account until he replaced every penny that he had withdrawn.[2]

After the Crash of 1929, with a grim sense of honor, Graham informed the participants in his investment partnership that he would abide by the original terms of the management contract. All losses would have to be made up in full before Graham and his partner, Jerome Newman, could receive any management fees. Only in 1933, under pressure from the clients themselves, did Graham agree to accept compensation while the partnership was still underwater.[3]

But Graham's definition of character goes beyond honesty and integrity. To him, the word "character" captures not just how you act but how you think. Although he never pairs the two words directly, Graham uses "character" as a synonym for "rationality." In 1949, Graham answered the rhetorical question of what it means to be an "intelligent" investor:

> The word "intelligent" . . . will be used . . . as meaning "endowed with the capacity for knowledge and understanding." It will not be taken to mean "smart" or "shrewd," or gifted with unusual foresight or insight. Actually the intelligence here presupposed is a trait more of the character than of the brain.[4]

And, in 1976, he summed up investing with these words: "The main point is to have the right general principles and the character to stick with them."[5]

In short, when Graham said an analyst must possess good character, he was thinking of a set of traits—what we might call a mental toolkit—that he so often praises throughout his writings:

- *A hunger for objective evidence*
  - As Graham put it, "operations for profit should be based not on optimism but on arithmetic."[6]
- *An independent and skeptical outlook that takes nothing on faith*

- ○ Your skepticism must also be directed at your own beliefs.
- *The patience and discipline to stick to your own convictions when the market insists that you are wrong*
  - ○ In Graham's words:
    "Have the courage of your knowledge and experience. If you have formed a conclusion from the facts and if you know your judgment is sound, act on it—even though others may hesitate or differ. (You are neither right nor wrong because the crowd disagrees with you. You are right because your data and reasoning are right.)"[7]
- *What the ancient Greek philosophers called ataraxia, or serene imperturbability—the ability to stay calm and keep your head when all investors about you are losing theirs*
  - ○ One of Graham's wives described him as "humane, but not human."[8] While it may have made Graham less than ideal as a husband, that quality of cool detachment made him a superb analyst.

"Good character" consists of these characteristics. Training, education, and experience can go only so far. No matter how thorough your analysis, you must also develop self-control and emotional discipline, or you will never be able to hold your views steadfastly against the whims of the market.

In "On Being Right in Security Analysis," Graham raises a question that sounds easy to answer: How should analysts (or their clients) determine whether their recommendations were valid?

Two factors combine to make the question far more difficult than it sounds.

First, the extent of learning depends on the quality of feedback: How much we can find out about the results of our actions depends on how well we can track them. Tennis players, anesthesiologists, and firefighters are among the many practitioners who can learn steadily through repetition and experience. Their work environments offer prompt and unambiguous feedback: They do not have to wait an indeterminate amount of time to learn whether the ball was in or out, the patient lived or died, or the fire was properly controlled. Security analysts, on the other hand, practice their craft in an environment that provides delayed and ambiguous feedback: You recommend a stock at 20. The next day it goes to 21; you seem right already. A week later it is at 18; now you seem wrong. The next month it is at 25; right again! Six months after your recommendation, it is at 14; wrong again, you start to check your earnings model for errors. A year after your recommendation, it is at 30; now you were right all along. Because market prices change so much so often, the feedback you get is in continuous flux, making it extraordinarily difficult to know what to conclude about the quality of your analysis.[9]

Second, humans are better at rationalizing than at being rational. When reality makes mincemeat of our forecasts, we do not say we were wrong. Instead, we say that we were right too soon, that we will be proven right in the end, that we were almost right, that we were closer to being right than anyone else was, or that uncontrollable forces that no one could have foreseen prevented our reasonable assumptions from being realized.[10]

Graham understands the human tendency to weasel out of responsibility for failed forecasts. In "On Being Right in Security Analysis," he also warns analysts that being right is not enough. You must also be right for the right reasons:

> If this is a sound recommendation, not only must it work out well in the market, but it must be based on sound reasoning also. . . . Professional standards for security analysis require that all recommendations indicate clearly both the type of recommendation made and the kind of analytical reasoning on which it is based.

Otherwise, neither you nor your clients will have any way of knowing whether you were right or merely lucky. Subsequent changes in market price can show whether your forecast was valid only if you clearly articulated the basis for your recommendation. Furthermore, you must be explicit about the time period over which your analysis applies.

In "The Hippocratic Method in Security Analysis," Graham warns that analysts who recommend high-yield securities, or growth stocks, or small stocks, on the basis of "rule-of-thumb, of vague impressions or even prejudices"—rather than on empirical evidence amassed from decades of data—run the risk of harming their clients instead of help-ing them.

Graham is too subtle even to point out that the Hippocratic oath enjoins doctors to "do no harm." But he does explicitly compare the practice of security analysis to the practice of medicine.[11] Doctors, he contends, have a deeper body of knowledge to draw on: decades of scientific evidence on symptoms, causes, and treatments. Analysts, in contrast, must contend with a lack of "systematic knowledge" about the performance of secu-rities with various characteristics.

That shortcoming has largely been cured, in the intervening years, by the publication of vast numbers of empirical papers in the *Financial Analysts Journal*, the *Journal of Finance*, the *Journal of Portfolio Man-agement*, and elsewhere. Indeed, many investors now regard the kinds of questions that Graham raised here as having been answered once and for all: Empirical research appears to have proven, for example, that small stocks will outperform large and that "value" will outperform "growth" stocks.[12]

For those who think this way, however, in "The Hippocratic Method in Security Analysis," Graham has another warning:

> By the time we have completed the cumbersome processes of inductive study, by the time our tentative conclusions have been checked and coun-terchecked through a succession of market cycles, the chances are that new economic factors will have supervened—and thus our hard won technique becomes obsolete before it is ever used.

The discovery of market anomalies lays the groundwork for their destruction: Once investors recognize that a strategy has outperformed reliably in the past, they rush into it, hampering its ability to excel in the future.

Thus, the security analyst must always ask not only whether his or her forecast is based on solid empirical evidence covering a large sample of the past but also whether the same patterns of performance will persist now that everyone knows about them. Validating the in-sample proof is one thing; obtaining the out-of-sample excess return is another thing entirely.

In "The S.E.C. Method of Security Analysis," Graham praises the U.S. Securities and Exchange Commission for following an orderly three-step procedure to appraise utility companies: first, formulate "standards of value"; second, gather "relevant data in the individual case"; and finally, apply "the standards to the data, to arrive at a definite valuation."[13]

You can sense Graham's frustration with the fact that government employees have forced themselves to think like "security appraisers," while sell-side analysts remain "reluctant" to do so. "There is no such thing as a sound investment regardless of the price paid," Graham says flatly. And yet, he notes, research departments continue to issue bullish reports based on generic arguments about industry growth rates or on naive extrapolations of historical earnings.

"There is only one objection to this procedure," writes Graham. Without a rigorous assessment of whether the value of the underlying business is above or below the current market price for the stock, this kind of analysis "is not good enough. It is not real analysis, but pseudo analysis."

That critique, written in 1946, still hits distressingly close to home today.

NOTES

1. Graham was flagrantly unfaithful to his first three wives. H. L. Mencken, "Art and Sex," in *A Mencken Chrestomathy* (New York: Alfred A. Knopf, 1949), p. 61.
2. Benjamin Graham, *The Memoirs of the Dean of Wall Street* (New York: McGraw-Hill, 1996), pp. 150–154. Note that $60 was a significant sum in 1916, worth approximately $1,200 today when adjusted for inflation (see www.measuringworth.com/ppowerus/).

3. Graham, *The Memoirs of the Dean of Wall Street*, pp. 267–268.

4. Benjamin Graham, *The Intelligent Investor* (New York: Harper & Brothers, 1949), p. 4.

5. Hartman Butler, Jr., "An Hour with Mr. Graham," in *Benjamin Graham, The Father of Financial Analysis*, by Irving Kahn and Robert D. Milne (Charlottesville, VA: The Financial Analysts Research Foundation, 1977), pp. 33–41.

6. Benjamin Graham, *The Intelligent Investor* (New York: HarperBusiness Essentials, 2003), p. 523.

7. Ibid., p. 524.

8. Graham, *The Memoirs of the Dean of Wall Street*, p. 311.

9. For an enlightening discussion of the importance of feedback for improving decisions, see Robin M. Hogarth, *Educating Intuition* (Chicago: University of Chicago Press, 2001).

10. Highly trained experts are especially adept at coming up with ex-post explanations of why their forecasts were valid even when the predicted outcomes did not occur. See Philip E. Tetlock, "Close-call Counterfactuals and Belief System Defenses: I Was Not Almost Wrong but I Was Almost Right," *Journal of Personality and Social Psychology*, vol. 75 (1998), pp. 639–652.

11. Characteristically, Graham's ideas, as presented in "The Hippocratic Method in Security Analysis," were well ahead of his time, even in a field that was not his own. Anticipating the "wellness" movement in medicine by several decades, he admonishes that physicians should not merely heal the sick but sustain the healthy: "the typical doctor who ministers only to the sick is fulfilling but a part of his function, as would a security analyst who was consulted only when investments went wrong."

12. Most researchers agree that market capitalization and valuation are risk factors; smaller stocks and those with depressed valuations should be riskier and thus should outperform, on average, over longer periods. But in the short run anything can happen, and the risks of holding these stocks at the wrong time are substantial. The premium on small and value stocks is neither a sure thing nor a free lunch.

13. Under the legal interpretation of the Public Utility Holding Company Act of 1935 that still prevailed in 1946, the SEC routinely determined whether a recapitalization proposed by a utility company was fair to shareholders. From 1940 through 1952, the SEC broke up the utility industry from an oligopoly of holding companies into a much larger number of independent enterprises. Graham refers to "the fertile fields of Philadelphia" because in 1942, as an agency deemed "nonessential to the war effort," the Commission was relocated from Washington, D.C., to Philadelphia. The agency moved back to Washington in 1948.

1

Should Security Analysts Have a Professional Rating?

The Affirmative Case

INTRODUCTORY STATEMENT

In 1942, the Committee on Standards of the New York Society of Security Analysts proposed to the membership that a rating or professional title be established for security analysts. This rating was designated tentatively as "Qualified Security Analyst" or "Q.S.A." The proposed machinery included the following: A Board of Qualifiers was to be set up by the Society and cooperating agencies—e.g., the Association of Stock Exchange Firms, insurance companies, investment counsel, etc. The Board would confer the rating upon applicants who met designated standards, including those relating to:

a—Character

b—Education and experience

c—Passing of an examination

Editors' Note: In part two of this article, Lucien O. Hooper made the case against a professional designation, "The Negative Case."

Reprinted from *The Analysts Journal*, vol. 1, no. 1 (1945): 37–41 with permission.

The latter test might be waived for suitable reasons. Application for the rating would be on a voluntary basis and would be motivated by the desire for prestige and practical advantage. Eventually, however, it might be expected that the Q.S.A. rating would become necessary for those doing the work of a senior security analyst having direct or indirect contact with the public.

No final action has been taken on the Committee's findings. The following articles analyze the arguments for and against the proposal. The Editors will welcome expressions of opinion from the members.

The issues involved in this rating proposal are comparatively simple and may be argued largely by analogy. Some fifty years ago, trained accountants were wrestling with a similar idea, and at that time the difficulties and drawbacks of the proposed C.P.A. designation no doubt appeared quite serious to many of them. Today the need for a professional rating in that field and in many others is taken for granted. It takes no prophet to predict that once we surmount the initial hurdles involved in a rating for security analysts, the procedure will establish itself firmly and will come to be considered as indispensable to the public interest.

For purposes of this discussion, a security analyst is defined as one whose function it is to advise others respecting the purchase and sale of specific securities. This definition would exclude the following:

1. Junior statisticians or analysts who merely assemble data
2. Business or financial analysts and economists who do not deal with specific security values
3. Teachers and students of theory as such

Strictly considered, this definition would also exclude stock market analysts since they ordinarily do not advise about specific securities. The writer believes, however, that ultimately, if not now, market analysis will be regarded as a special department of security analysis and that every competent market analyst will be grounded in security analysis.

In any event, by security analysts in this context are meant those giving advice or suggestions on security transactions to customers (and partners) of brokerage houses, investment bankers, banks, and trust companies; those engaged in investment counsel; and those having similar functions on the staff of investment companies, insurance companies, other corporations, philanthropic organizations, and the like. The field is wide and undoubtedly includes several thousand practitioners in this country.

Advantages of a Rating System

The advantages of a rating system may be summarized thus: Those dealing with a Q.S.A. will know he has met certain minimum requirements in regard to knowledge of his field and has professional competence. They will know also that to retain his designation of Q.S.A., the analyst will have to observe rules of ethical conduct which no doubt will become increasingly definite and stringent as time unfolds. These benefits will apply both to the direct employers of security analysts and to the clients of such employers.

The analyst who qualifies for the rating will have the obvious advantages of prestige, improved ability to get a job, and the chance for higher pay. In addition, he is likely to develop a more professional attitude towards his work and a keener interest in maintaining and advancing the standards of his calling.

Answers to Some Possible Objections

It would seem advisable to list the various objections advanced against the proposed rating and to comment briefly on them. These objections apply both to the underlying soundness of the idea and to its practical application.

OBJECTION 1. It is basically impossible to distinguish between qualified and nonqualified analysts, since skill in this field rests largely on judgment rather than on specific knowledge or technique. Good judgment cannot be tested by ordinary examinations.

ANSWER. While judgment plays an important role in security analysis, it requires the aid of well-established methods and of specialized knowledge and experience. More and more emphasis is being laid on sound techniques in analysis—by employers, by teachers, by those entering the field, and by the work of this Society.

Technical ability and adequate information may, of course, be determined by suitable tests, and this applies also to some of the more obvious judgment factors entering into security analysis.

OBJECTION 2. The Q.S.A. rating may mislead the public, because it indicates but cannot guarantee that its holder is a capable analyst.

ANSWER. This objection has a certain validity, but no more than the observation that an M.D. may be a poor doctor. As in similar fields, the Q.S.A. rating will purport to guarantee only that the holder has met certain minimum tests—not that he possesses maximum abilities. The chance of misconception is smaller here than in other fields because the typical analyst is employed by an executive with considerable practical knowledge of his own, and not by unsophisticated members of the general public.

OBJECTION 3. The Q.S.A. rating is a step in the direction of privilege for some and limited opportunity for others. It is a closed shop or cartel development.

ANSWER. There is no reason why the Q.S.A. rating should be denied to anyone who deserves it and wants it. It might result in the exclusion of unqualified practitioners from the field, but this would not be unfair or unsound. The right of every individual to practice his chosen trade is subject to the higher right of society to impose standards of fitness where these are advisable.

OBJECTION 4. The plan has administrative difficulties. Who would judge the competence of others and by what right? Who would give the necessary time to the task?

ANSWER. This rating proposal involves no more difficulties than are found in similar requirements imposed in other fields. Suitable people will be found to act as Qualifiers, as they are found for the Character Committees of the Bar Associations, for the Board of Psychiatric Examiners, etc. Public-spirited analysts of reputation will devote time to this task as to other nonprofit work.

The initiation of the program presents certain special problems. It might appear presumptuous for some analysts to pass on the qualifications of others of similar experience and standing. This hurdle might be overcome, if advisable, by waiving the examination at the outset for those with practical experience of not less than ten or fifteen years. With the passage of time, a constantly larger percentage of analysts will have been subject to the test.

The level of competence necessary to qualify for the rating will have to be determined by the Board of Qualifiers. If precedent in other fields is followed, it will probably be set rather on the low side at first and gradually raised thereafter. It is the writer's personal view that the test may be equivalent to that given for students completing a full year's college or graduate school course in Security Analysis. Character and experience requirements would be set up separately, but some interchange of credit for academic work as against business experience would be advisable.

CONCLUSION. There is in this discussion no desire to minimize the practical difficulties faced by the rating proposal. However, it does not seem that these problems are essentially different from those met in the fields of accounting, law, medicine, and other professions. If these analogies appear too elevated, we can point to the licenses or Certificates of Fitness required, in various areas, for real estate brokers, insurance salesmen, and customers' brokers employed by Stock Exchange houses. It is hard to see why it is sound procedure to examine and register customers' brokers but not sound to apply corresponding standards to security analysts. The crux of the question is whether security analysis as a calling has enough of the professional attribute to justify the requirement that its practitioners present to the public evidence of fitness for their work. The publication of this *Journal* is in itself an assertion of professional status for security analysts. It would seem to follow, almost as an axiom, that security analysts would welcome a rating of quasi-professional character, and will work hard to develop this rating into a universally accepted warranty of good character and sound competence.

2

On Being Right
in Security Analysis

The most interesting and important work of the senior analyst leads up to and includes the recommendation that one or more common stocks be purchased. How can we tell whether such a recommendation has been right or wrong? This seems like a simple question, but a really satisfactory answer is not so easy to find. When a department store buyer recommends the purchase of certain merchandise, he implies that all—or nearly all—of it can be sold at the standard mark-up during the current season. In most cases the soundness of such recommendations can be readily checked by the sequel. When a stock market analyst recommends the purchase of stock at 80, on the grounds that its technical action indicates an upward move is imminent, it should not be too difficult to check the "rightness" of such a proposal. Most of us would agree that for the market analyst to be proved right the stock must advance, say, not less than four points in not more than, say, sixty days.

But if a security analyst should recommend the purchase of United States Steel at 80, as "a good buy," what criteria of corresponding definiteness can we apply to test his wisdom? Obviously we cannot ask that the stock go up four points in sixty days.

Reprinted from *The Analysts Journal*, vol. 2, no. 1 (First Quarter 1946): 18–21 with permission.

Shall we require that it advance 10% in a year? Or that it do 10% better than "the general market"? Or that, regardless of market action, the stock should meet certain requirements with respect to dividends and earnings, over, say, a five-year period?

We have no scoring system for security analysts, and hence no batting averages. Perhaps that is just as well. Yet it would be anomalous indeed if we were to devote our lives to making concrete recommendations to clients without being able to prove, either to them or to ourselves, whether we were right in any given case. The worth of a good analyst undoubtedly shows itself decisively over the years in the sum total results of his recommendations, even though precise criteria for evaluating them be lacking. But it is unlikely that security analysis could develop professional stature in the absence of reasonably definite and plausible tests of the soundness of individual or group recommendations. Let us try, tentatively, to formulate such tests.

We return to our assumption that a security analyst is now recommending that United States Steel common be bought at 80. If this is a sound recommendation, not only must it work out well in the market, but it must be based on sound reasoning also. For without such reasoning we may have a good market tip but we cannot have a good security analysis. The reasoning, however, may take various forms, and the meaning of the recommendation itself will vary with the reasoning behind it. Let us illustrate by four alternatives:

1. Steel should be bought because its future earning power is likely to average about $13 per share.[1]
2. Steel should be bought because it is fundamentally cheaper at 80 than is the Dow Jones Industrial Average at 190.
3. Steel should be bought at 80 because next year's earnings will show a substantial increase.

4. Steel should be bought at 80 because that price is
far below the top figure reached in the last two bull
markets.

Reason 1 implies that Steel will prove a satisfactory long pull investment. That does not mean necessarily that it will average earnings of $13 over the next twenty-five years, but certainly over the next five years. If this analysis proves correct, the purchaser will have both satisfactory earnings and dividends and an undoubted opportunity to sell out at a good advance. The correctness of the analysis and the consequent recommendation can be proved only over a five-year period or longer.

Suppose that the same suggestion, with similar reasoning, had been made in January 1937, when Steel was also selling at 80? Would that analysis have been right? No; even though the stock promptly advanced 57% to 126. For in no five-year period since 1936 have the earnings averaged $7 per share. And the 1937–44 average was about $5 per share. The rise to 126 within sixty days did not establish the rightness of this analysis, any more than the decline to 38 in the following twelve months would necessarily have proved it to be wrong.

The recommendation to buy United States Steel because it is cheaper than the Dow Jones Industrial Average (reason 2) would represent a valid and standard form of analytical argument. It may or may not be coupled with the statement that Steel is attractive in its own right. In the former case, it would be equal to recommendation 1, plus the assertion that Steel is cheaper than other standard issues. But the analyst properly may recommend Steel common on a comparative basis only, without claiming that it is intrinsically cheap. In that case he will be proved right if Steel performs better than the average, even though it may not do well by itself. For example, if Steel declines to 70 within a year from now, while the Dow Jones Industrials decline to 140, the comparative recommendation should be called right—provided (a) it was originally couched in comparative terms, and (b) it was backed by plausible analytical reasoning. Proviso (b) would seem necessary in every case where a single recommendation is tested, in order to make sure that the rightness is not due obviously to mere luck.

Recommendations to buy a stock for the main reason that next year's earnings are going to be higher (reason 3) are among the most common in Wall Street. They have the advantage of being subject to rather simple tests. Such a recommendation will be right if both (a) the earnings increase and (b) the price advances—say, at least 10%—within the next twelve months.

The objection to this type of recommendation is a practical one. It is naive to believe that in the typical case the market is unaware of the prospects for improved earnings next year. If this is so, the favorable factor is likely to be discounted, and the batting average of recommendations based on this simple approach can scarcely be very impressive.

Steel should be bought at 80 because it sold considerably higher in the last two bull markets (reason 4). Is this a valid type of reasoning for security analysis? Opinions may differ on this point, but in any case we can readily tell if such a recommendation proves right. The stock must advance substantially—say, 20% at least—in the current bull market.

Conclusions

The preceding discussion leads to some general conclusions, which are put forward on a tentative basis and as a starting point for controversy:

1. In most cases the rightness of an analyst's recommendation can be tested by the sequel, provided he indicates the type and basis of his recommendation.

2. Different types of recommendation—even though they all may call for the same action, for example, to buy Steel at 80—will be tested for rightness in different ways.
3. Where a recommendation is made on a group basis, only the group result should be tested. Individual issues may be expected to go counter to the group trend.
4. Professional standards for security analysis require that all recommendations indicate clearly both the type of recommendation made and the kind of analytical reasoning on which it is based.

Analysts recommend bonds and preferred issues as well as common stocks. The warranty behind each such suggestion is that the issue has quality at least commensurate to the yield. Such recommendations may be tested two ways: either by the review of the analysis of quality or by the subsequent market action of the issues approved, preferably as compared with a suitable group index. This field of activity does not raise serious problems of testing, except where very refined results are required.

Assuming we can test the analyst's performance on individual recommendations, we can develop a crude batting average for his work, based solely on the percentage of times he is right out of total number of recommendations made. How high should this average be for a good analyst? And is it necessary to refine this test by distinguishing between "very right" or "very wrong" and just "rightish" or "wrongish"?

These are questions for others to answer.

NOTES

1. See C. J. Collins, "Estimating Earnings of an Active Post-War Year," *The Analysts Journal* (July 1945), p. 23.

3

The Hippocratic Method
in Security Analysis

That excellent compendium of reflective thinking known as
"The Practical Cogitator"—from which our own pseudonym
may have been filched—contains an interesting account by L. J.
Henderson of the method of Hippocrates, "the most famous of
physicians." This procedure is described as follows:

> The first element of the method is hard, persistent, intelligent,
> responsible, unremitting labor in the sick-room, not in the
> library; the complete adaptation of the doctor to his task, an
> adaptation that is far from being merely intellectual. The second
> element of that method is accurate observation of things and
> events; selection, guided by judgment born of familiarity and
> experience, of the salient and the recurrent phenomena, and their
> classification and methodical exploitation. The third element
> of that method is the judicious construction of a theory—not
> a philosophical theory, nor a grand effort of the imagination,
> nor a quasi-religious dogma, but a modest pedestrian affair, or
> perhaps I had better say, a useful walking-stick to help on the
> way—and the use thereof.

Henderson goes on to suggest that this procedure, so successful
in the study of sickness, may well be employed in studying "the
other experiences of everyday life." That phrase would scarcely
suggest our special line of endeavor; yet the temptation to draw

Reprinted from *The Analysts Journal*, vol. 2, no. 2 (Second Quarter 1946): 47–50 with
permission.

parallels between security analysis and medicine is almost irresistible.[1] Both medicine and security analysis partake of the mixed nature of an art and a science; in both the outcome is strongly influenced by unknown and unpredictable factors; in both we may find—in Henderson's phrase—"the concealment of ignorance, probably more or less unconsciously, with a show of knowledge."

If we give our imagination a little rein we can develop systematic analogies between the work of the physician and that of the analyst. We can set off the client, with his cash resources and his security holdings, good and bad, against the patient with his constitution and his physical vigors or ailments. This suggests that the typical doctor who ministers only to the sick is fulfilling but a part of his function, as would a security analyst who was consulted only when investments went wrong. The full duty of the physician, as of the analyst, should be to assist the patient-client to make the most effective use of all his resources—in one case physical, in the other financial.

Another analogy, more forced yet perhaps more useful, may be drawn between the individual patient and the individual security. Suppose doctors were asked by insurance companies to tell at what rate they should insure given applicants against sickness and death. This would involve an appraisal of each applicant's health factors in quantitative terms, perhaps as a percent of "par." Is not this at bottom what the security analyst does, or should do, with respect to the stock or bond issues he examines? He must judge whether they are good risks at going prices, or, conversely, name the price at which they would be good risks. Both the physician and the analyst must consider a host of factors in arriving at these judgments; they must expect unforeseeable events to play hob with some of them; they must rely on sound methods, experience, and the law of averages to vindicate their work.

We have pursued our analogies farther than is prudent, in order to gain a better hearing from security analysts for the Hippocratic method. The first element listed at the outset—"unremitting labor in the sick-room"—we shall concede is followed by our responsible analysts. We do work hard and persistently; we do gain our knowledge of securities at first hand—in the board room, if not in the sick room.

It is the second and third steps that invite our self-critical attention. To what extent do we address ourselves to the "classification and methodical exploitation . . . of the salient and recurrent phenomena"? Of this we have as yet only the rudiments. Very little effort has been made to construct systematic inductive studies of our experience with various types of securities, or security situations. The experience we draw upon in forming our judgments is largely a matter of rule-of-thumb, of vague impressions or even prejudices, rather than the resultant of many recorded and carefully studied case histories.

What warrant have we for our views on questions such as the following: Do higher yielding bonds or stocks show better overall results than low yielders? Are (statistically shown) upward earnings trends reliable enough to warrant the payment of substantial price premiums? Are the mathematical odds in favor of low priced stocks (in normal markets) sufficient to warrant giving preference to this group? Can the near term earnings outlook be used soundly as a primary basis for common stock selection? And countless others.

It is amazing to reflect how little systematic knowledge Wall Street has to draw upon as regards the historical behavior of securities with defined characteristics. We do, of course, have charts showing the long term price movements of stock groups and of individual stocks. But there is no real classification here, except by type of business. (An exception is Barron's index of low priced stocks.) Where is the continuous evergrowing body of knowledge and techniques handed down by the analysts of the past to those of the present and the future? When we contrast the annals of medicine with those of finance, the paucity of our recorded and digested experience becomes a reproach.

There are explanations and answers in rebuttal. Security analysis is a fledgling science; give it (and the *Analysts Journal*) time to spread its wings. Contrariwise, many of us believe, perhaps unconsciously rather than consciously, that there is not enough permanence in the behavior of security patterns to justify a laborious accumulation of case histories. If physicians and research men keep on investigating cancer, they will probably end by understanding and controlling it—because the nature of cancer does not change during the years it is being studied. But the factors underlying security values and the price behavior of given types of securities do suffer alteration through the years. By the time we have completed the cumbersome processes of inductive study, by the time our tentative conclusions have been checked and counterchecked through a succession of market cycles, the chances are that new economic factors will have supervened—and thus our hard won technique becomes obsolete before it is ever used.

That is what we may think, but how do we know whether, or to what extent, it is so? We lack the codified experience which will tell us whether codified experience is valuable or valueless. In the years to come we analysts must go to school to [study] the older established disciplines. We must study their ways of amassing and scrutinizing facts and from this study develop methods of research suited to the peculiarities of our own field of work.

The final element of the Hippocratic method is "the judicious construction of a theory." In our initial quotation, Henderson emphasizes the modest nature of any such theory based on medical observation. It is to be "only a useful walking-stick to help on the way."

So, too, in security analysis, we need theories which stem from experience and close observation but which are appropriately limited in their scope and modest in their pretensions. We must steer a middle course between starry eyed doctrinairism on the one hand and vacillating optimism on the other. It is precisely this judicious admixture of the theoretical and the practical approach which characterizes the truly successful security analyst—and the outstanding physician.

The idea of "theory" applied to security analysis is almost equivalent to the idea of "standard." It means some specific quantitative technique by which securities are to be valued or selected. If we assert that railroad fixed charges must be covered twice over on the average, as a necessary addition for bond safety, we are advancing the theory that the class of railroads showing a (substantially) lower coverage will not prove a satisfactory field for ordinary bond investment. This would be roughly equivalent to the medical "theory" that people who show a specific degree of overweight are likely to die sooner than others.

The Dow theory affords an excellent model for the theories which security analysts should develop, test out, publish, and actively discuss. This is true, regardless of the intrinsic soundness or unsoundness of the Dow theory, and despite the fact that it does not itself lie within the field of security analysis proper. For the Dow theory has grown out of protracted observation; it lends itself to definite quantitative formulation; and its value can be tested and retested over the years.

All those devoted to the advancement of security analysis realize that it is as yet a largely undisciplined calling. In the Hippocratic method, with its three elements, there may lie a first-rate formula for attaining our needed discipline.

NOTES

1. Witness the Editor's analogy between the spread of respiratory ailments and that of security gambling, in our last issue. Nor can we forbear recalling the popular anecdote of the early 1930s: Speculator A, asking B why he looks so sad, is told: "I'm a very unlucky man. I've got diabetes at 40." To which A replies: "That's nothing. I've got Consolidated Treacle at 187½."

4

The S.E.C. Method
of Security Analysis

In our last essay dealing with the Hippocratic method, we strayed pretty far from Wall Street. Now we return to our own back yard—if thus we may designate the fertile fields of Philadelphia. The most careful and complete work in security analysis during recent years has undoubtedly been done by the S.E.C. This has included—at least in part—the three stages of a thorough-going analysis, viz.: (a) the formulation of standards of value; (b) the gathering of relevant data in the individual case; and (c) the application of the standards to the data, to arrive at a definite valuation.

The S.E.C. has done all this work not with the idea of breaking new paths to security analysis, nor of prescribing higher standards for analysts to follow—but because it could not help itself. The law gave it specific duties, and these it could perform only by indulging in full-scale security analysis. Such duties include: first, primary jurisdiction over recapitalization plans and security deals of public utility holding company systems; second, supplying advisory reports, when requested, on the fairness and feasibility of Chapter 10 reorganization plans; third (and less important), jurisdiction over security deals between Investment Companies and so-called affiliated persons.

Reprinted from *The Analysts Journal*, vol. 2, no. 3 (Third Quarter 1946): 32–35 with permission.

In order to determine whether a given plan or deal is fair, the Commission has found it necessary to arrive at a more or less exact valuation of the securities affected. This in turn has required the adoption of methods and standards of security analysis. It is important to realize that these valuation responsibilities apply only in a limited area of the S.E.C.'s activities; it has no such duties with respect to new security offerings in general, nor with respect to the level of prices established on the exchanges. Yet enough of these special assignments have fallen to the Commission's lot to create by now quite a respectable volume of security analyses and valuations for which it must take praise or blame.

This is no place to write a critical history of the security valuations arrived at by the S.E.C. No doubt that job is already under way for some Ph.D. thesis. Let us limit ourselves to a reference to a recent and interesting case—namely, the recapitalization of American States Utilities Corp. Here the company submitted a plan under which the preferred would get 77% and the common 23% of the new all common capitalization. This was contested by a preferred stockholders' group who asked for a larger share of the total. It is not clear from the opinion whether any common holders claimed more for their side. Nevertheless, the Commission actually decided that the common was not being given enough; it cut down the preferred to 65% and increased the common to 35% of the total. And on this basis the exchange was finally made.

How did it happen that the Commission here departs from its traditional role of champion of preferred stockholders' claims and raises up the common man from the dust?[1] Answer: Security Analysis. After studying the relevant facts, the S.E.C. reached the conclusion that the fair value of the new common stock issues would exceed the full claim of the old preferred by more than 50%; hence the preferred was entitled to only 65% of the total. In its opinion, the Commission set forth its method of analysis quite clearly. First, it examined past earnings for the period 1934–44; then it considered estimates of future earnings made by four witnesses—these ranging between \$282,000 and \$350,000. Then it discussed certain factors bearing on future earnings, such as power supply, income taxes, invested capital—and concluded that such earnings should be set at \$335,000, for purposes of recapitalization. It then suggests various rates at which these prospective earnings might be capitalized; asserts negatively that the rate implied in giving 77% to the preferred (say 8¼%) would be too high; and decides affirmatively on a capitalization rate of about 6.90%—i.e., a multiplier of about 14½.[2]

Here then we find the S.E.C., impelled not by choice but by its statutory duties, using certain procedures of security analysis to determine the fair value of stocks of a going concern. Most of the enterprises are public utilities, but similar valuations have been made for industrials—notably in the McKesson & Robbins reorganization. Is this the direction in which security analysts as a whole are tending? Will they—or should they—sit down before every security presented to them, and proceed likewise to determine a fair value for it, which may be compared or contrasted with the current market price? If the Commission's procedure is sound in the area of reorganization plans, etc.—to which they are limited by law—why should it not be appropriate for Wall Street analysts to employ it for every security?

This prospect is not likely to appeal to the typical analyst of long experience. To write his name under a specific value for a stock, which value may differ widely from the current price, would seem to him to be a repellently hazardous undertaking. The more definite he is about the factors which result in his valuation, the more likely he is to be proven wrong by subsequent events. Analysts don't mind so much being wrong in general but they hate being wrong in particular.

Furthermore, this synthetic figure—sometimes called "intrinsic value" or "justified selling price"—is a rather unsubstantial affair. It is neither today's market price nor tomorrow's true value—for by tomorrow the basis of true value will have changed. Rather than meddle with such a troublesome concept, it is easier and more comfortable merely to present the relevant facts, and then to conclude that "the stock appears attractive as a speculation at current levels," or that "it has a good measure of appeal as a sound investment equity."[3]

There is only one objection to this procedure: It is not good enough. It is not real analysis, but pseudo analysis. There is no such thing as a sound investment regardless of the price paid, and if there are attractive speculations independent of the price quotation, the recommendations would have to come from stock market analysts and not from security analysts.

Let us be concrete. A brokerage house circular recommends American Radiator at 22 because of the promising outlook for the building industry. The "analysis" gives the capitalization and ten-year data on earnings and working capital. Why are these figures given? If the stock is a good speculation because of its prospects, and if this is so *regardless of price*, then the statistical details are mere surplusage. But if the figures are intended to inform and guide the purchaser, is it not the duty of the security analyst to evaluate them? Does he not have to reach the conclusion in his own mind that, with reasonable allowance for the good prospects, the business of American Radiator is fairly priced at $225 million or more (its current market quotation) before he can sponsor it as an attractive speculation? In the end, this would mean that the analyst must arrive at some range of fair value for every stock he recommends, and must be satisfied that the price does not exceed the top of the range.

I venture to predict that the same logical events which have made security appraisers out of a reluctant S.E.C. will make security appraisers out of the equally reluctant Wall Street analysts. There are signs of such developments in the public utility field, where our senior analysts are assigning specific values to stocks of operating companies which are to come on the market in the future.

These calculated values often take the form of minimum and maximum figures—a prudent and common-sense device, since no appraisal can be better than an approximation. The Commission, wherever possible, also prefers to think in terms of a range of value; where it is compelled to adopt a single figure, it probably prefers the midpoint of its range.

The S.E.C. method of security analysis is not beyond criticism, and doubtless it is still in the development stage. The final product—if there is one—may differ strikingly from present appearances. But we should be grateful to the Philadelphians for wrestling manfully with problems that face not only them but ourselves as well.

NOTES

1. Similarly, in the recent case of American Gas & Power, the S.E.C. gave more stock to the common than the company had proposed.
2. The Commission skirts around the minor question whether the claim of the preferred should be taken at par or call price—hence, its exact valuation cannot be stated in certainty.
3. We do not imply that this is representative of all Wall Street analysis. A good deal of truly thoughtful work is now being done which gives full recognition to the factor of market price. But most of these studies are of semi-private character—e.g., by investment-trust analysts—hence they rarely appear amid the large mass of brokerage house circulars.

PART 2

Defining the New Profession

The earliest essays in this section show another side to Benjamin Graham that few readers may be aware of: his passion for justice and his sense of outrage at poor corporate governance. He did not believe that companies could be poorly run only from the inside; he knew that poor governance also came from the outside, whenever owners failed to exert their legitimate rights.

In the classic series of three articles that he wrote for *Forbes* magazine in the summer of 1932, Graham fulminates against the imperial behavior of corporate insiders who pay no heed to their public shareholders.[1] In the wake of the Crash of 1929, corporate managements kept cash piled high, both as a cushion against any future calamity and to protect themselves from the consequences of their own potential misjudgments. And shareholders, stupefied by their own losses and overly deferential to the will of management, did nothing about it.

Graham describes the problem in simple, stark language, with devastating logic and the passion of a Biblical prophet. Graham was furious that companies sat on cash even as the American public suffered through the depths of the Great Depression. "Treasurers are sleeping soundly these nights," he wrote, "while the stockholders walk the floor in worried desperation."

The cash policy of the corporation, Graham makes clear, is the central issue of corporate governance. The cash belongs to the shareholders, but it is controlled by management. Shareholders, if they understand their rights and responsibilities, recognize that they cannot afford to take for granted the belief that management will always do the right thing with the cash.

While Graham heaps scorn on management, he regards the majority of investors with outright disgust for abdicating their ethical responsibilities. In "Inflated Treasuries and Deflated Stockholders: Are Corporations Milking Their Owners?" Graham says that stockholders

> have forgotten also that they are *owners of a business* and not merely owners of a quotation on the stock ticker. It is time, and high time, that the millions of American shareholders turned their eyes from the daily market reports long enough to give some attention to the enterprises themselves of which they are the proprietors, and which exist for their benefit and at their pleasure.[2]

The attitude Graham highlights is what has sometimes been called "Daddy-knows-best," a chronic deference toward management by even the most powerful institutional investors, who assume that insiders know more about running the business than outsiders ever could. As Graham understood, Daddy may know best—but that does *not* mean he will always act accordingly.

Graham's warnings boil down to a single message: To be an intelligent investor, you must also be an intelligent owner. The analyst's responsibility to understand all relevant information about a company does not cease at the moment of purchase; arguably, that is when it finally begins in earnest. Having established the value of the underlying business, the analyst must now monitor the quality of management's actions and the wisdom of its capital-allocation decisions.

It is tempting to blame management for actions that hurt shareholders, but analysts should always remember that when you point your index finger at someone else, at least three of your own fingers are likely pointing back at you. In 2006 and 2007 alone, U.S. nonfinancial corporations borrowed roughly $1.3 trillion—much of it for the express purpose of funding share repurchases at a time when stock prices were nearing record highs.[3] Too few analysts asked management to justify its view that the shares were cheap enough to be worth repurchasing or to explain why such massive borrowing could possibly be wise. This buyback binge left many leading companies overindebted and undercapitalized. Should the blame lie with the borrowers, or with those who permitted—or even encouraged—them to borrow?

Other companies clung, white-knuckled, to the cash they had raised through operations and borrowings. By November 2009, U.S. corporations were sitting on no less than $840 billion in cash and marketable securities—an all-time record.[4] Most analysts seem to have concluded that these piles of cash, like sandbags in a flood, would protect the companies and their shareholders. But even a glance at Graham's articles from the depths of the Great Depression shows that there is a fine line between being prudent and depriving investors of their right to redeploy capital as they see fit. Establishing where that line ought to be drawn is not the job of management alone; outside investors, led by analysts, must also speak up.

The analyst's job, in short, is to evaluate not merely whether a company's securities are valued fairly but also whether its owners are treated fairly. As Graham wrote in 1949:

> there are just two basic questions to which stockholders should turn their attention:
>
> 1. Is the management reasonably efficient?
>
> 2. Are the interests of the average *outside* shareholder receiving proper recognition?[5]

Graham is often regarded, by those who do not know his work, as a doctrinaire thinker who believed in ramming securities mechanically through rigid valuation filters. Nothing could be further from the truth.

Instead, as the other essays in this section show, Graham was profoundly curious, always flexible, and constantly in search of new insights and better methods. Like any good scientist, he revised his own thinking whenever the facts warranted it. As Graham shaped the field of security analysis in its formative years, he urged his colleagues to look, as he had done, to the prevailing standards in other respected professions, such as medicine, accounting, and law.

Graham reminds his readers not to think only of analyzing each security as a unique case; in addition, they must apply a consistent set of standards to each of their judgments and all of their actions. That, he insists, is the only way a young profession can convey seriousness and engender respect. Even more importantly, a systematic process is essential if the field is to progress toward the status of "a scientific discipline."

"Toward a Science of Security Analysis" is an extension of the essays included in Part 1. Here, Graham takes as a given that analysts should be guided by the scientific method; in summary, they should establish specific facts by observation, develop theories (or "formulas") based on those observations, and test them through predictions about future results.

Graham cites four investment categories, each of which can be analyzed by the scientific method:

- Bonds
- Value stocks
- Growth stocks
- "Near-term opportunities" (securities with the potential for quick trading profits)

Graham excludes technical analysis (which he calls "stock market analysis" here), although he leaves open the question of whether it might be able to complement fundamental research.[6]

Again Graham emphasizes the importance of collecting—and preserving—large samples of data, without which the observation, theory, and testing of the scientific method are impossible.[7] In "Toward a Science of Security Analysis," he writes:

> The greatest weakness of our profession, I have long believed, is our failure to provide really comprehensive records of the results of investments initiated or carried on by us under various principles and techniques. We have asked for unlimited statistics from others covering the results of their operations, but we have been more than backward in compiling fair and adequate statistics relating to the results of our own work.

Graham is making a profound point: Most investment professionals do not scrutinize the workings of their own firms nearly as rigorously as they analyze the companies they invest in. But they should. In this same article, he goes on to say that only continuous, systematic self-examination can "show what methods and approaches are sound and fruitful and which ones fail to meet the test of experience."

To give just a few examples: When you say that your sell discipline is effective, how do you know? Does your firm continue to track the performance of all the stocks you have sold, *after you sold them,* to measure whether the sells have actually added value? If you believe that meetings with management improve your security selection, how do you know? Have you recorded systematic data over the years that could prove or disprove that proposition? If you think it pays to focus on companies that invest heavily in research and development, how do you know? Does published empirical research demonstrate that increased R&D correlates to higher equity returns?

Graham also warns, in a striking passage, that scientifically based conclusions about broad samples of data can lead to dangerous decisions. Graham comments on what we now call the "equity risk premium," or the amount by which the returns on stocks exceed those of bonds and cash in order to compensate investors for the greater risks of holding stocks. Graham points out that the premium has consistently been too big in the past—a conclusion that is "both scientifically valid and psychologically dangerous." If everyone comes to believe in the superiority of stocks, then prices will be bid unsustainably high and future returns will, in fact, automatically be lower. No amount of historical evidence can ever mean that stocks are attractive "regardless of how high they sell."[8]

In "Two Illustrative Approaches to Formula Valuations of Common Stocks," Graham points out that the present value of a stock depends most crucially on the very things that no one can ever know for certain: its future earnings and dividends.

Graham develops two techniques for estimating these unknowable quantities. The first takes a historical view in applying five factors—growth in earnings per share, "stability" (or minimal shrinkage in retained earnings during hard times), dividend payout, return on invested capital, and net assets per share—and combines each of them at a 20% weight to arrive at a composite score. This model may seem like too blunt an instrument to work, but experimental psychologists have shown that simple models often work better in the real world than more complicated and theoretically accurate ones—precisely because people can implement simple models more consistently, without compulsive alterations to the variables and the weights. The investment firm that scoffs at Graham's simple first model should first try adapting its own version and testing it; the results might be surprising.[9]

Graham recognizes that what really matters in security valuation is the expected future performance, which may differ markedly from the past. He recognizes that "the real determinants of the value" are "the earnings and dividends of the future." Graham's second method then takes the market price itself as the best means of estimating future growth. Over the period he analyzed, he devises a formulaic method for relating the earnings growth of the past to that anticipated by the market. He suggests using such a formula as "a point of departure" for assessing whether the market price is too enthusiastic or pessimistic.

In "The New Speculation in Common Stocks," a speech Graham gave to the annual convention of the National Federation of Financial Analysts Societies (a forerunner to CFA Institute) in May 1958, he revisits the distinction he developed in the 1930s between "investment" and "speculation." His original definition of a speculation was simply a negative one: anything that did not fulfill the rigorous standards Graham set for an investment.[10] Now, however, a speculation was not merely any security that did not happen to qualify as an investment: It was the attempt by analysts to apply the certainty of higher mathematics to the profound uncertainty of the future. Graham warns that measuring imprecise variables with highly precise tools is no better than using crude tools. In fact, it may well be worse because overprecise formulas tend to trigger overconfidence in those who wield them—creating the illusion of certainty in areas where no certainty is ever possible.

Graham's warning from "The New Speculation in Common Stocks" has acquired fresh resonance in the wake of the devastation wrought by complex derivative securities in the 2008–09 financial crisis:

> [T]he combination of precise formulae with highly imprecise assumptions can be used to establish, or rather to justify, practically any value one wishes. . . . Mathematics is ordinarily considered as producing precise and dependable results; but in the stock market the more elaborate and abstruse the mathematics the more uncertain and speculative are the conclusions we draw therefrom. In 44 years of Wall Street experience and study I have never seen dependable calculations made about common-stock values, or related investment policies, that went beyond simple arithmetic or the most elementary algebra. Whenever calculus is brought in, or higher algebra, you could take it as a warning signal that the operator was trying to substitute theory for experience, and usually also to give to speculation the deceptive guise of investment.

Five decades before investors used Gaussian copula functions and other complex formulas to justify the purchase of bundled mortgage derivatives, Graham foresaw the dangers. The slightest flaw in the assumptions, the smallest error in the measurements, and the formulas can explode.

In "Special Situations," Graham describes a variety of arbitrage opportunities and how to analyze them. He defines a special situation as "one in which a particular development is counted upon to yield a satisfactory profit in the security even though the general market does not advance." Bankruptcy reorganizations, preferred stocks with large dividend arrears, mergers and acquisitions, significant litigation, the regulatory breakup of holding companies, and convertible-bond arbitrage are all examples of special situations. On the one hand, Graham insists that a special situation requires that "the particular development is already under way." On the other hand, despite that certainty, he reminds his readers that they must estimate a probability for the chance of success and a likely loss "in the event of failure."

Graham came early to special situations and never lost his interest in them. When he was only twenty-one, the Guggenheim Exploration Company announced that it would dissolve. The company owned major stakes in four publicly traded copper mines; as part of the wind-up, it would distribute the interests in those mines to its shareholders. Graham calculated that the sum of the parts was worth almost 11% more than the whole, so he bought Guggenheim and simultaneously sold shares in the four mines.[11] Nearly four decades later, in 1954, Graham asked a bright analyst new to his firm, a fellow named Warren Buffett, to investigate the arbitrage possibilities in Rockwood & Company. This chocolate company, based in Brooklyn, New York, was proposing an unusual tender offer: 80 pounds of cocoa beans for each common share. Graham liked the deal, sending Buffett off to buy the shares and sell the beans.[12]

In "Some Investment Aspects of Accumulation through Equities," published in 1962, Graham looks at the arguments claiming that "a new stock-market era" justified "the present unprecedented level of stock prices and earnings multipliers." Many investors believed that the stock market was then blessed with "a permanently changed character and future," thanks to such factors as robust and stable economic growth, sound fiscal and monetary policy, the recognition that stocks are a durable hedge against inflation, and the floods of new cash from mutual funds and pension-plan sponsors.

Graham patiently and fairly spells out the case that the bulls may be right. He recognizes that there is at least some validity to the contention that stocks deserve higher valuations than in the past. In the end, however, he concludes that "the fundamental character of the stock market must be as unchanging as that of human nature."

Graham points out that the latest bullish arguments are, in essence, no different from those of earlier "new eras," like the late 1920s. Of course, they returned in almost identical form in 1999 and 2000. And they will again, among future investors—at least those who do not heed Graham's warnings.

Finally, he considers whether dollar-cost averaging—systematically purchasing equal amounts of shares at equal time intervals—can work even if it is undertaken when the market is overvalued. He concludes that "such a policy will pay off ultimately, regardless of when it is begun, *provided* that it is adhered to conscientiously and courageously under all intervening conditions." As he points out, that takes extraordinary emotional discipline. To prevail in the end, the investor who dollar-cost averages must "be a different person from the rest of us . . . not subject to the alternations of exhilaration and deep gloom." Graham understood that no technique or tool can ever impose complete external discipline on an investor who lacks internal discipline.

NOTES

1. These essays, bristling with anger, constitute a working first draft for the more logical and detailed arguments that Graham fleshed out in Chapters 43 and 44 of the 1934 edition of *Security Analysis*.
2. Italics in original.
3. www.federalreserve.gov/releases/z1/Current/z1r-2.pdf, Table D2.
4. Personal communication, Howard Silverblatt, senior index analyst, Standard & Poor's, Nov. 16, 2009.
5. Benjamin Graham, *The Intelligent Investor* (New York: Harper & Row, 1949), p. 218.
6. Graham was not nearly as charitable in *Security Analysis*, where he wrote that "chart reading cannot possibly be a science," that "it has not proved itself in the past to be a dependable method of making profits in the stock market," and that "its theoretical basis rests upon faulty logic or else upon mere assertion" (Benjamin Graham and David Dodd, *Security Analysis*, New York: McGraw-Hill, 1934, p. 609).

7. *The Global Body of Investment Knowledge,* the compendium of information that is compiled and updated by CFA Institute, corresponds closely to Graham's call for "a continuous, ever-growing body of knowledge and technique."

8. For a more recent discussion of these issues, see the proceedings of the CFA Institute forum on the equity risk premium, www.cfapubs.org/toc/cp.1/2002/2002/7, and Rajnish Mehra (ed.), *Handbook of the Equity Risk Premium* (Amsterdam and Oxford: Elsevier, 2008).

9. See, for example, Robyn M. Dawes, "The Robust Beauty of Improper Linear Models in Decision Making," *American Psychologist,* vol. 34, no. 7 (1979), pp. 571–582, an article that has been cited more than 1,600 times in psychology journals but rarely if ever in the literature on applied finance.

10. Graham and Dodd, *Security Analysis,* p. 54.

11. Irving Kahn and Robert D. Milne, *Benjamin Graham: The Father of Financial Analysis* (Charlottesville, VA: Financial Analysts Research Foundation, 1977), p. 4; Benjamin Graham, *The Memoirs of the Dean of Wall Street* (New York: McGraw-Hill, 1996), p. 145.

12. Berkshire Hathaway Annual Letter to Shareholders, 1988 and 2007.

5

Toward a Science
of Security Analysis

The Scientific Method

As H. D. Wolfe pointed out in his paper in the last *Journal* ("Science as a Trustworthy Tool"),[1] scientific method includes among its factors the wide observation and recording of events, the construction of rational and plausible theories or formulas, and their validation through the medium of reasonably dependable predictions. There are many varieties of scientific or quasi-scientific disciplines, and the character of the predictions based on them will vary greatly from one to another.

At one extreme take the microphone. An electrical engineer, having rigged it up carefully, can predict that a word spoken into it will be immediately amplified. The prediction is precise, the verification prompt and unquestionable. At the other extreme let us take psychoanalysis—a discipline sometimes compared with our own security analysis. Here prediction and verification are less definite. A layman who finances psychoanalytical treatment for one of his family is apt to be slightly in the dark about such details as the nature of the illness, the method and duration of the treatment, and the extent of the cure, if any. About the only thing he can predict with certainty is how much it will cost per

Reprinted from *The Analysts Journal*, vol. 8, no. 4 (August 1952): 96–98 with permission.

hour. Between these two extremes lies actuarial science, which to my mind is more relevant than the others to the scientific possibilities of security analysis. The life insurance actuary makes predictions concerning mortality rates, the rate of earnings on invested reserves, and factors of expense and profit—in all instances based largely on carefully analyzed past experience, with allowance for trends and new factors. Out of these predictions, with the aid of mathematical techniques, he fashions suitable premium schedules for various types of insurance. What is most important for us about his work and his conclusions is that he deals not with individual cases but with the probable *aggregate result* of a large number of similar cases. Diversification is of the essence in actuarial science.

Thus our first practical question about "scientific security analysis" is whether it is actuarial in character and has diversification as its essential ingredient. One plausible answer may be that diversification is essential for certain types and objectives of security analysis but not for others. Let us classify the things that security analysis tries to do and see how the element of diversification applies to each. At the same time we may raise other questions concerning the scientific methods and predictions operating in each of the classes.

I suggest that the end product of our work falls into four different categories, as follows:

1. The selection of safe securities, of the bond type
2. The selection of undervalued securities
3. The selection of growth securities, that is, common stocks that are expected to increase their earning power at considerably better than the average rate
4. The selection of "near-term opportunities," that is, common stocks that have better-than-average prospects of price advance, within, say, the next twelve months

This list does not include stock market analysis and predictions based thereon. Let me comment briefly on this point. If security analysis is to be scientific, it will have to be so in its own right and not by depending on market techniques. It is easy to dismiss this point completely by saying that, if market analysis is good, it doesn't need security analysis; and, if it isn't good, security analysis doesn't want *it*. But this may be too cavalier an attitude toward an area of activity that engages the interest of a host of reputable security analysts. That stock market analysis and security analysis combined may be able to do a *better* job than security analysis by itself is at least a conceivable proposition and perhaps a plausible one. But the burden is on those who would establish this thesis to demonstrate it to the rest of us in unequivocal and convincing fashion. Certainly the published record is far too meager, as yet, to warrant conceding a scientific standing to a combination of the two analyses.

Four Categories

To return to our four categories of security analysis, choosing safe bonds and preferred stocks is certainly the most respectable if not the most exciting occupation of our guild. Not only has it major importance of its own, but also it can offer useful analogies and insights for other branches of our work. The emphasis of bond analysis is on past performance, tempered by a conservative view of future changes and dangers. Its chief reliance is on a margin of safety that grows out of a small ratio of debt to total real value of the enterprise. It requires broad diversification to assure a representative or average overall result. These viewpoints have made bond investment, as practiced by our financial institutions, a soundly scientific procedure. In fact, bond investment now appears to be almost a branch of actuarial science. There are interesting similarities (as well as differences) between insuring a man's life for $1,000 against a premium of $34 per year, and lending $1,000 on a long-term bond also paying $35 per year. The calculated mortality rate for men aged 35 is about 4 out of 1,000, or 0.4% per year. A comparable "mortality rate" might be applied to corporate enterprises in the best financial and operating health, to estimate the risk attaching to high-grade bond investment. Such a figure, say 0.5%, might then properly measure the risk and yield differential between the strongest corporate bonds and U. S. government obligations.

Bond Investment: A Scientific Procedure

Bond investment should take on more of the character of a scientific procedure when the monumental corporate bond study, carried on by the National Bureau of Economic Research and other agencies, is finally completed and the mass of statistical data and findings is made available to security analysts. The greatest weakness of our profession, I have long believed, is our failure to provide really comprehensive records of the results of investments initiated or carried on by us under various principles and techniques. We have asked for unlimited statistics from others covering the results of their operations, but we have been more than backward in compiling fair and adequate statistics relating to the results of our own work. I shall have a suggestion to make on that point a little later.

Selection of Undervalued Securities

The selection of undervalued securities appears next on my list because of its logical relationship to investment in safe bonds or preferred stocks. The margin-of-safety concept is the dominant one in both groups. A common stock is undervalued, typically, if the analyst can soundly establish that the enterprise as a whole is worth well above the market price of all its securities. There is a close analogy here with bond selection, which also requires an enterprise value well in excess of the debt. But the rewards for establishing that a common stock is undervalued are, of course, incomparably greater; for in the average case all or a good part of the margin of safety should eventually be realized as a profit to the buyer of a truly undervalued issue.

In this connection I want to throw out a broad and challenging idea—that from a scientific standpoint common stocks *as a whole* may be regarded as an essentially undervalued *security form*. This point grows out of the basic difference between individual risk and overall or group risk. People insist on a substantially higher dividend return and a still larger excess in earnings yield for common stocks than for bonds, because the risk of loss in the average *single* common stock issue is undoubtedly greater than in the average *single* bond. But the comparison has not been true historically of a *diversified group* of common stocks, since common stocks as a whole have had a well-defined upward bias or long-term upward movement. This in turn is readily explicable in terms of the country's growth, plus the steady reinvestment of undistributed profits, plus the strong net inflationary trend since the turn of the century.

Fire and Casualty Rates

The analogy here is with fire and casualty insurance rates. People pay about twice as much for fire insurance as their own actuarially determined exposure would indicate—because they cannot soundly afford to carry the individual risk themselves. For similar reasons the overall return on common stocks appears to have been at least twice as much as their true overall risk has required. An interesting relationship at this point appears from the Keystone chart showing the trend of the Dow Jones Industrial Average since 1899. Both the upper and lower lines happen to rise at the rate of one-third every ten years. You will recognize this as the 2.90% rate of compound interest realized on U. S. Savings Bonds, Series E. What this means is the consistent Dow Jones investor has obtained the same increase in *principal value* as the savings bonds offer in lieu of interest; and in addition the Dow Jones stock investor has obtained all the annual dividends from his holdings as a bonus above the government bond interest rate.

The reasoning I have just indulged in is, I believe, both scientifically valid and psychologically dangerous. Its validity depends on the maintenance in the stock market of the substantial disparity between bond yields and the price-earnings ratios on stocks. If—as happened in the 1920s—this very thesis is twisted into the slogan that common stocks are attractive investments, regardless of how high they sell, then we would find ourselves beginning as scientists and ending as heedless and ill-starred gamblers. It may be a fair generalization to assert that the top levels of most "normal" bull markets are characterized by a tendency to equate stock risks with bond risks. These high valuations may indeed have some justification in pure theory, but the important thing for us to bear in mind as practicing analysts is that, when you pay full value for common stocks, you are in great danger of later appearing to have paid too much.

Individual Undervaluations

Turning now to the field of *individual* undervaluations, we find ourselves on more familiar ground. Our work with this group readily admits of the scientific processes of wide observation and the testing out of predictions or hypotheses by their sequels. The theory of undervalued issues must necessarily require an explanation of their origin. The explanations are in truth quite varied and taken together form what may be called a "pathology of market prices." They range from obvious causes, such as an unduly low dividend or a temporary setback in earnings, to more subtle and special conditions such as too much common stock in the capital structure or even too much cash in the bank. In between lie numerous other causes such as the presence of important litigation, or the combination of two dissimilar businesses, or the use of the now discredited holding company setup.

Origins of Undervaluation Understood

The origins of undervaluation are pretty well understood by now and could no doubt be set forth in an acceptably scientific study. We do not know as much about the cure of undervaluations. In what proportion of cases is the discrepancy corrected? How or why does the correction occur? How long does the process take? These questions remind us somewhat of those we raised about psychoanalysis at the outset. But one thing of importance we do know, and that is that the purchase of undervalued issues on a diversified basis does produce consistently profitable results. Thus we have a worthwhile field for more scientific cultivation. Here inductive studies carried on intelligently and systematically over a period of years are almost certain to be rewarding.

Selection of Growth Stocks

The third objective of security analysis is the selection of growth stocks. How scientific a procedure is this now, and how scientific can it be made to be? Here I enter difficult waters. Most growth companies are themselves tied in closely with technological progress; by choosing their shares the security analyst latches on, as it were, to the coattails of science. In the forty or more plant inspections that are on your scheduled field trips for this convention week, no doubt your chief emphasis will be placed on new products and new process developments; and these in turn will strongly influence your conclusions about the long-pull prospects of the various companies. But in most instances this is primarily a *qualitative* approach. Can your work in this field be truly scientific unless it is solidly based on dependable *measurements*, that is, specific or minimum projections of future earnings, and a capitalization of such projected profits at a rate or multiplier that can be called reasonably conservative in the light of past experience? Can a definite *price* be put on future growth—below which the stock is a sound purchase, above which it is dear, or in any event speculative? What is the risk that the expected growth will fail to materialize? What is the risk of an important downward change in the market's evaluation of favorable prospects? A great deal of systematic study in this field is necessary before dependable answers to such questions will be forthcoming.

Stock Investment in Prescientific Stage

In the meantime I cannot help but feel that growth stock investment is still in the prescientific stage. It is at the same time more fascinating and less precise than the selection of safe bonds or undervalued securities. In the growth stock field, the concept of margin of safety loses the clarity and the primacy it enjoys in those other two classes of security analysis. True, there is safety in growth, and some of us will go so far as to declare that there can be no real safety except in growth. But these sound to me more like slogans than scientifically formulated and verified propositions. Again, in the growth field the element of selectivity is so prominent as to place diversification in a secondary and perhaps dubious position. A case can be made for putting all your growth eggs in the one best or a relatively few best baskets. Thus in this branch of security analysis the actuarial element may be missing, and that circumstance undoubtedly militates against truly scientific procedures and results.

Inverted Relationship

There is undoubtedly an organic but inverted relationship between the growth stock concept and the theory of undervalued securities. The attraction of growth is like a tidal pull which causes high tides in one area, the assumed growth companies, and low tides in another area, the assumed nongrowth companies. We can measure, in a sense, scientifically the distorting effect of this influence by using as our standard the *minimum business value* of enterprises in the nonfavored group. By way of illustration let us apply that thought to three California concerns. The shares of Roos Brothers, a local retail enterprise, will in the nature of things tend to sell below their analytically determined value for basically the same reasons that are bound to produce overvaluations in the shares of Superior Oil or Kern County Land.

I come finally to the standard occupation of brokerage house analysts and advisory services, namely, the selection of issues favorably situated for a near-term market advance. The usual assumption here is that, if the earnings will improve or the dividend will be raised, then the price will improve. Thus the process consists essentially of locating and recommending those companies that are likely to increase their earnings or dividends in the near term. You all know the three basic hazards encountered in this work: that the expected improvement will not take place, that it is already discounted in the current price, that for some other reason or for no known reason the price will not move the way it should.

It may be that despite these hazards it is possible to obtain worthwhile results on the average from competent short-term analyses and predictions. Who of us can say whether or not this is true? In view of the importance of this analytical work, in terms of time, energy, and money cost, it might not be a bad idea to subject it to a thorough-going evaluation.

Searching Self-Examination

This brings me to my conclusion and my one concrete proposal. Security analysis has now reached the stage where it is ready for a continuous and searching self-examination by the use of established statistical tools. We should collect the studies and recommendations of numerous analysts, classify them in accordance with their objectives (perhaps in the four groups suggested in this paper), and then do our best to evaluate their accuracy and success. The purpose of such a record would not be to show who is a good security analyst and who is a poor one, but rather to show what methods and approaches are sound and fruitful and which ones fail to meet the test of experience.

This suggestion was originally made in the articles published under the pseudonym of *Cogitator* in *The Analysts Journal* six years ago. At that time I wrote: "It is unlikely that security analysis could develop professional stature in the absence of reasonably definite and plausible tests of the soundness of individual and group recommendations."[2] The New York Society is now taking the first positive steps to establish a quasi-professional rating or title for security analysts who meet specified requirements. It is virtually certain that this movement will develop ultimately in full-fledged professional status for our calling. The time may well be ripe for the Federation and its constituent Societies to begin a systematic accumulation of case histories, which should make possible the transmission of a continuous, ever-growing body of knowledge and technique from the analysts of the past to those of the future.

When this work is well under way security analysis may begin—modestly, but hopefully—to refer to itself as a scientific discipline.

NOTES

1. H. D. Wolfe, "Science as a Trustworthy Tool," *The Analysts Journal* (March 1952): 45–49.
2. Cogitator, "On Being Right in Security Analysis," *The Analysts Journal* (First Quarter 1946): 18–21, especially at p. 18 for quoted material.

6

Two Illustrative Approaches
to Formula Valuations
of Common Stocks

Of the various basic approaches to common-stock valuation, the most widely accepted is that which estimates the average earnings and dividends for a period of years in the future and capitalizes these elements at an appropriate rate. This statement is reasonably definite in form, but its application permits of the widest range of techniques and assumptions, including plain guesswork. The analyst has first a broad choice as to the future period he will consider; then the earnings and dividends for the period must be estimated and, finally, a capitalization rate selected in accordance with his judgment or his prejudices. We may observe here that since there is no *a priori* rule governing the number of years to which the valuer should look forward in the future, it is almost inevitable that in bull markets investors and analysts will tend to see far and hopefully ahead, whereas at other times they will not be so disposed to "heed the rumble of a distant drum." Hence arises a high degree of built-in instability in the market valuation of growth stocks, so much so that one might assert with some justice that the more dynamic the company the more inherently speculative and fluctuating may be the market history of its shares.[1]

Reprinted from *The Analysts Journal*, vol. 13, no. 5 (November 1957): 11–15 with permission.

When it comes to estimating future earnings few analysts are willing to venture forth, Columbus-like, on completely uncharted seas. They prefer to start with known quantities—e.g., current or past earnings—and process these in some fashion to reach an estimate for the future. As a consequence, in security analysis the past is always being thrown out of the window of theory and coming in again through the back door of practice. It would be a sorry joke on our profession if all the elaborate data on past operations, so industriously collected and so minutely analyzed, should prove in the end to be quite unrelated to the real determinants of the value—the earnings and dividends of the future.

Undoubtedly there are situations, not few perhaps, where this proves to be the rueful fact. But in most cases the relationship between past and future proves significant enough to justify the analyst's preoccupation with the statistical record. In fact the daily work of our practitioner consists largely of an effort to construct a plausible picture of a company's future from his study of its past performance, the latter phrase inevitably suggesting similar intensive studies carried on by devotees of a very different discipline. The better the analyst he is, the less he confines himself to the published figures and the more he adds to these from his special study of the company's management, its policies, and its possibilities.

The student of security analysis, in the classroom or at home, tends to have a special preoccupation with the past record as distinct from an independent judgment of the company's future. He can be taught and can learn to analyze the former, but he lacks a suitable equipment to attempt the latter. What he seeks, typically, is some persuasive method by which a company's earnings record—including such aspects as the average, the trend or growth, stability, etc.—plus some examination of the current balance sheet, can be transmuted first into a projection of future earnings and dividends, and secondly into a valuation based on such projection.

A closer look at this desired process will reveal immediately that the future earnings and dividends need not be computed separately to produce the final value. Take the simplest presentation:

1. Past earnings times X equal future earnings.
2. Future earnings times Y equal present value.

This operation immediately foreshortens to:

3. Past earnings times XY equal present value.

It is the XY factor, or multiplier of past earnings, that my students would dearly love to learn about and to calculate. When I tell them that there is no dependable method of finding this multiplier they tend to be incredulous or to ask, "What good is security analysis then?" They feel that if the right weight is given to all the relevant factors in the past record, at least a reasonably good present valuation of a common stock can be produced, one that will take probable future earnings into account and can be used as a guide to determine the attractiveness or the reverse of the issue at its current market price.

In this article I propose to explain two approaches of this kind which have been developed in a Seminar on Common-Stock Valuation. I believe the first will illustrate reasonably well how formula operations of this kind may be worked out and applied. Ours is an endeavor to establish a comparative value in 1957 for each of the thirty stocks in the Dow Jones Industrial Average, related to a base valuation of 400 and 500, respectively, for the composite or group. (The 400 figure represented the approximate "Central Value" of the Dow Jones Average, as found separately by a whole series of formula methods derived from historical relationships. The 500 figure represented about the average market level for the preceding twelve months.)

As will be seen, the valuations of each component issue take into account the four "quality elements" of profitability, growth, stability, and dividend payout, applying them as multipliers to the average earnings for 1947–56. In addition, and entirely separately, a weight of 20% is given to the net asset value.

The second approach is essentially the reverse of that just described. Whereas the first method attempts to derive an independent value to be compared with the market price, the second starts with the market price and calculates therefrom the rate of future growth expected by the market. From that figure we readily derive the earnings expected for the future period, in our case 1957–66, and hence the multiplier for such future earnings implicit in the current market price.

The place for detailed comment on these calculations is after they have been developed and presented. But it may be well to express the gist of my conclusions at this point, viz.:

1. Our own "formula valuations" for the individual stocks, and probably any others of the same general type, have little if any utility in themselves. It would be silly to assert that Stock A is "worth" only half its market price, or Stock B twice its market price, because these figures result from our valuation formula.

2. On the other hand, they may be suggestive and useful as composite reflections of the past record, taken by itself. They may even be said to represent what the value would be, assuming that the future were merely a continuation of past performances.

3. The analyst is thus presented with a "discrepancy" of definite magnitude, between formula "value" and the price, which it becomes his task to deal with in terms

of his superior knowledge and judgment. The actual size of these discrepancies, and the attitude that may possibly be taken respecting them, are discussed below.

Similarly, the approach which starts from the market price, and derives an implied "growth factor" and an implied multiplier therefrom, may have utility in concentrating the analyst's attention on just what the market seems to be expecting from each stock in the future, in comparison or contrast with what it actually accomplished in the past. Here again his knowledge and judgment are called upon either to accept or reject the apparent assumptions of the market place.

METHOD 1. A Formula Valuation Based Solely on Past Performance in Relation to the Dow Jones Industrial Average as a Group.

The assumptions underlying this method are the following:

1. Each component issue of the Dow Jones Industrial Average may be valued in relation to a base value of the average as a whole by a comparison of the statistical records.
2. The data to be considered are the following:
   a. *Profitability*—as measured by the rate of return on invested capital. (For convenience this was computed only for the year 1956.)
   b. *Growth of per-share earnings*—as shown by two measurements: 1947–56 earnings vs. 1947 earnings, and 1956 earnings vs. 1947–56 earnings.

      (It would have been more logical to have used the 1954–56 average instead of the single year 1956, but the change would have little effect on the final valuations.)
   c. *Stability*—as measured by the greatest shrinkage of profits in the periods 1937–38 and 1947–56.

(The calculation is based on the percentage
of earnings retained in the period of maximum
shrinkage.)

d. *Payout*—as measured by the ratio of 1956 dividends
to 1956 earnings. In the few cases where the 1956
earnings were below the 1947–56 average we substituted the latter for the former, to get a more realistic
figure of current payout.

These criteria demonstrate the quality of the company's
earnings (and dividend policy) and thus may control the multiplier to be applied to the earnings. The figure found under
each heading is divided by the corresponding figure for the
Dow Jones group as a whole, to give the company's relative performance. The four relatives were then combined on the basis of
equal weights to give a final "quality index" of the company as
against the overall quality of the group.

The rate of earnings on invested capital is perhaps the most
logical measure of the success and quality of an enterprise. It
tells how productive are the dollars invested in the business. In
studies made in the relatively "normal" market of 1953, I found
a surprisingly good correlation between the profitability rate and
the price-earnings ratio, after introducing a major adjustment
for the dividend payout and a minor (moderating) adjustment
for net asset value.

It is not necessary to emphasize the importance of the growth
factor to stock-market people. They are likely to ask rather why
we have not taken it as the major determinant of quality and
multipliers. There is little doubt that the expected future growth
is in fact the major influence upon current price-earnings ratios,
and this truth is fully recognized in our second approach, which
deals with growth expectations as reflected in market prices. But
the correlation between market multipliers and past growth is by
no means close.

Some interesting figures worked out by Ralph A. Bing show this clearly.[2] Dow Chemical, with per-share earnings growth of 31% (1955 vs. 1948) had in August 1956 a price-earnings ratio of 47.3 times 1955 earnings. Bethlehem Steel, with corresponding growth of 93%, had a multiplier of only 9.1. The spread between the two relationships is thus as wide as fourteen to one. Other ratios in Mr. Bing's table show similar wide disparities between past growth and current multipliers.

It is here that the stability factor asserts its importance. The companies with high multipliers may not have had the best growth in 1948–55, but most of them had greater than average stability of earnings over the past two decades.

These considerations led us to adopt the simple arithmetical course of assigning equal weight to past growth, past stability, and current profitability in working out the quality coefficient for each company. The dividend payout is not strictly a measure of quality of earning power, though in the typical case investors probably regard it in some such fashion. Its importance in most instances is undeniable, and it is both convenient and plausible to give it equal weight and similar treatment with each of the other factors just discussed.

Finally we depart from the usual Wall Street attitude and assign a weight of 20% in the final valuation to the net assets per share. It is true that in the typical case the asset value has no perceptible influence on current market price. But it may have some long-run effect on future market price, and thus it has a claim to be considered seriously in any independent valuation of a company. As is well known, asset values invariably play some part, sometimes a fairly important one, in the many varieties of legal valuations of common stocks, which grow out of tax cases, merger litigation, and the like. The basic justification for considering asset value in this process, even though it may be ignored in the current market price, lies in the possibility of its showing its weight later, through competitive developments, changes in management or its policies, merger or sale eventuality, etc.

The above discussion will explain, perhaps not very satisfactorily, why the four factors entering into the quality rating and the fifth factor of asset value were finally assigned equal weight of 20% each.

The actual application of our illustrative method can now be explained by working through the figures for the first company in the group, Allied Chemical & Dye. Following are data used in computing the "value" of ACD relative to a 400 and a 500 valuation for the Dow Jones Industrial Average:

	D.J. Ind. Avg.	Allied C. & D.	"Quality" Factors: Ratio of ACD to D.J.
Earned per share 1956	$36.00	$4.74	
1947–56	27.50	4.50	
1947–49	21.80	3.73	
1938 (unadjusted)	6.01	5.92	
1937 (unadjusted)	11.49	11.19	
Dividends 1956	23.15	3.00	
Net Asset Value 1956	275.00	40.00	
Profitability:			
1956 earnings/1956 net assets	13.0%	11.85%	91%
Growth-A: 1947–56 vs. 1947–49	26.0%	21.00%	
B: 1956 vs. 1947–56	30.0%	5.00%	
A plus B.	56.0%	26.00%	46%
Stability:			
1938 earnings/1937 earnings	52.3%	53.00%	101%
Payout:			
1956 dividend/1956 earnings	64.3%	64.00%	100%
	Average of four Quality Factors		84%

Formula to produce value of 400 for D.J. Ind. Av.:

"Value" equals $^1/_5$ Net Assets plus 12.5 × 1947–56 earnings

   or 55 plus 12.5 × 27.50

   or 400.

Corresponding "Valuation" of Allied Chem. & Dye (including Quality Factor of 84%):

Value equals $^1/_5$ × 40 plus .84 × 12.5 × 4.50

   or 55.

Formula to produce value of 500 for D.J. Ind. Av.:

Value equals $^1/_5$ Net Assets plus 16.2 × 1947–56 earnings

   or 500.

Corresponding "Valuation" of Allied Chem. & Dye (including Quality Factor of 84%):

Value equals $^1/_5$ × 40 plus .84 × 16.2 × 4.50

   or 69.

In Table 1 we supply the "valuation" reached by this method for each of the thirty stocks in the Dow Jones Industrial Average. Our table includes the various quality factors, the average earnings, and the asset values used to arrive at our final figures.

Table 1

Formula Valuations of Dow Jones Industrial Issues

| Company | Quality Factors | | | | Av. Factor | Earns. 1947–56 | Book Value | Indicated Value Basis | | Price Aug. 5 |
	Profit-ability	Growth	Stability	Payout				D.J. 400	D.J. 500	1957
Allied Ch.	91	46	94	100	84	4.50	40	55	69	89
Am. Can	81	70	137	107	99	2.61	28	39	48	44
Am. S. & Ref.	101	39	100	81	80	5.43	51	65	85	54
Am. T. & T.	54	40	163	130	97	9.90	150	151	185	173
Am. Tob.	98	27	111	104	85	6.58	59	82	102	72
Beth. St.	95	138	0	97	83	2.88	31	36	45	49
Chrysler	*91	0	38	51	45	8.15	74	66	80	77
Corn. Prod.	100	65	114	98	94	1.96	40	31	37	31
Du Pont	154	198	100	109	140	5.60	41	107	136	199
East. Kod.	136	100	148	85	117	3.49	28	57	63	104
Gen. Elec.	139	129	84	127	120	1.87	14	31	39	68
Gen. Foods	138	99	141	79	114	2.42	20	39	49	49
Gen. Motors	160	119	95	104	120	2.48	20	42	53	45
Goodyear T.	108	207	129	83	132	4.18	43	78	98	76
Int. Harv.	*58	0	91	98	62	3.70	49	39	47	35
Int. Nickel	164	263	119	90	159	3.86	31	83	105	92
Int. Paper	100	46	0	101	62	6.40	55	61	76	101
Johns Man.	93	96	44	100	83	3.07	29	38	47	45
Nat. Dist.	*73	0	62	118	63	2.47	26	25	31	26
Nat. Steel	95	96	101	88	95	5.71	68	79	99	75
Proc. & Gam.	110	46	105	103	91	2.61	21	34	42	49
Sears Roe.	112	56	144	84	99	1.82	15	26	32	28
S. O. Cal.	124	113	134	65	109	3.09	24	47	59	58
S. O. N.J.	130	166	97	80	118	2.85	24	47	59	67
Texas Corp.	126	171	81	66	111	3.48	34	56	70	74
Un. C. & C.	138	92	108	100	110	3.73	27	53	67	117
Un. Aircr.	158	361	181	66	192	3.65	35	96	121	62
U. S. Steel	99	239	0	67	101	3.51	47	54	67	69
Westinghouse	*65	0	0	83	37	3.79	43	27	32	64
Woolworth	*69	0	116	109	74	3.58	40	41	51	42
D.J. Ind. Av.	**(13.0)**	**(56)**	**(52.3)**	**(64.3)**	**100**	**27.50**	**275**	**400**	**500**	**500**

* Based on 1947–56 Av. Earns. vs. 1956 Book Value plus adj.

In about half the cases these "valuations" differ quite widely from the prices ruling on August 5 last, on which date the D. J. Average actually sold at 500. Seven issues were selling at 20% or more above their formula value, and an equal number at 20% or more below such value. At the extremes we find Westinghouse selling at a 100% "premium," and United Aircraft at about a 50% "discount." The extent of these disparities naturally suggests that our method is technically a poor one, and that more plausible valuations could be reached—i.e., ones more congruous with market prices—if a better choice were made of the factors and weights entering into the method.

A number of tests were applied to our results to see if they could be "improved" by some plausible changes in the technique. To give these in any detail would prolong this report unnecessarily. Suffice it to say that they were unproductive. If the asset-value factor had been excluded, a very slight change would have resulted in favor of the issues which were selling at the highest premium over their formula value. On the other hand, if major emphasis had been placed on the factor of past growth, some of our apparently undervalued issues would have been given still larger formula values, for Table 1 shows that more of the spectacular growth percentages occur in this group than in the other—e.g., United Aircraft, International Nickel, and Goodyear.

It is quite evident from Table 1 that the stock market fixes its valuation of a given common stock on the basis not of its past statistical performance but rather of its expected future performance, which may differ significantly from its past behavior. The market is, of course, fully justified in seeking to make this independent appraisal of the future, and for that reason any automatic rejection of the market's verdict because it differs from a formula valuation would be the height of folly. We cannot avoid the observation, however, that the independent appraisals made in the stock market are themselves far from infallible, as is shown in part by the rapid changes to which they are subject. It is possible, in fact, that they may be on the whole a no more dependable guide to what the future will produce than the "values" reached by our mechanical processing of past data, with all the latter's obvious shortcomings.

METHOD 2. Let us turn now to our second mathematical approach, which concerns itself with future growth, or future earnings, as they appear to be predicted by the market price itself. We start with the theory that the market price of a representative stock, such as any one in the Dow Jones group, reflects the earnings to be expected in a future period, times a multiplier which is in turn based on the percentage of future growth. Thus an issue for which more than average growth is expected will have this fact shown to a double degree, or "squared," in its market price—first in the higher figure taken for future earnings, and second in the higher multiplier applied to those higher earnings.

We shall measure growth by comparing the expected 1957–66 earnings with the actual figures for 1947–56. Our basic formula says, somewhat arbitrarily, that where no growth is expected the current price will be 8 times both 1947–56 earnings and the expected 1957–66 earnings. If growth G is expected, expressed as the ratio of 1957-66 to 1947–56 earnings, then the price reflects such next decade earnings multiplied by 8 times G.

From these assumptions we obtain the simple formula:

$$\text{Price equals } (E \times G) \times (8 \times G), \text{ or } 8G^2 \times E,$$
where E is the per-share earnings for 1947–56.

To find G, the expected rate of future growth, we have only to divide the current price by 8 times 1947–56 earnings, and take the square root.

When this is done for the Dow Jones Average as a whole, using its August 5, 1957, price of 500, we get a value of 1.5 for G—indicating an expected growth of 50% for 1957–66 earnings vs. the 1947–56 actuality. This anticipates an average of $41 in the next decade, as against $27.50 for the previous ten years and about $36 in 1956. This estimate appears reasonable to the writer in relation to the 500 level. (In fact he started with this estimate and worked back from it to get the basic multiplier of 8 to be applied to issues with no expected growth.) The price of 500 for the D. J. Average would represent in turn a multiplier of 8 × 1.5, or 12, to be applied to the expected future earnings of $41. (Incidentally, on these assumptions the average current formula value of about 400 for the Dow Jones Average would reflect expectations of a decade-to-decade growth of 35%, average earnings of $37.1 for 1957–66, and a current multiplier of 10.8 for such future earnings.)

In Table 2 we set forth the results of applying this second approach to the thirty Dow Jones issues. (The figures for Am. Tel. & Tel. might well be ignored, since utility issues should take a different basic formula.) The main interest in the table lies in the disparities it indicates between the expected future growth, implicit in the market prices, and the actual growth during the past decade. Ten of the companies (plus ATT) sold at prices anticipating at least twice the Dow Jones Average rate of growth, comparing 1957–66 with 1956. Of these only two, Du Pont and General Electric, had actually shown distinctly better than average growth in the last ten years. Conversely, eight of the companies were indicating less than half the average expected rate of growth, including five for which actual declines from 1956 levels were apparently predicted. Yet of these eight companies, no less than five had actually shown far greater than average growth in the past decade.

Table 2

Formula Calculations of Expected Growth of Earnings of Dow Jones Ind. Issues, as Indicated by August 5, 1957 Price

Company	Price 8/5/57	Average Earnings 1947–56	Expected Growth 1957–66 vs. 1947–56	Indicated Earnings 1957–66	Indicated Multiplier*	Earnings 1956	Expected Increase 1957–66 vs. 1956	Actual Increase 1956 vs. 1947–56
Allied Ch.	89	$4.50	+58%	$7.22	12.6	$4.74	+52%	+6%
Am. Can	44	2.61	46	3.83	11.6	2.92	33	12
Am. S. & R.	54	5.43	12	6.10	9.0	6.67	(−8)	23
Am. T. & T.**	173	9.90	47	14.70	11.8	10.74	36	14
Am. Tob.	72	6.58	18	7.80	9.4	7.51	4	14
Beth. St.	49	2.88	44	4.15	11.5	3.83	8	33
Chrysler	77	8.95	4	9.28	8.30	2.29	(large)	(−76)
Corn Prod.	31	1.96	41	2.76	11.4	2.36	18	12
Du Pont	199	5.60	112	11.85	17.0	8.20	45	47
East. Kod.	104	3.49	93	6.62	15.4	4.89	36	37
Gen. Elec.	68	1.87	113	4.00	17.0	2.45	62	31
Gen. Foods	49	2.42	59	3.86	12.7	3.56	9	45
Gen. Motors	45	2.48	51	3.74	12.1	3.02	24	22
Goodyear T.	76	4.18	42	5.96	11.4	6.03	(−1)	47
Int. Harv.	35	3.70	8	4.02	8.6	3.14	29	(−15)
Int. Nickel	92	3.86	62	6.30	13.0	6.50	(−3)	68
Int. Paper	101	6.40	40	9.03	11.2	7.05	28	11
Johns Man.	45	3.07	36	4.21	10.9	3.50	20	14
Nat. Dist.	26	2.47	15	2.86	9.2	2.11	36	(−15)
Nat. Steel	75	5.71	28	7.32	10.2	7.09	3	25
Proc. & Gam.	49	2.61	53	3.99	12.2	3.05	30	20
Sears Roebuck	28	1.82	38	2.53	11.0	2.20	16	18
S. O. Cal.	58	3.09	55	4.78	12.4	4.24	12	39
S. O. N. J.	67	2.85	72	4.99	13.8	4.11	21	44
Texas Corp.	74	3.48	62	5.66	13.0	5.51	3	59
Un. C. & C.	117	3.73	99	7.43	15.9	4.86	53	32
Un. Air.	62	3.65	45	5.31	11.6	7.66	(−32)	93
U. S. Steel	69	3.51	57	5.55	12.6	6.01	(−8)	73
Westinghouse	64	3.79	45	5.53	11.6	.10	(large)	(−97)
Woolworth	42	3.58	22	4.39	9.8	3.57	23	0
D.J. Ind. Av.	500	$27.50	50	$41.25	12.0	$35.80	15	30

* Dec. 1956 price ÷ Indic. 1957–66 Earns.

** The basic formula is less applicable to A. T. & T. than to industrial issues.

This leads us to our final observations, which tie our two tables together. The ten companies previously mentioned, for which unusually rapid growth is anticipated, includes seven of those shown in Table 1 as selling significantly above their formula valuation. Again, the eight for which subnormal or no growth is expected include six which were selling substantially below their formula valuations.

We conclude that a large part of the discrepancies between carefully calculated formula values and the market prices can be traced to the growth factor, not because the formulas underplay its importance, but rather because the market often has concepts of future earnings changes which cannot be derived from the companies' past performance. The reasons for the market's breaking with the past are often abundantly clear. Investors do not believe, for example, that United Aircraft will duplicate its brilliant record of 1947–56, because they consider that a company with the United States Department of Defense as its chief customer is inherently vulnerable. They have the opposite view with regard to Westinghouse. They feel its relatively mediocre showing in recent years was the result of temporary factors, and that the electric manufacturing industry is inherently so growth-assured that a major supplier such as Westinghouse is bound to prosper in the future.

These cases are clear cut enough, but other divergencies shown in our table are not so easy to understand or to accept. There is a difference between these two verbs. The market may be right in its general feeling about a company's future, but the price tag it sets on that future may be quite unreasonable in either direction.

It is here that many analysts will find their challenge. They may not be satisfied merely to find out what the market is doing and thinking, and then to explain it to everyone's satisfaction. They may prefer to exercise an independent judgment—one not controlled by the daily verdict of the market place, but ready at times to take definite issue with it. For this kind of activity one or more valuation processes, of the general type we have been illustrating, may serve a useful purpose. They give a concrete and elaborated picture of the past record, which the analyst may use as a point of departure for his individual exploration and discoveries in the field of investment values.

NOTES

1. On this point the philosophically inclined are referred to the recent article of David Durand on "Growth Stocks and the Petersburg Paradox" in the September 1957 issue of the *Journal of Finance*. His conclusion is "that the growth-stock problem offers no great hope of a satisfactory solution."

2. "Can We Improve Methods of Appraising Growth Stocks?" by R. A. Bing, *Commercial and Financial Chronicle*, Sept. 13, 1956. Table on p. 24.

7

The New Speculation
in Common Stocks

I asked Hartley Smith, in introducing me to you, to lay chief stress upon my advanced age. What I shall have to say will reflect the spending of many years in Wall Street, with their attendant varieties of experience. This has included the recurrent advent of new conditions, or a new atmosphere, which challenge the value of experience itself. It is true that one of the elements that distinguish economics, finance, and security analysis from other practical disciplines is the uncertain validity of past phenomena as a guide to the present and future. Yet we have no right to reject the lessons of the past until we have at least studied and understood them. My address today is an effort toward such understanding in a limited field—in particular, an endeavor to point out some contrasting relationships between the present and the past in our underlying attitudes toward investment and speculation in common stocks.

Let me start with a summary of my thesis. In the past the speculative elements of a common stock resided almost exclusively in the company itself; they were due to uncertainties, or fluctuating elements, or downright weaknesses in the industry, or the corporation's individual setup. These elements of speculation still exist, of course; but it may be said that they have been sensibly diminished by a number of long-term developments to

Reprinted from *The Analysts Journal*, vol. 14, no. 3 (June 1958): 17–21 with permission.

which I shall refer. But in revenge a new and major element of speculation has been introduced into the common-stock arena from *outside* the companies. It comes from the attitude and viewpoint of the stock-buying public and their advisers—chiefly us security analysts. This attitude may be described in a phrase: primary emphasis upon future expectations.

Nothing will appear more logical and natural to this audience than the idea that a common stock should be valued and priced primarily on the basis of the company's expected future performance. Yet this simple-appearing concept carries with it a number of paradoxes and pitfalls. For one thing, it obliterates a good part of the older, well-established distinctions between investment and speculation. The dictionary says that "speculate" comes from the Latin "specula," a look-out or watch-tower. Thus it was the speculator who looked out from his elevated watch-tower and saw future developments coming before other people did. But today, if the investor is shrewd or well-advised, he too must have his watch-tower looking out on the future, or rather he mounts into a common watch-tower where he rubs elbows with the speculator.

Secondly, we find that, for the most part, companies with the best investment characteristics—i.e., the best credit rating—are the ones which are likely to attract the largest speculative interest in their common stocks, since everyone assumes they are guaranteed a brilliant future. Thirdly, the concept of future prospects, and particularly of continued growth in the future, invites the application of formulae out of higher mathematics to establish the present value of the favored issues. But the combination of precise formulae with highly imprecise assumptions can be used to establish, or rather to justify, practically any value one wishes, however high, for a really outstanding issue. But, paradoxically, that very fact on close examination will be seen to imply that no one value, or reasonably narrow range of values, can be counted on to establish and maintain itself for a given growth company; hence at times the market may conceivably value the growth component at a strikingly *low* figure.

Returning to my distinction between the older and newer speculative elements in common stock, we might characterize them by two outlandish but convenient words, viz.: endogenous and exogenous. Let me illustrate briefly the old-time speculative common stock, as distinguished from an investment stock, by some data relating to American Can and Pennsylvania Railroad in 1911–13. (These appear in *Security Analysis*, 1940 Edition, pp. 2–3.)

In those three years the price range of "Pennsy" moved only between 53 and 65, or between 12.2 and 15 times its average earnings for the period. It showed steady profits, was paying a reliable $3 dividend, and investors were sure that it was backed by well over its par of $50 in tangible assets. By contrast, the price of American Can ranged between 9 and 47; its earnings between 7¢ and $8.86; the ratio of price to the average earnings moved between 1.9 times and 10 times; it paid no dividend at all; and sophisticated investors were well aware that the $100 par value of the common represented nothing but undisclosed "water," since the preferred issue exceeded the tangible assets available for it. Thus American Can common was a representative speculative issue, because American Can Company was then a speculative-capitalized enterprise in a fluctuating and uncertain industry. Actually, American Can had a far more brilliant long-term future than Pennsylvania Railroad; but not only was this fact not suspected by investors or speculators in those days, but even if it had been it would probably have been put aside by the investors as basically irrelevant to investment policies and programs in the years 1911–13.

Now, to expose you to the development through time of the importance of long-term prospects for investments, I should like to use as my example our most spectacular giant industrial enterprise—none other than International Business Machines, which last year entered the small group of companies with $1 billion of sales. May I introduce one or two autobiographical notes here, in order to inject a little of the personal touch into what otherwise would be an excursion into cold figures? In 1912 I had left college for a term to take charge of a research project for U. S. Express Co. We set out to find the effect on revenues of a proposed revolutionary new system of computing express rates. For this purpose we used the so-called Hollerith machines, leased out by the then Computing-Tabulating-Recording Co. They comprised card-punches, card-sorters, and tabulators— tools almost unknown to businessmen, then, and having their chief application in the Census Bureau. I entered Wall Street in 1914, and the next year the bonds and common stock of C.-T.-R. Co. were listed on the New York Stock Exchange. Well, I had a kind of sentimental interest in that enterprise, and besides I considered myself a sort of technological expert on their products, being one of the few financial people who had seen and used them. So early in 1916 I went to the head of my firm, known as Mr. A. N., and pointed out to him that C.-T.-R. stock was selling in the middle 40s (for 105,000 shares); that it had earned $6.50 in 1915; that its book value—including, to be sure, some nonsegregated intangibles—was $130; that it had started a $3 dividend; and that I thought rather highly of the company's products and prospects. Mr. A. N. looked at me pityingly. "Ben," said he, "do not mention that company to me again. I would not touch it with a ten-foot pole. (His favorite expression.) Its 6% bonds are selling in the low 80s, and they are no good. So how can the stock be any good? Everybody knows there is nothing behind it but water." (Glossary: In those days that was the ultimate of condemnation. It meant that the asset-account on the balance sheet was fictitious. Many industrial companies—notably U. S.

Steel—despite their $100 par, represented nothing but water, concealed in a written-up plant account. Since they had "nothing" to back them but earning power and future prospects, no self-respecting investor would give them a second thought.)

I returned to my statistician's cubby-hole, a chastened young man. Mr. A. N. was not only experienced and successful, but extremely shrewd as well. So much was I impressed by his sweeping condemnation of Computing-Tabulating-Recording that I never bought a share of it in my life, not even after its name was changed to IBM in 1926.

Now let us take a look at the same company with its new name in 1926, a year of pretty high stock markets. At that time it first revealed the goodwill item in its balance sheet, in the rather large sum of $13.6 million. A. N. had been right. Practically every dollar of the so-called equity behind the common in 1915 had been nothing but water. However, since that time the company had made an impressive record under the direction of T. L. Watson, Sr. Its net had risen from $691,000 to $3.7 million— over fivefold—a greater percentage gain than it was to make in any subsequent eleven-year period. It had built up a nice tangible equity for the common and had split it 3.6 for one. It had estab- lished a $3 dividend rate for the new stock, while earnings were $6.39 thereon. You might have expected the 1926 stock market to have been pretty enthusiastic about a company with such a growth history and so strong a trade position. Let us see. The price range for that year was 31 low, 59 high. At the average of 45 it was selling at the same 7-times multiplier of earnings and the same 6.7% dividend yield as it had done in 1915. At its low of 31 it was not far in excess of its tangible book value, and in that respect was far more conservatively priced than eleven years earlier.

These data illustrate, as well as any can, the persistence of the old-time investment viewpoint until the culminating years of the bull market of the 1920s. What has happened since then can be summarized by using ten-year intervals in the history of IBM. In 1936 net expanded to twice the 1926 figures, and the average multiplier rose from 7 to 17½. From 1936 to 1946 the gain was 2½ times, but the average multiplier in 1946 remained at 17½. Then the pace accelerated. The 1956 net was nearly 4 times that of 1946, and the average multiplier rose to 32½. Last year, with a further gain in net, the multiplier rose again to an average of 42, if we do not count the unconsolidated equity in the foreign subsidiary.

When we examine these recent price figures with care, we see some interesting analogies and contrasts with those of forty years earlier. The one-time scandalous water, so prevalent in the balance sheets of industrial companies, has all been squeezed out—first by disclosure and then by write-offs. But a different kind of water has been put back into the valuation by the stock market—by investors and speculators themselves. When IBM now sells at 7 times its book value, instead of 7 times earnings, the effect is practically the same as if it had no book value at all. Or the small book-value portion can be considered as a sort of minor preferred-stock component of the price, the rest representing exactly the same sort of commitment as the old-time speculator made when he bought Woolworth or U. S. Steel common entirely for their earning power and future prospects.

It is worth remarking, in passing, that in the thirty years which saw IBM transformed from a 7-times earnings to a 40-times earnings enterprise, many of what I have called the endogenous speculative aspects of our large industrial companies have tended to disappear, or at least to diminish greatly. Their financial positions are firm, their capital structures conservative; they are managed far more expertly, and even more honestly, than before. Furthermore, the requirements of complete disclosure have removed one of the important speculative elements of years ago—that derived from ignorance and mystery.

Another personal digression here. In my early years in the Street one of the favorite mystery stocks was Consolidated Gas of New York, now Consolidated Edison. It owned as a subsidiary the profitable New York Edison Co., but it reported only dividends received from this source, not its full earnings. The unreported Edison earnings supplied the mystery and the "hidden value." To my surprise I discovered that these hush-hush figures were actually on file each year with the Public Service Commission of the state. It was a simple matter to consult the records and to present the true earnings of Consolidated Gas in a magazine article. (Incidentally, the addition to profits was not spectacular.) One of my older friends said to me then: "Ben, you may think you are a great guy to supply those missing figures, but Wall Street is going to thank you for nothing. Consolidated Gas with the mystery is both more interesting and more valuable than ex-mystery. You youngsters who want to stick your noses into everything are going to ruin Wall Street."

It is true that the three M's which then supplied so much fuel to the speculative fires have now all but disappeared. These were Mystery, Manipulation, and (thin) Margins. But we security analysts have ourselves been creating valuation approaches which are so speculative in themselves as to pretty well take the place of those older speculative factors. Do we not have our own "three M's" now—none other than Minnesota Mining and Manufacturing Co.—and does not this common stock illustrate perfectly the new speculation as contrasted with the old? Consider a few figures. When M.M. & M. common sold at 101 last year, the market was valuing it at 44 times 1956 earnings, which happened to show no increase to speak of in 1957. The enterprise itself was valued at $1.7 billion, of which $200 million was covered by net assets, and a cool $1½ billion represented the market's appraisal of "goodwill." We do not know the process of calculation by which that valuation of goodwill was arrived at; we do know that a few months later the market revised this appraisal downward by some $450 million, or about 30%. Obviously it is impossible to calculate accurately the intangible component of a splendid company such as this. It follows as a kind of mathematical law that the more important the goodwill or future earning-power factor the more uncertain becomes the true value of the enterprise, and therefore the more speculative inherently the common stock.

It may be well to recognize a vital difference that has developed in the valuation of these intangible factors, when we compare earlier times with today. A generation or more ago it was the standard rule, recognized both in average stock prices and in formal or legal valuations, that intangibles were to be appraised on a more conservative basis than tangibles. A good industrial company might be required to earn between 6% and 8% on its tangible assets, represented typically by bonds and preferred stock; but its excess earnings, or the intangible assets they gave rise to, would be valued on, say, a 15% basis. (You will find approximately these ratios in the initial offering of Woolworth Preferred and Common stock in 1911, and in numerous others.) But what has happened since the 1920s? Essentially the exact reverse of these relationships may now be seen. A company must now typically earn about 10% on its common equity to have it sell in the average market at full book value. But its excess earnings, above 10% on capital, are usually valued more liberally, or at a higher multiplier, than the base earnings required to support the book value in the market. Thus a company earning 15% on the equity may well sell at 13½ times earnings, or twice its net assets. This would mean that the first 10% earned on capital is valued at only 10 times, but the next 5%—what used to be called the excess—is actually valued at 20 times.

Now there is a logical reason for this reversal in valuation procedure, which is related to the newer emphasis on growth expectations. Companies that earn a high return on capital are given these liberal appraisals not only because of the good profitability itself, and the relative stability associated with it, but perhaps even more cogently because high earnings on capital generally go hand and hand with a good growth record and prospects. Thus what one is really paying for nowadays in the case of highly profitable companies is not the goodwill in the old and restricted sense of an established name and a profitable business, but rather for their assumed superior expectations of increased profits in the future.

This brings me to one or two additional mathematical aspects of the newer attitude toward common-stock valuations, which I shall touch on merely in the form of brief suggestions. If, as many tests show, the earnings multiplier tends to increase with profitability—i.e., as the rate of return on book value increases— then the arithmetical consequence of this feature is that value tends to increase directly as the square of the earnings, but *inversely* with book value. Thus in an important and very real sense tangible assets have become a drag on average market value rather than a source thereof. Take a far from extreme illustration. If Company A earns $4 a share on a $20 book value, and Company B also $4 a share on $100 of book value, Company A is almost certain to sell at a higher multiplier, and hence at a higher price than Company B—say $60 for Company A shares and $35 for Company B shares. Thus it would not be inexact to declare that the $80 per share of greater assets for Company B are responsible for the $25 per share lower market price, since the earnings per share are assumed to be equal.

But more important than the foregoing is the general relationship between mathematics and the newer approach to stock values. Given the three ingredients of (a) optimistic assumptions as to the rate of earnings growth, (b) a sufficiently long projection of this growth into the future, and (c) the miraculous workings of compound interest—and the security analyst is supplied with a new kind of Philosopher's Stone which can produce or justify any desired valuation for a really "good stock." I have commented in a recent article in *The Analysts Journal* on the vogue of higher mathematics in bull markets, and quoted David Durand's exposition of the striking analogy between value calculations of growth stocks and the famous St. Petersburg Paradox, which has challenged and confused mathematicians for more than 200 years. The point I want to make here is that there is a special paradox in the relationship between mathematics and investment attitudes on common stocks, which is this: Mathematics is ordinarily considered as producing precise and dependable results; but in the stock market the more elaborate and abstruse the mathematics the more uncertain and speculative are the conclusions we draw therefrom. In forty-four years of Wall Street experience and study, I have never seen dependable calculations made about common-stock values, or related investment policies, that went beyond simple arithmetic or the most elementary algebra. Whenever excalculus is brought in, or higher algebra, you could take it as a warning signal that the operator was trying to substitute theory for experience, and usually also to give to speculation the deceptive guise of investment.

The older ideas of common-stock investment may seem quite naive to the sophisticated security analyst of today. The great emphasis was always on what we now call the defensive aspects of the company or issue—mainly the assurance that it would continue its dividend unreduced in bad times. Thus the strong railroads, which constituted the standard investment commons of fifty years ago, were actually regarded in very much the same way as the public-utility commons in recent years. If the past record indicated stability, the chief requirement was met; not too much effort was made to anticipate adverse changes of an underlying character in the future. But, conversely, especially favorable future prospects were regarded by shrewd investors as something to look for but not to pay for.

In effect this meant that the investor did not have to pay anything substantial for superior long-term prospects. He got these, virtually without extra cost, as a reward for his own superior intelligence and judgment in picking the best rather than the merely good companies. For common stocks with the same financial strength, past earnings record, and dividend stability, all sold at about the same dividend yield.

This was indeed a short-sighted point of view, but it had the great advantage of making common-stock investment in the old days not only simple but also basically sound and highly profitable. Let me return for the last time to a personal note. Somewhere around 1920 our firm distributed a series of little pamphlets entitled "Lessons for Investors." Of course it took a brash analyst in his middle twenties like myself to hit on so smug and presumptuous a title. But in one of the papers I made the casual statement that "If a common stock is a good investment it is also a good speculation." For, reasoned I, if a common stock was so sound that it carried very little risk of loss it must ordinarily be so good as to possess excellent chances for future gains. Now this was a perfectly true and even valuable discovery, but it was true only because nobody paid any attention to it. Some years later, when the public woke up to the historical merits of common stocks as long-term investments, they soon ceased to have any such merit, because the public's enthusiasm created price levels which deprived them of their built-in margin of safety, and thus drove them out of the investment class. Then, of course, the pendulum swung to the other extreme, and we soon saw one of the most respected authorities declaring (in 1931) that no common stock could *ever* be an investment.

When we view this long-range experience in perspective we find another set of paradoxes in the investor's changing attitude toward capital gains as contrasted with income. It seems a truism to say that the old-time common-stock investor was not much interested in capital gains. He bought almost entirely for safety and income, and let the speculator concern himself with price appreciation. Today we are likely to say that the more experienced and shrewd the investor, the less attention he pays to dividend returns, and the more heavily his interest centers on long-term appreciation. Yet one might argue, perversely, that precisely because the old-time investor did not concentrate on future capital appreciation he was virtually guaranteeing to himself that he would have it, at least in the field of industrial stocks. And, conversely, today's investor is so concerned with anticipating the future that he is already paying handsomely for it in advance. Thus what he has projected with so much study and care may actually happen and still not bring him any profit. If it should fail to materialize to the degree expected, he may in fact be faced with a serious temporary and perhaps even permanent loss.

What *lessons*—again using the pretentious title of my 1920 pamphlets—can the analyst of 1958 learn from this linking of past with current attitudes? Not much of value, one is inclined to say. We can look back nostalgically to the good old days when we paid only for the present and could get the future for nothing—an "all this and Heaven too" combination. Shaking our heads sadly we mutter, "Those days are gone forever." Have not investors and security analysts eaten of the tree of knowledge of good and evil prospects? By so doing have they not permanently expelled themselves from that Eden where promising common stocks at reasonable prices could be plucked off the bushes? Are we not doomed always to run the risk either of paying unreasonably high prices for good quality and prospects, or of getting poor quality and prospects when we pay what seems a reasonable price?

It certainly looks that way. Yet one cannot be sure even of that pessimistic dilemma. Recently, I did a little research in the long-term history of that towering enterprise, General Electric—stimulated by the arresting chart of fifty-nine years of earnings and dividends appearing in their recently published 1957 report. These figures are not without their surprises for the knowl-edgeable analyst. For one thing they show that prior to 1947 the growth of G.E. was fairly modest and quite irregular. The 1946 earnings, per share adjusted, were only 30% higher than in 1902—52¢ vs. 40¢—and in no year of this period were the 1902 earnings as much as doubled. Yet the price-earnings ratio rose from 9 times in 1910 and 1916 to 29 times in 1936 and again in 1946. One might say, of course, that the 1946 multiplier at least showed the well-known prescience of shrewd investors. We analysts were able to foresee then the really brilliant period of growth that was looming ahead in the next decade. Maybe so. But some of you remember that the next year, 1947, which estab-lished an impressive new high for G.E.'s per share earnings, was marked also by an extraordinary fall in the price-earnings ratio. At its low of 32 (before the 3-for-1 split) G.E. actually sold again at only 9 times its current earnings, and its average price for the year was only about 10 times earnings. Our crystal ball certainly clouded over in the short space of twelve months.

This striking reversal took place only eleven years ago. It casts some little doubt in my mind as to the complete dependability of the popular belief among analysts that prominent and promising companies will now always sell at high price-earnings ratios—that this is a fundamental fact of life for investors and they may as well accept and like it. I have no desire at all to be dogmatic on this point. All I can say is that it is not settled in my mind, and each of you must seek to settle it for yourself.

But in my concluding remarks I can say something definite about the structure of the market for various types of common stocks, in terms of their investment and speculative characteristics. In the old days the investment character of a common stock was more or less the same as, or proportionate with, that of the enterprise itself, as measured quite well by its credit rating. The lower the yield on its bonds or preferred, the more likely was the common to meet all the criteria for a satisfactory investment, and the smaller the element of speculation involved in its purchase. This relationship, between the speculative ranking of the common and the investment rating of the company, could be graphically expressed pretty much as a straight line descending from left to right. But nowadays I would describe the graph as U-shaped. At the left, where the company itself is speculative and its credit low, the common stock is of course highly speculative, just as it has always been in the past. At the right extremity, however, where the company has the highest credit rating because both its past record and future prospects are most impressive, we find that the stock market tends more or less continuously to introduce a highly speculative element into the common shares through the simple means of a price so high as to carry a fair degree of risk.

At this point I cannot forbear introducing a surprisingly relevant, if quite exaggerated, quotation on the subject which I found recently in one of Shakespeare's sonnets. It reads:

"Have I not seen dwellers on form and favor
Lose all and more by paying too much rent?"

Returning to my imaginary graph, it would be the center area where the speculative element in common-stock purchases would tend to reach its minimum. In this area we could find many well-established and strong companies, with a record of past growth corresponding to that of the national economy and with future prospects apparently of the same character. Such common stocks could be bought at most times, except in the upper ranges of a bull market, at moderate prices in relation to their indicated intrinsic values. As a matter of fact, because of the present tendency of investors and speculators alike to concentrate on more glamorous issues, I should hazard the statements that these middle-ground stocks tend to sell on the whole rather below their independently determinable values. They thus have a margin-of-safety factor supplied by the same market preferences and prejudices which tend to destroy the margin of safety in the more promising issues. Furthermore, in this wide array of companies there is plenty of room for penetrating analysis of the past record and for discriminating choice in the area of future prospects, to which can be added the higher assurance of safety conferred by diversification.

When Phaethon insisted on driving the chariot of the Sun, his father, the experienced operator, gave the neophyte some advice which the latter failed to follow—to his cost. Ovid summed up Phoebus Apollo's counsel in three words:

"Medius tutissimus ibis"
"You will go safest in the middle course"

I think this principle holds good for investors and their security-analyst advisers.

8

Special Situations

The period 1939–42 was a heyday for operators in special situations and undervalued securities. During these years the trend was unfavorable to those owning standard issues, and the brokerage business also was on the quiet side. By contrast, many bargain industrial stocks scored substantial advances—especially since the early war years brought proportionately greater business improvement to the secondary companies than to the leaders. In addition, quite a number of railroad and utility reorganizations were taking shape, and developing good profits for those who had bought their issues at unpopular times and consequently at basement prices.

By 1942 many in Wall Street had come to believe that the real and dependable income was to be made in special situations. As usually happens, this generalization proved wide of the mark. In the ensuing four years there have been good profits in almost everything, and the spectacular returns have lately been shown in essentially speculative, as distinct from "special," operations. But perhaps enough interest remains in the latter type of activity to warrant an article on the subject.

The Meaning of Special Situations

First, just what is meant by a "special situation"? Convention has not jelled sufficiently to permit a clear-cut and final definition.

Reprinted from *The Analysts Journal*, vol. 2, no. 4 (Fourth Quarter 1946): 31–38 with permission.

In the broader sense, a special situation is one in which a particular development is counted upon to yield a satisfactory profit in the security even though the general market does not advance. In the narrow sense, you do not have a real "special situation" unless the particular development is already under way.

This distinction is readily apparent by reference to the wide fields of bankrupt corporations and preferred stocks with large back dividends. In the former case, "the particular development" would be reorganization; in the latter, it would be discharge of the arrears, usually by a recapitalization. Many practitioners will say that a company in trusteeship does not constitute a special situation until a reorganization plan has actually been submitted; similarly, there must be a definite plan on foot for taking care of dividend accumulations. Thus, American Woolen Preferred may have had interesting possibilities for years because of its very large back dividends, but it became a true special situation only when the buyer knew that a plan of repayment had been or was soon to be announced.

There is a logical and important reason for favoring this narrower definition of a special situation. By doing so we are able to conceive of these commitments in terms of an expected annual return on the investment. As will be seen, such a calculation involves quite a number of estimates in each case, and thus the final figure bears little resemblance to the bond yields taken out of a basis book. Nevertheless, this technique is valuable as a guide to the operator in special situations, and it gives him an entirely different attitude toward his holdings than that of the trader, speculator, or ordinary investor.

In one respect, however, the calculation goes beyond the lore of the yield book. If we are willing to make the necessary assumptions, the attractiveness of any given special situation can be expressed as an indicated annual return in percent *with allowance for the risk factor*. Here is the general formula:

Let   **G** be the expected gain in points in the event of
        success;

        L be the expected loss in points in the event of
        failure;

        C be the expected chance of success, expressed
        as a percentage;

        Y be the expected time of holding, in years;

        P be the expected current price of the security.

Then:

$$\text{Indicated annual return} = \frac{G\,C - L(100 - C)}{Y\,P}$$

We may take as a current example the Metropolitan West Side Elevated 5s selling at 23. It is proposed to sell the property to the City of Chicago on terms expected to yield in cash about 35 for the bonds. For illustrative purposes only (and without responsibility) let us assume (a) that if the plan fails the bonds will be worth 16; (b) that the chances of success are two out of three—i.e., 67%; (c) that the holding period will average one year.

Then by the formula:

$$\text{Indicated annual return} = \frac{12 \times 67 - 7 \times 33}{1 \times 23} = 24.7\%$$

Note that the formula allows for the chance and the amount of possible loss. If only possible gain were considered, the indicated annual return would be 34½%.

Classes of Special Situations

Let us turn now to a condensed description and discussion of the various types of special situations. These could be divided into two main categories: (I) Security exchanges or distributions, (II) Cash payouts. Only in a rare case does a special situation, as we use the term, work itself out in a higher market without a cash or security distribution occurring somewhere in the picture. However, a more conventional classification may better serve our present purpose.

Class A: Standard Arbitrages, Based on a Reorganization, Recapitalization, or Merger Plan

In bankruptcy reorganizations, particularly those of railroads, the operation consists of buying old and selling "when-issued" securities. Railroad arbitrage has had a curious history in the past five years. In more than half of the cases the plans have been consummated and the expected profit realized—although almost always after a longer time lag than was originally anticipated. In the remainder the plans have been changed or dropped and the when-issued trades cancelled; or else such cancellation is now expected, chiefly as a result of the Wheeler Bill. Nevertheless, large profits were made by many arbitragers, even in the unsuccessful plans, because the old securities advanced greatly above the price they paid, in spite of the plan's failure. Thus what was intended to be an old-fashioned arbitrage turned into a successful bond speculation.

This experience illustrates one pleasing aspect of the special situation operation, which is that if your deal works out you are sure to make a profit, but if it doesn't, you may still make a profit. The hazards of arbitraging increase as the general market level rises, because your chances of loss in the event of the plan's failure become correspondingly greater. To this important extent many types of special situations are tied in with general market conditions; but it is still true that in the average or representative case the result depends upon corporate and not on market price developments.

Arbitrages in industrials generally grow out of mergers or recapitalizations and involve the sale of existing rather than when-issued securities. In the recent Raytheon-Submarine Signal merger, one could buy Submarine Signal and sell Raytheon on announcement at an indicated spread of about 18%. That arbitrage was successfully consummated within sixty days. Similarly, when the General Cable Recapitalization Plan was announced, one could buy a share of A stock at 52 and sell four shares of common for 59—a spread of about 13%—with consummation in forty-five days. However, such operations have as a prerequisite the ability to borrow the stock for the duration of the arbitrage. Under present conditions of no margin trading, such borrowing is so difficult as to prevent many (though not all) of these deals.

In the utility field, somewhat similar arbitrages have been available as a result of exchange offers made by holding companies for their preferred stocks. Recent examples are United Corporation and American Superpower.

There are, of course, various hazards involved in all these arbitrages. They include possible rejection by stockholders; possible legal action by minority holders; possible disapproval by the. S.E.C., etc. The experienced operator does not ignore these hazards, but attempts to measure them carefully in the particular circumstances of each case.

It will be noted that the industrial, utility, and rail arbitrages fall respectively into three distinct classes with regard to the time element. One might almost say that the first is usually a matter of weeks, the second of months, and the third of years.

An exception to this rule was the United Light & Power arbitrage. Here one bought a share of old preferred and sold five shares of new common when issued against it, at an initial spread of about 10% net. Because of litigation that reached the Supreme Court, this utility recapitalization took fully two years between proposal and consummation. Though it yielded the expected profit in dollars, the time element made the outcome far from brilliant.

Class B: Cash Payouts, in Recapitalizations or Mergers

A recent example of this type is Central and Southwestern Utilities 2nd Preferred. Under a recapitalization and merger plan, presented to the S.E.C. on Feb. 5, 1946, the holders were given the option of taking the full redemption value in cash or the equivalent in new common stock at the syndicate offering price. The current redemption value was $220 per share, against the market price of 185. Thus the expected profit would be 19%, plus interest at about 3% per annum for the duration of the operation. The hurdles to be surmounted here include (a) S.E.C. approval; (b) court approval; (c) ability to secure an underwriting of new common stock at a specified minimum price; (d) miscellaneous delays, most frequently caused by litigation. If the plan should fail, the buyer risks a fall in the price of his shares; but contrariwise in the typical preferred stock or bond payout, there is virtually no chance of getting more than the redemption value accorded under the plan. We must recognize here an inherent weakness in this type of operation.

The experienced analyst knows that the chance of ultimate loss diminishes to the extent that the preferred stock is cushioned by the presence of a proportionately large common-stock equity. Thus he should feel differently as regards Cities Service 1st Preferred selling at 132, with total claim of 181 (or 193 at call price), as compared with American Power & Light $6 Preferred selling at 117 with a total claim of 145 (or 160 at call price). The maximum indicated gain for Cities Service Preferred is 46%, against 37% for American P. & L. Preferred. The latter, however, has the advantage, first, of paying a current dividend ($4.50) and, second, of having an actual plan on file for paying off the issue. On the other side of the picture is the important fact that each dollar paid for Cities Service Preferred is now (October 5th) backed by $1.20 in market value of common stock; while each dollar paid American P. & L. Preferred is backed by only 20 cents of common stock. If continued weakness in the stock market should result in the definite postponement of the American P. & L. plan, the purchaser of Cities Service Preferred will undoubtedly fare the better of the two.

Class C: Cash Payments on Sale or Liquidation

In most cases where a company sells out its business to another or merely liquidates its assets piecemeal, the ultimate amount received by the security holder exceeds the market price at the time the sale or liquidation is proposed. (This condition grows out of the nature of the price making factors in the security market; we do not have space to discuss the reasons in detail.) In the case of a sale for cash on a going concern basis, the large profits are most often to be made by those who buy before the negotiations are begun or completed. But even after the terms are announced, there is often an interesting spread to be realized if the sale is consummated.

Quite a number of such sales have recently taken place in the textile-mill field. At this time the most recent example is a bid of $365 per share for stock of the Luther Mfg. Co., contingent on acceptance by not less than 95% of the stock. A week before the purchase offer was made public, the stock was quoted at $150 bid. Most of these purchase offers, even though contingent on acceptance by a large majority, have become effective; and those which failed generally did so because a still higher bid was forthcoming from other quarters.

A vote to liquidate assets by piecemeal sale is rather infrequent, except that we have had a number of such liquidations of public utility holding companies under statutory pressure. In such cases the amount of cash to be realized for the assets, less the corporate liabilities and expenses, is subject to estimation and consequent error. Where estimates are made by the management, they are customarily on the conservative side. In most instances, the market price at the time of the vote to liquidate proves to be appreciably less than the amount recovered. A protracted liquidation of this kind has been under way in Ogden Corp., showing a very good percentage profit for those who bought at an early stage. Brewster Corp. is an example in the industrial field. At this writing the tax liabilities of Brewster have not been determined. As against a stated book value of 5 and a market price of about 4¼, the current "expert" estimate of ultimate realization ranges between 5½ and 6.

Class D: Litigated Matters

There are fairly numerous cases in which the value of a security depends largely on the outcome of litigation. This may involve a damage or subordination suit (e.g., International Hydro Electric, Inland Gas Co.); disputed income tax liability (e.g., Gold and Stock Telegraph, Pittsburgh Incline Plane); an appeal from a reorganization plan wiping out stock issues (e.g., St. Louis Southwestern Ry., New Haven R. R.). In general, the market undervalues a litigated claim as an asset and overvalues it as a liability. Hence the students of these situations often have an opportunity to buy into them at less than their true value, and to realize attractive profits—on the average—when the litigation is disposed of.

Class E: Public Utility Breakups

These have been a very important group of special situations in recent years. They are an essentially temporary phenomenon in that they will pass out of the picture when compliance with Section 11 of the Public Utility Holding Company Act has been completed for the industry.

Their unique feature is that the profit in them depends upon the principle that a holding company is worth more dead than alive—i.e., that its separate assets, net, will sell for more than the parent company securities. This has brought about the paradoxical situation that the stocks of holding companies bitterly fighting dissolution—presumably for the sake of their owners, the shareholders—have been depressed in price by this valiant battle and have advanced when they lost their fight.

The technical quality which sets these situations apart from others is the fact that they usually depend upon an estimate or forecast of the market value of securities which are to be distributed and are not now traded in. In some cases there is a narrow market for existing minority shares, but it may not be too informing in relation to conditions after the majority shares come on the market. (An example of this is Philadelphia Co., which is the central factor in the valuation of Standard Gas and Electric Preferred issues. The curb-market price for the 3.2% minority interest may or may not be representative of the value of the entire issue.)

Improvement in the art of utility analysis, favored by the relative infrequency of unlooked for developments in the field, makes it possible to calculate fairly dependably what any operating company stock is likely to sell at under current market conditions. Thus the hazard in exploiting these breakup situations grows largely out of the uncertain time element, with the attendant possibility of an unfavorable change in market conditions before the distributions are received.

Class F: Miscellaneous Special Situations

This catch-all category includes everything we have not already classified. There is no point in trying to make our descriptions comprehensive since a good deal depends on one's personal definition of "special situation." We may suggest two additional varieties by way of example only. A peculiar one would be the rather major field of hedging operations—most characteristically the sale of a common stock against ownership of a convertible bond or preferred stock. (Here the security-exchange feature operates to protect against loss rather than to create the profit.) Another, more limited, would be the purchase of a guaranteed security on the expectation that it will later be made exchangeable into a bond on attractive terms, in order to save a heavy corporate income tax. (This occurred in the case of Delaware and Hudson and D. L. & W. leased-line stocks.)

Conclusion

At the outset of this article we grouped special situations and undervalued securities together. The reader will have noticed that we do not consider these terms as synonymous—although it may be held that special situations constitute a major subdivision of undervalued securities. The essence of a special situation is an expected corporate (not market) development within a time period estimable in the light of past experience. Thus here, as almost everywhere else in finance, wide experience is a major factor in lasting success; it must be supplemented by careful study of each situation and the possession of sound though somewhat specialized judgment.

Special situations, as we define them, appeal mightily to one class of temperament for the very reason that they leave other people cold. They lack industrial glamour, speculative dynamite, or more sober growth prospects. But they do afford the analyst an opportunity to deal with security values very much as the merchant deals with his inventory, calculating in advance his average profits and his average holding period. In this sense they occupy an interesting middle ground between security purchases for ordinary speculation or investment and security purchases for resale in syndicate or dealership operations.

9

Some Investment Aspects of
Accumulation through Equities

I

The terms of reference for this paper relate to systematic plans for saving or accumulation through common stocks. Such plans might include (a) a pension plan concentrating on equities, such as the CREF arrangement for college professors; (b) the very similar mechanics of the newly developing variable annuities; (c) systematic purchases of mutual-fund or closed-end investment company shares; and (d) an individual dollar-averaging plan, such as the monthly purchase program of the New York Stock Exchange.

The chairman has asked me to consider investment aspects of such plans in longer perspective and to give my views on the following questions: What results can be expected from them in the future as compared with the results either of the shorter-term past—i.e., since 1949—or of the longer-term past, going back into the last century and farther? How good will common stocks be as an inflation hedge in the future? Can dollar-averaging be counted on infallibly to produce satisfactory results? More specifically, can the much better performance of common stocks as against bonds be counted on to repeat itself in the next fifteen years?

© American Finance Association. Reprinted from *The Journal of Finance*, vol. 17, no. 2 (May 1962): 203–214 with permission.

I shall leave the chances and the effects of atomic war out of the following discussion, except for some observations regarding the indefinite continuance of the Cold War. Which of the two past periods will the future stock market resemble more closely— that of 1949–61 or that of, say, 1871–1961?

The latter comprises the ninety years for which we have common-stock indexes of earnings, dividends, and prices, as compiled first by the Cowles Commission and then continued by Standard & Poor's. In discussing equity experience in terms of the future behavior of these indexes, we are assuming that the various equity-accumulation plans within our purview are likely to show results, in the aggregate, approximating those of the S&P Composite or 500-Stock Index. It would seem easy enough to equal these average results; all that is needed is a representative diversification "across the board" and without that selectivity which is a watchword of today. But, paradoxically, if it is easy to equal the averages, it seems almost impossible for the average skilled investor to beat them.

We have very full information regarding the operations and achievements of the investment funds. For the 1949–60 period, as in the earlier years, they have not managed as a group to outperform the S&P 500-Stock Composite. It may be that professionally managed funds are too large a part of the total picture to be able to outperform the market as a whole; it may also be true, as I suspect, that certain weaknesses in their basic principles of stock selection tend to offset the superior training, intelligence, and effort that they bring to this task. But our main point is to establish that what happens to the stock market in general is going to happen to the typical or average accumulator of equities by any plan or under any auspices.

Let us attempt to summarize briefly the chief characteristics of the two market periods to which we are turning for clues to the future and among which we may have to choose. Table 1

Table 1*

A Picture of Stock-Market Performance, 1871–1960 and 1947–61

Period	Average Price	Average Earnings	Average P/E Ratio	Average Dividend	Average Yield (Percent)	Average Payout (Percent)	Annual Growth Rate** Earnings (Percent)	Dividend (Percent)
1871–80	3.58	0.32	11.3×	0.21	6.0	67	....	....
1881–90	5.00	0.32	15.6	0.24	4.7	75	−0.64	−0.66
1891–1900	4.65	0.30	15.5	0.19	4.0	64	−1.04	−2.23
1901–10	8.32	0.63	13.1	0.35	4.2	58	+6.91	+5.33
1911–20	8.62	0.86	10.0	0.50	5.8	58	+3.85	+3.94
1921–30	13.89	1.05	13.3	0.71	5.1	68	+2.84	+2.29
1931–40	11.55	0.68	17.0	0.78	5.1	85	−2.15	−0.23
1941–50	13.90	1.46	9.5	0.87	6.3	60	+10.60	+3.25
1951–60	39.20	3.00	13.1	1.63	4.2	54	+6.74	+5.90
1951	22.34	2.45	9.1	1.41	6.3	58	....	....
1961(H)	72.20	3.10	23.2	1.97	2.7	64	+2.5	+3.5
1947–49	15.71	2.18	7.1	0.97	6.4	45	....	....
1953–55	31.64	3.02	10.1	1.51	4.8	50	+5.7	+7.8
1959–61	59.70	3.24	18.3	1.91	3.2	58	+3.5	+5.9

* The above data are based largely on figures appearing in N. Molodovsky's article "Stock Values and Stock Prices," Financial Analysts Journal, May, 1960. These, in turn, are taken from the Cowles Commission book Common Stock Indexes for years before 1926 and from the spliced-on Standard & Poor's 500-Stock Composite Index for 1926 to date.

** The annual growth-rate figures are Molodovsky compilations covering successive twenty-one-year periods ending in 1890, 1900, etc. The lower growth-rate figures cover the ten years ended 1961, the six years ended 1953–55, and the twelve years ended 1959–61. The 1961 price is the high to December 7.

gives some data covering the three salient factors of earnings, dividends, and price behavior. We bring down the 1949–61 period into two six-year halves. The longer span can be handled in a variety of ways; we have decided to supply average computations for each of the nine decades between 1871 and 1961.

A cursory study of our table shows a number of striking differences between the exhibits of the two periods. Molodovsky has demonstrated that the overall gain to investors for the eighty-eight years, 1871–1959, has averaged about 5% per annum in dividend return and 2½% per annum in price appreciation—both taken against annual market prices. The 2½% annual increase, compounded, in market price was closely paralleled by the annual rate of growth in both earnings and dividends.[1]

But between 1947–49 and 1959–61 the growth rates for the various components have been quite diverse, and they have also varied sharply between the first and the second halves of the period. Thus we get very different indications of recent performance if we consider earnings rather than market price and if we consider the last six years rather than the last twelve.

The behavior of the stock market itself has been significantly different in the last twelve years from any previous period of equal length covered by our records. We have experienced what appears to be a single bull market, beginning at 13.55 for the composite index and rising to a current high of 72. The advance has been interrupted by three recessions, each on the order of some 20%. Under the usual terminology, these would be characterized as corrections or setbacks within a bull market.

As is well known, the long-term history of the stock market has been completely different. The picture, shown in Table 2, is one of a succession of bull and bear markets of varying duration and amplitude. Between 1899 and 1949 there were ten such well-defined cycles, thus averaging five years in length. (The longest period between peaks was ten years, from 1919 to 1929, and the shortest was two years, from 1899 to 1901 and from 1937 to 1939.) Most of the declines in the industrial averages were in the range of 40% to 50%; in the earlier years the composite average had somewhat smaller losses. The largest, of course, was the shocking fall of the Composite Index from 31.92 in 1929 to a low of only 4.40 in 1932, a loss of 86%. About the same proportionate decline was shown by the Dow Jones Industrial Average.

It should be pointed out also that the gyrations of past stock markets may not properly be viewed as taking place around a well-defined and persistent upward trend line, sloped at 2½% per annum. Both the price record and the earnings record disclose an irregular, rather than a regular, trend line. This should be evident from an inspection of our successive ten-year average figures between 1871 and 1950 and the Molodovsky growth rates appended thereto.

Table 2

Major Stock-Market Swings between 1871 and 1949

Year	Cowles-Standard 500-Composite			Dow Jones Industrial Average		
	High	Low	Percent Decline	High	Low	Percent Decline
1871	....	4.74	....	....	....	....
1881	6.58	....	....	....	....	....
1885	....	4.24	28	....	....	....
1887	5.90	....	....	....	....	....
1893	....	4.08	31	....	....	....
1897	....	....	....	....	38.85	....
1899	....	....	....	77.6	....	....
1900	....	....	....	....	53.5	31
1901	8.50	....	....	78.3	....	....
1903	....	6.26	26	....	43.2	45
1906	10.03	....	....	103	....	....
1907	....	6.25	38	....	53	48
1909	10.30	....	....	100.5	....	....
1914	....	7.35	29	....	53.2	47
1916	10.21	....	....	110.2	....	....
1917/8	....	6.80	33	....	73.4	33
1919	9.51	....	....	119.6	....	....
1921	....	6.45	32	....	63.9	47
1929	31.92	....	....	381	....	....
1932	....	4.40	86	....	41.2	89
1937	18.68	....	....	197.4	....	....
1938	....	8.50	55	....	99	50
1939	13.23	....	....	158	....	....
1942	....	7.47	44	....	92.9	41
1946	19.25	....	....	212.5	....	....
1949	....	13.55	30	....	161.2	24

The price-earnings ratio has also shown wide fluctuations. Since earnings have been even more unstable than prices—because of the recurrent business cycles—there has been a clear-cut tendency for the highest earnings multipliers to be established in years of depression, when profits tended toward the vanishing point. Our average figures by decades smooth out this type of variation; but they do not show the upward trend in price-earnings ratios that we might have expected to accompany improvement in the underlying strength of our corporations and in the dependability of published earnings figures. Actually, the ratio of 6.2 times for 1949–50, at the beginning of the present bull market, was the lowest for any two-year period in our ninety-year history of stock prices and earnings. A devotee of the pendulum-swing theory of economic phenomena might well explain the current record-high multiplier as a reaction to the opposite extreme from the 1949–50 depreciation of the earnings dollar.

II

With these two quite diverse stock-market pictures before us, let us now inquire what are the respective arguments for considering the 1949–61 period as an integral continuation of the 1871–1949 span or for recognizing it as a new dispensation which will determine the character of the markets of the future. It is not too difficult for the student to fit the pattern of the recent market into that of the longer past. True, both the duration and the extent of its rise are already greater than those of any other.[2] But that a pattern of many decades should establish new records of various kinds from time to time is only to be expected. A new record does not create a new pattern or character.

Is it possible, then, that we are living through a modified, but not essentially different, version of the experience of the 1920s?

That there must be impressive differences goes without saying; for otherwise all of us would have been so struck by the incipient similarity as to make its continuation impossible. What may be more likely–speaking in abstract terms–is that the original differences have convinced us that the 1929 experience is irrelevant but that the similarities have been developing later, gradually, and so insidiously as to find us psychologically incapable of recognizing them. Let us attempt an enumeration of the major differences and resemblances between the current market and that of the 1920s, as they appear to this observer.

The two major internal differences relate to financial manipulation of various sorts and to excessive borrowing for speculation. The bull-market heights of 1929 were made possible by a huge wave of buying on thinner margins than are now permitted. Brokers' loans rose from $2.769 million in 1926 to $8.549 million in 1929, at which time they constituted about half of total member-bank loans. By contrast, the corresponding rise to date has been relatively much smaller. (Borrowings on smaller margins through other sources are no doubt significant at present but not sufficiently so to change the broad picture.) In the field of financial practices, the major abuses of the 1920s consisted of crass manipulation of stock prices by speculative pools and of corporate pyramiding through successive tiers of holding companies of various types. Both stock-market manipulation and corporate-structure manipulation have been greatly restricted by the S.E.C. legislation and by tighter stock-exchange supervision. The amount that escapes detection is comparatively small, in my view. Although the various investigations now under way produce some startling exposés, whatever abuses now exist will not be found to have permeated the whole fabric of finance as was the case thirty years ago.

An exception to the above reassuring statement may have to be made in the field of new offerings of common stocks. Here I think a set of at least semi-manipulative practices has developed in handling so-called hot issues. The number of such offerings has been increasing steadily in the last two years, and their quality has been retrogressing at an equal rate. It is in this speculative area that I sense the closest parallel between the internal market conditions of the late 1920s (and particularly of 1919) and those of today. Whether the new-issue financing of dubious merit will prove to be so heavy in aggregate dollars as ultimately to turn the market scales definitely downward, I shall not venture to guess. It is not impossible.

The widespread belief that we are in a new stock-market era, differing in its essential character from the bull-and-bear sequences of the past, rests on a number of claimed differences between then and now. These go well beyond the reforms in stock trading and in corporate financial practices. The case to justify the present unprecedented level of stock prices and earnings multipliers is essentially that which would justify the concept of a permanently changed character and future for the stock market. The safety and attractiveness of common-stock investment today is thought to be solidly grounded on a complex of favorable factors. Among them are (a) assured growth of population and GNP; (b) a rate of expansion more rapid than formerly, created by technological progress and the rivalry with Russia; (c) an assurance against major depressions provided by the government's new responsibility to prevent or quickly terminate them; (d) the public's recognition that common-stock investment is a necessary protection against continued inflation; and (e) the emergence of mutual funds, pension trusts, and other institutional investors as the chief source of demand and continuous support for common stocks.

Those who study the record of the 1920s will find that reasons similar to most, but not all, of the above were advanced to justify the ill-fated market rise of those years. The doctrine of "Common

Stocks as (the Best) Long-Term Investments" emerged in 1924 and was made the cornerstone of the market's philosophy and its excesses. There was the same optimism about the future growth of the country and perhaps a better-founded confidence in the share of common-stock earnings in that growth. (The rate of return on invested capital was better maintained between 1922 and 1929 than between 1950 and 1961.) Old standards of value—particularly the once normal relationship between bond yields and common-stock yields—were thrown aside then as now, on the grounds that they had no relevance to the new economic climate. There was great confidence, also, in the future stability of business and its immunity from severe depressions. This was founded on the idea that scientific management, careful control of inventories, the absence of inflation, and other factors would help our business leaders avoid the costly mistakes of the past.

In my view, there are three major differences between the economic realities of the 1920s and the present. The first relates to the inflation factor, the second to the Cold War, and the third to the role of government in business. The bull market of the 1920s ran its course without the aid of commodity-price inflation; the market rise since 1949 has been accompanied by an irregular, but virtually continuous, advance in wholesale and consumer prices. It is difficult to say whether the investor's current emphasis on future inflation possibilities should be considered primarily as a recognition on his part of objective fact or rather as a strong *subjective* reaction to an element that is by no means new to the financial scene. We had more inflation in wholesale prices from 1900 to 1910 than from 1950 to 1960; the rise from 1900 to 1920 also exceeded that from 1940 to 1960 (the equivalent of from 36 to 100 versus from 51 to 120). Most of us believe that inflation is the path of least resistance for governments, labor leaders, and business heads and that hence it will be followed. But the record of the past will not help us much to determine what the amount of inflation will be over future decades, whether its course will be regular or interspersed with sharp deflations, as in 1921 and 1932, and whether investors will remain as inflation-conscious in the future as they are today. The reaction to inflation, like almost every other investment and speculative attitude, seems to be more the result of the stock market's behavior than the cause of it.

My view of the effects of the Cold War on common-stock values is quite a personal one, not shared by many, I am sure. In the first place, I think that it has contributed a good deal to the business expansion and relative stability of the past decade. But, in a contrary sense, I cannot see how the kind of Cold War we are now living through can continue throughout "our lifetime and that of our children." Sometime within the present decade, a way will have to be found to terminate the Cold War, or it will be transformed into large-scale hostilities, with all their nuclear implications. If our prosperity since 1949 has, in fact, rested rather heavily on our defense expenditures and if, in truth, we must fairly soon have either no war or nuclear war in place of Cold War, then today's international situation cannot be termed more favorable for common stocks than the cloudless one of 1929.

The government's commitment to prevent large-scale unemployment and serious depressions is both a new factor and one of major importance. The most logical reason for expecting a different kind of stock-market cycle in the future than in the long-term past would appear to be by analogy with the business cycle. The record since 1949 strongly supports this thesis. The new material on "Business Cycle Developments," now available monthly, shows four periods of business contraction since 1948—in 1949, 1953–54, 1957–58, and 1960. All these were very moderate, as compared with the sharp recession of 1937–38 and the major depressions after 1919 and 1929. The three declines of about 20% each in the stock averages since 1950 appear to correspond fairly well to the three setbacks of about 10% in the index of industrial production. If we have now entered a new era that excludes old-time business depressions, it seems reasonable to deduce that we are also in a new era that precludes old-fashioned bear markets.

III

Both my analysis and my instinct warn me that there may be a catch in this plausible and reassuring parallel. If the recent picture had been one of the stock market's advancing in step with the national product and in close proportion with it also, then the observer might conclude—somewhat to his amazement—that not only has the economy been reformed but human nature as well. But here the facts part company with the hypothesis. The stock-market level has not been governed primarily by the level of business but rather by the development of new investment theories and attitudes and by a typical growth of speculative interest and activity. Some of the old financial abuses that characterized former bull markets have, indeed, been virtually eliminated. But some have again raised their heads, and some new ones have appeared and are spreading apace. These are in the areas of corporate reporting, corporate financing, the quality of the enterprises offered for public sale, and the ways in which new issues of common stocks are offered and subsequently traded.

Equally important and dangerous, in my eyes, is the ready acceptance by security analysts of the going market levels and earnings-multipliers as the proper standard of value and of comparison for any issue under study. The new analytical concepts of growth-stock valuation, of "cash flow," of the desirability of tax-free dividends from companies which are triumphantly able to report earnings *deficits*—all have enough plausibility

and lack of inner discipline to lead both investors and speculators far astray. In sum, the new investment theories and techniques remind me very much of 1928–29, and the outpouring of
common-stock issues of secondary and lower-degree enterprises
reminds me equally of 1919. If the relative stability of general
business and corporate profits produces an unlimited enthusiasm
and demand for common stocks, then it must eventually produce
instability in stock prices. We have already seen the working of
this paradox in the area of growth stocks. The price of a successful and promising concern such as Texas Instruments can be
driven up so high by speculative emphasis on its prospects that the
ensuing reaction has cut the price in half—with no change in the
underlying worth of the business. Examples of this sort are now
numerous. Conceivably, this behavior of issues in the growth-
stock class may give us a preview of the ultimate behavior of the
general market—as represented by comprehensive averages—if
common-stock investment becomes essentially identical with
common-stock speculation. In that case the stock market will
have a life-cycle of its own, quite independent of the business
cycle. The market cycle will once more prove to be the human-
nature cycle; its economic background will have changed but not
its basic character or the consequences of its character.

These arguments against a new character for the stock market
are not necessarily arguments that the present levels are too high,
although they certainly would be adjudged so by older standards.
Conceivably and even probably, new factors in the economic
figure have moved upward the central value of the average dollar
of corporate earnings and justify a more favorable relationship
than heretofore between stock yields and bond yields. This would
certainly be true if the general business picture can be counted
on to continue indefinitely the relative immunity to depression
it has shown since as far back as 1941. What we are concerned
with here is not the future central value of the stock market but

rather the amplitude and the consequences of possible future variations around this value.

To soften a possible charge of old-fogyism and prejudice against new standards of value, may I take this paragraph to show how the recent record level of stock prices may be justified by some not implausible calculations. Let us assume that the investor wants an overall return of 7½% annually, as a composite of dividend income and average market appreciation. (This 7½% target is itself taken from the long-term record of dividend yields and price advances; it seems reasonable as a guide to the future.) Assume, next, that earnings and dividends will grow in the indefinite future at the annual rate of 4½%, which appears to be the projection for this decade. Then the investor should be satisfied with a 3% dividend return. This would justify a current level of 65 for the S&P Composite, only 10% below the recent high. A small adjustment here or there would put us over the top.

It is by no means impossible to assume a permanent growth rate of 4½%; we have been told that we must increase our GNP faster than this or lose out in the race with Russia. The basic objection is that it is only an assumption, that the experience of the longer past puts the figure rather at 2½% and that the difference between 4½% and 2½% in this calculation means the difference between 65 and 39 for the value of the S&P Composite. My experience leads me to predict that the action of the market will govern the investor's choice as to probable future growth rates rather than vice versa.

This completes my case for and against a new era and character for the stock market. If the market since 1949 foreshadows the stock markets of the future, the investment aspects of equity accumulation are unbelievably favorable. All that will be needed will be the funds to buy a representative assortment of common stocks and a little patience to sit through periods of mild reaction.

The annually compounded rate of overall return from the 500-Stock Composite has been about 13%—curiously enough, this has been about the same as the average from a selected list of growth stocks.[3] A much lower annual rate, without severe interruptions, will prove amply rewarding.

IV

But if, as I deem more likely, the fundamental character of the stock market must be as unchanging as that of human nature, then the accumulator of equities who starts today is faced with quite a different prospect. The new appearance of the variable annuity suggests a broad analogy with the 1920s. It was during that bull market that investment trusts had their first important development in this country. Most of the arguments in their favor were the same as those now used for the sale of mutual-fund shares and for equity accumulation in general. The collapse of 1929 resulted in a severe and protracted setback for the investment-trust movement, as part of a widespread loss of faith in common stocks generally. It is true that many—although perhaps less than half—managed to survive the bitter subsequent experience and to reestablish themselves more firmly than before in public esteem. Furthermore, the principle of dollar-cost averaging—which is the most systematic of the equity-accumulation techniques—was able to vindicate itself in the end, after perhaps twenty years of unsatisfactory-to-mediocre results.[4]

The computations made of theoretical dollar-averaging experience in the past embolden us to predict that such a policy will pay off ultimately, regardless of when it is begun, *provided* that it is adhered to conscientiously and courageously under all intervening conditions. This is by no means a minor proviso. It presupposes that the dollar-cost-averager will be a different sort of person from the rest of us, that he will not be subject to the alternations of exhilaration and deep gloom that have accompanied the gyrations of the stock market for generations past. This, I greatly doubt—particularly because most of the dollar-cost-averagers we are speaking of will be typical members of the public who have been persuaded to embark on an equity-accumulation program by the arts of salesmanship now so highly developed in the mutual-fund field.

Let me return once again to the problem of the proper perspective for viewing the character of the stock market and the investment aspects of equity accumulation. At the outset I presented a statistical comparison of the market's behavior over the last twelve years and over the last ninety years. But our knowledge of stock-market behavior goes back a good deal more than ninety years—a full two centuries and a half, in fact, to the inception of the South Sea Company in 1711. In our first edition of *Security Analysis,* published in 1934, we characterized the stock-market madness of the 1920s as a repetition or rerun of the famous South Sea Bubble. By comparison, the behavior of our present market appears more rational, dignified, and reassuring. No one today, not even ingrained conservatives (like this speaker), expects consequences to this market and the economy even faintly resembling the catastrophe of 1929–32. Yet I have a feeling that the financial world has become too complacent about the future, too confident of the invulnerability of common stocks as a whole to a drastic change in their fortunes.

A great corporation can withstand great vicissitudes; the same is true of great institutions, among which not the least important is common-stock investment and equity accumulation over a span of time. But a bull market has never become a financial institution, and I have great doubts whether this attractive development is an admissible possibility, when the frailty of human nature is taken into account.

My own inward picture of the present stock market is that of an institution cut adrift from old standards of value without having found dependable new standards. (In this respect present-day investment may be in somewhat the same position as present-day painting.) The market may either return to the old measures of central value or—as is perhaps more probable—eventually establish a new and more liberal basis for evaluating equities. If the first happens, common stocks will prove highly disappointing over a long period for many accumulators of equities. If the newer and higher value levels are to be established on a sound basis, I envisage this working out by a process of trial and error, covering an unpredictable period of time and a number of pendulum swings of unforeseeable magnitude. I do not know whether bonds will do better than stocks over the next fifteen years, but I do know that the people behind College Retirement Equity Fund (CREF) are eminently wise in insisting that its beneficiaries have at least an equal dollar stake in bond as in stock investment.

NOTES

1. See N. Molodovsky, "Stock Values and Stock Prices," *Financial Analysts Journal,* March, 1960.
2. These statements refer to the S&P Composite Index. The percentage rise in the industrials was somewhat larger from 1921 to 1929 than from 1949 to date, because it started from a relatively lower level.
3. See, for example, J. F. Bohmfalk, Jr., "The Growth Stock Philosophy," *Financial Analysts Journal,* November, 1960, Table A.
4. For calculated results of dollar-cost-averaging results for ten-year periods ending from 1929 through 1952, see Lucile Tomlinson, *Practical Formulas for Successful Investing* (New York: Wilfred Funk, 1953), Table 3, p. 62.

10

Inflated Treasuries and Deflated Stockholders: Are Corporations Milking Their Owners?

Selling America for 50 Cents on the Dollar

More than one-third of all industrial stocks are selling in the open market for less than the companies' net quick assets.

Scores of common stocks are selling for less than their pro rata of cash in the company's treasury.

Corporations who are good risks for commercial loans do not need to borrow. They still have large unused cash balances furnished by their stockholders in the New Era days.

Corporation treasurers sleep soundly while stockholders walk the floor.

Banks no longer lend directly to big corporations. They lend to stockholders who have overfinanced the companies through rights to buy stock at inflated prices.

What are the responsibilities of the corporation, its directors, its stockholders? What is the proper way out? Are stockholders part-owners of their companies, or just suckers?

Shall companies reverse the 1929 method—give the stockholder rights to sell back the stock he bought, reduce capitaliza-

This article is part one of a three-part series titled Is American Business Worth More Dead Than Alive? Reprinted by permission of Forbes Media LLC © 1932. Reprinted from *Forbes* (June 1, 1932).

tion, and equalize the burden between the corporations and the stockholder?

If market quotations discount huge cash reserves due to probable long-continued future losses then should not the stockholder demand liquidation before his money is thus dissipated?

Are corporations playing fair with their stockholders?

Suppose you were the owner of a large manufacturing business. Like many others, you lost money in 1931; the immediate prospects are not encouraging; you feel pessimistic and willing to sell out—*cheap*. A prospective purchaser asks you for your statement. You show him a very healthy balance sheet, indeed. It shapes up something like this:

Cash and U. S. Gov. Bonds	$ 8,500,000
Receivables and Merchandise	15,000,000
Factories, Real Estate, etc.	14,000,000
	$37,500,000
Less owing for current accounts	1,300,000
Net Worth	$36,200,000

The purchaser looks it over casually, and then makes you a bid of $5 million for your business—the cash, Liberty Bonds, and everything else included. Would you sell? The question seems like a joke, we admit. No one in his right mind would exchange $8.5 million in cash for $5 million, to say nothing of the $28 million more in other assets. But preposterous as such a transaction sounds, the many owners of White Motors stock who sold out between $7 and $8 per share did that very thing—or as close to it as they could come.

The figures given above represent White Motors' condition on December 31 last. At $7.37 per share, the low price, the company's 650,000 shares were selling for $4.8 million—about 60% of the cash and equivalent alone, and only *one-fifth of the net quick assets*. There were no capital obligations ahead of the common stock, and the only liabilities were those shown above for current accounts payable.

The spectacle of a large and old established company selling in the market for such a small fraction of its quick assets is undoubtedly a startling one.

But the picture becomes more impressive when we observe that there are literally dozens of other companies which also have a quoted value less than their cash in bank. And more significant still is the fact that an amazingly large percentage of *all* industrial companies are selling for less than their *quick* assets alone—leaving out their plants and other fixed assets entirely.

This means that a great number of American businesses are quoted in the market for much less than their liquidating value; that, in the best judgment of Wall Street, these *businesses are worth more dead than alive.*

For most industrial companies should bring, in *orderly* liquidations, at least as much as their quick assets alone. Admitting that the factories, real estate, etc., could not fetch anywhere near their carrying price, they should still realize enough to make up the shrinkage in the proceeds of the receivables and merchandise below book figures. If this is not a reasonable assumption, there must be something radically wrong about the accounting methods of our large corporations.

A study made at the Columbia University School of Business under the writer's direction, covering some 600 industrial companies listed on the New York Stock Exchange, disclosed that over 200 of them—or nearly one out of three—have been selling at less than their net quick assets.

Over 50 of them have sold at less than their cash and marketable securities alone. In the appended table [Table 1] is given a partial list, comprising the more representative companies in the latter category.

TABLE 1

Some Stocks That Are Selling for Less Than Their Cash Assets

Company	1932 Market Low	Market Value of Company at Low Price	Cash and Marketable Seurities	Current Assets Less All Liabilities	Cash Assets per Share	Net Quick Assets per Share
			(000 omitted)			
*Am. Car & Fdry	20¼	$ 9,225	$14,950	$32,341	$ 50	$108
*Am. Locomotive	30¼	14,709	14,829	22,630	41	63
*Am. Steel Foun.	60	8,021	8,046	11,720	128	186
*Am. Woolen	15¼	8,354	14,603	40,769	30½	85
Congoleum	7	10,078	10,802	16,288	7	12
Howe Sound	6	2,886	4,910	5,254	10	11
Hudson Motors	4⅛	6,377	8,462	10,712	5½	7
Hupp Motors	2	2,664	7,236	10,000	5½	7½
Lima Locomotive	8½	1,581	3,620	6,772	19	36
Magma Copper	4½	1,836	3,771	4,825	9	12
Marlin Rockwell	7½	2,520	3,834	4,310	11½	13
Motor Products	13	2,457	2,950	3,615	15½	19
Munsingwear	10⅞	1,805	2,888	5,769	17	34
Nash Motors	10	27,000	36,560	37,076	13½	14
N.Y. Air Brake	4½	1,170	1,474	2,367	5	9
Opp'hm Collins	5	1,050	2,016	3,150	9½	15
Reo Motors	1½	2,716	5,321	10,332	3	5½
S. O. of Kansas	7	2,240	2,760	4,477	8½	14
Stewart Warner	2⅜	3,023	4,648	8,303	3½	7
White Motors	7¾	4,938	8,620	22,167	13	34

Preferred stock.

What is the meaning of this situation? The experienced financier is surely to answer that stocks always sell at unduly low prices after a boom collapses. As the president of the New York Stock Exchange testified, "in times like these frightened people give this United States of ours away."

Stated differently, it happens because those with enterprise haven't the money, and those with money haven't the enterprise, to buy stocks when they are cheap. Should we not have had the same phenomenon existing in previous bear markets—for example, 1921?

The facts are quite otherwise, however. Stocks sold at low prices in the severe postwar depression, but very few of them could be bought on the stock exchange for less than quick assets, and not one for less than the company's available cash.

The comparative figures for both periods, covering representative companies, are little short of astounding especially when it is noted that they showed no materially poorer operating results in 1931 than in 1921. Today these companies are selling in the aggregate for half their working capital; ten years ago working capital was only half the bottom prices. With respect to cash assets the present prices are relatively *six* times lower than in 1921.

We must recognize, therefore, that the situation existing today is *not* typical of all bear markets. Broadly speaking, it is new and unprecedented. It is a strange, ironical aftermath of the New Era madness of 1928–29. It reflects the extraordinary results of profound but little understood changes in the financial attitude of the people and the financial fabric of the country.

Two plausible and seemingly innocent ideas—the first, that good stocks are good investments; the second, that values depend on earning power—were distorted and exploited into a frenzied financial gospel which ended by converting all our investors into speculators, by making our corporations rich and their stockholders poor, by reversing the relative importance of commercial loans and Wall Street loans, by producing topsy-turvy accounting policies and wholly irrational standards of value—and in no small measure was responsible for the paradoxical depression in which we find ourselves submerged.

Behind the simple fact that a great many stocks are selling for much less than their working capital lies a complex of causes, results, and implications. The remainder of this article will deal with the causes of the present unique situation, while other ramified aspects will be developed in succeeding articles.

The current contrast between market prices and liquid assets is accounted for in large measure by the huge flood of new cash which stockholders in recent years have poured into the treasuries of their corporations by the exercise of subscription rights. This phenomenon, which was one of the distinguishing features of the 1928–29 bull market, had two quite opposite consequences. On the one hand the additional funds received greatly improved the companies' cash and working capital position; on the other hand the additional shares issued greatly increased the supply of stocks, weakened their technical position, and intensified their market decline. The same circumstance, therefore, served both to improve the *values* behind stock and to depress the *price*.

It is doubtful, however, that the declines would have gone to the current extraordinary lengths if during the last decade investors had not lost the habit of looking at balance sheets. Much of the past year's selling of stocks has been due to fear rather than necessity. If these timid holders were thoroughly aware that they were selling out at only a fraction of the liquid assets behind their share, many of them might have acted differently.

But since value has come to be associated exclusively with earning power, the stockholder no longer pays any attention to what his company owns—not even its money in the bank.

It is undoubtedly true that the old-time investor laid too much stress upon book values and too little upon what the property could earn. It was a salutary step to ignore the figures at which the plants were carried on the books, unless they showed a commensurate earning power.

But like most sound ideas in Wall Street, this one was carried too far. It resulted in excessive emphasis being laid on the reported earnings—which might only be temporary or even deceptive—and in a complete eclipse of what had always been regarded as a vital factor in security values, namely, the company's working capital position.

Businesses have come to be valued in Wall Street on an entirely different basis from that applied to private enterprise. In good times the prices paid on the stock exchange were fantastically high, judged by ordinary business standards; and now, by the law of compensation, the assets of these same companies are suffering an equally fantastic undervaluation.

A third reason that stocks now sell below their liquid asset value is the fear of future operating losses. Many readers will assert that this is the overshadowing cause of the present low market level. These quotations reflect not only the absence of earning power, but the existence of "losing power" which threatens to dissipate the working capital behind the shares today.

Is it true that one out of three American businesses is destined to continue losing money until the stockholders have no equity remaining? This is what the stock market says in no uncertain tones.

In all probability it is wrong, as it always has been wrong in its major judgments of the future. The logic of Wall Street is proverbially weak. It is hardly consistent, for example, to despair of the railroads because the trucks are going to take most of their business, and at the same time to be so despondent over the truck industry as to give away shares in its largest units for a small fraction of their liquid capital alone.

But since even in prosperous times many undertakings fall by the wayside, it is certain that the number of such ill-starred ventures must now be greatly increased. The weakly situated business will find it difficult, perhaps impossible, to survive. Hence in a number of individual cases the market's prophecy of extinction will be borne out. Nevertheless, there must still be a basic error in this wholesale dumping of shares at a small fraction of liquidating value.

If a business is doomed to lose money, why continue it? If its future is so hopeless that it is worth much less as a going concern than if it were wound up, why not wind it up?

Surely the owners of a business have a better alternative than to give its present cash away, for fear that it is later going to be dissipated. We are back to the contract between the White Motors stockholder and the individual factory owner, with which we started our article.

The issue is merely one of simple logic. Either White Motors is worth more as a going concern than its cash in bank, or it is not. If it is worth more, the stockholder is foolish to sell out for much less than this cash, unless he is compelled to do so. If it isn't, the business should be liquidated and each stockholder paid out his share of the cash plus whatever the other assets will bring.

Evidently stockholders have forgotten more than to look at balance sheets. They have forgotten also that they are *owners of a business* and not merely owners of a quotation on the stock ticker. It is time, and high time, that the millions of American shareholders turned their eyes from the daily market reports long enough to give some attention to the enterprises themselves of which they are the proprietors, and which exist for their benefit and at their pleasure.

The supervision of these businesses must, of course, be delegated to directors and their operation to paid officials. But whether the owners' money should be dissipated by operating losses, and whether it should be tied up unproductively in excessive cash balances while they themselves are in dire need of funds, are questions of major policy which each stockholder must ponder and decide for himself.

These are not management problems; these are *ownership problems.* On these questions the management's opinion may be weighty but it is not controlling.

What stockholders need today is not alone to become *balance sheet conscious,* but more than that, to become *ownership conscious.* If they realized their rights as business owners, we would not have before us the insane spectacle of treasuries bloated with cash and their proprietors in a wild scramble to give away their interest on any terms they can get. Perhaps the corporation itself buys back the shares they throw on the market, and by a final touch of irony, we see the stockholders' pitifully inadequate payment made to them with their own cash.

The waggish barber of the legend painted on his sign:

What, do you think—
We shave you for nothing and give you a drink!

That, without the saving comma, might as well be blazoned as the motto of the stock seller of today, who hands over his share in inventories and receivables for less than nothing, and throws in real estate, buildings, machinery, and what-not as a lagniappe or trading stamp.

The humor of the situation could be exploited further, but the need is not for witticism but for a straightforward presentation of the vitally important issues that face stockholders, managements, and bankers. These will be dealt with in succeeding articles.

11

Should Rich Corporations Return Stockholders' Cash?

In our first article, the present disparity between the cash asset position of many companies and the price of their stocks was ascribed in part to the huge issues of additional shares which transferred money from stockholders' pockets into corporate treasuries. According to the New York Stock Exchange's compilation, the funds so absorbed by listed companies alone, between 1926 and 1930, amounted to no less than $5 billion.

The total sale of corporate securities to the public in this period exceeded $29 billion, of which a small part perhaps was turned over to private individuals, but the major portion was paid into the businesses, and either expended in plant additions or added to working capital.

It must not be forgotten that other enormous sums have also been accumulated in the form of undistributed earnings. After this tremendous influx of cash, it is no wonder that corporate treasuries are still bulging, despite all the money that has been spent, or lost, or paid in dividends.

But what of the people who supplied the bulk of this money, the investor who bought new offerings, the stockholder who subscribed to additional shares? They are not rolling in wealth today, nor burdened with a plethora of idle funds. They stripped themselves of cash to enrich their corporations' treasuries; they

This article is part two of a three-part series titled Is American Business Worth More Dead Than Alive? Reprinted by permission of Forbes Media LLC © 1932. Reprinted from *Forbes* (June 15, 1932).

borrowed heavily in order that these corporations might be able to pay off their debts.

The grotesque result is that the people who own these rich American businesses are themselves poor, that the typical stockholder is weighed down by financial problems while his corporation wallows in cash. Treasurers are sleeping soundly these nights, while their stockholders walk the floor in worried desperation.

True, the public has more stock certificates to represent the new shares which it paid for, and each certificate carries ownership in the cash held by the company. But somehow this doesn't help the stockholder very much. He can't borrow from the bank, or margin his existing loans, on the basis of the cash behind his shares. If he wants to sell, he must accept the verdict of the ticker. If he should appeal to the officers of the company for a little of his own cash, they would probably wave him away with a pitying smile. Or perhaps they may be charitable enough to buy his stock back at the current market price—which means a small fraction of its fair value.

Meanwhile, the prodigal transfer of cash by the public to corporations in the New Era days has not only made infinite trouble for the security holder, but it has seriously demoralized our banking structure. Commercial loans have always been the heart and the bulwark of our credit system. Loans on securities have been secondary in volume and drastically subordinated in their standing.

But what have the corporations and the public done between them in recent years? They have paid off the cream of the country's commercial borrowings and substituted security loans in their place. Instead of lending directly to big business, the banks have been forced to lend to their stockholders against pledges of their shares, or to purchase securities on their own account.

Some idea of the extent of this shift of banking accommodation can be gleaned from the comparative figures of the reporting member banks of the Federal Reserve System [see Table 2].

The whole development has proved most disastrous to stockholders and most embarrassing to the banks. The best form of borrowing has been replaced by the worst. The safety of the loans, and to some extent the solvency of the banks making them, has been placed at the mercy of stock market fluctuations, instead of resting on the financial strength of our large corporations.

Table 2

Change in the Composition of Banking Resources, 1920–32 (in millions)

	Commercial Loans	Loans on Securities	Total
Oct. 1920	$9,741	$ 7,451	$17,192
May 1932	6,779	12,498	19,277

Thousands of stockholders—the owners of their company's business—find themselves today in an absurd position. The market value of their stock may be, for instance, only $10 million, its borrowing value at best $8 million. Yet not only may the company have $15 million in the treasury, but it could borrow large additional amounts against its many millions of other quick assets. If the owners of the business really controlled such a company, they could draw out not only the $15 million in cash but another $5 million from bank loans, and still have a business in sound condition with substantial equities.

The very banks which hesitate to lend $10 per share on a stock would probably be glad to lend the company itself enough to enable it to pay out $15 per share to the stockholders.

Consider on the one hand a typical standard business with its enormous cash and credit resources; and then consider the people who own this business and who poured millions into its treasury, unable to realize or borrow more than a miserable fraction of the cash value of their own property.

This is the result of undue generosity by stockholders toward their corporations in good times—and of undue parsimony by the corporations toward their stockholders today.

The banks may seem like co-villains in such a situation, but in fact they, too, are victims of circumstance—handicapped by a soundly conceived system which is out of harmony with the actualities of the present situation. They have been educated and they are directed to give first consideration to commercial loans.

But who now are the commercial borrowers? Strong corporations with good past (if not recent) records, requiring money for seasonal requirements? Not at all. Such corporations don't need the banks; they raised all the money they could use from the stockholders when the raising was good.

There are left three classes of bank borrowers: (a) Small or privately owned enterprises—maybe good, maybe not; (b) Large industrial corporations with poor records even in the late prosperity; (c) Railroads and utilities needing temporary (cash) accommodation, to be paid off by permanent financing—a fruitful source of trouble for all concerned.

It must be recognized, therefore, that the replacement of good commercial loans on stock collateral has been harmful alike to our banking system and to the vast army of stockholders. Is there a remedy for this condition? There certainly is, and a very simple one:

Let corporations return to their stockholders the surplus cash holdings not needed for the normal conduct of their business.

The immediate result of such a movement would be to benefit the individual stockholder, by placing funds in his hands to meet his urgent needs or to use as he sees fit. The secondary result would be to improve the price of the shares affected and the stock market generally, as the public is made aware in this forceful fashion of the enormous cash values behind American business today. The third result would be to improve the balance of our banking structure, making for a larger proportion of sound commercial loans (especially when business again expands) and permitting the repayment of a certain quantity of frozen security loans.

How should this return of cash be accomplished? Preferably by the direct retracing of the financial steps which have led to the present predicament. Instead of rights to buy stocks, let companies offer their stockholders the right to sell stock in a fixed proportion and at a stated price. This price should be above the current market but in most cases below the net quick assets per share and therefore far below the book value. From the corporation's point of view the result of such repurchases at a discount will be an increase both in the surplus and in the net current assets per share of stock remaining.

A few corporations have followed this procedure, one of the earliest being Simms Petroleum. Recently Hamilton Woolen has offered to buy one-sixth of the outstanding shares pro rata $65, which is about equal to the net quick assets and considerably above the previous market price. This represents the return of a large portion of the new money paid in by stockholders in 1929.

Other companies have returned surplus cash to stockholders in the form of special distributions without cancellation of stock. Peerless Motors is a case in point, and another is Eureka Vacuum Cleaner, which accompanied its action by a statement recommending a similar move to other corporations as an aid in relieving the depression. A few companies, notably the Standard Oil pipe lines and some New England mills, have returned surplus cash capital to shareholders by reducing the par value of the stock.

All these methods accomplish the same purpose and the differences between them are largely technical. The repurchase of shares pro rata, which we recommend, is more practical in most cases than a reduction in par value, and it has certain bookkeeping advantages over a straight special dividend. Furthermore, as a direct reversal of the process of taking money from stockholders by issuing subscription rights, this method undoubtedly has a strong logical appeal.

A sizable number of enterprises have been employing surplus funds to acquire stock by purchase in the open market. This also represents a transfer of corporate funds to stockholders. It is undoubtedly helpful to the market price and hence to those constrained to sell, and the repurchase of shares at bargain prices presumably benefits the surviving stockholders. Certainly, corporations using excess cash in this manner are acting more liberally than those who hold on like grim death to every dollar in the bank.

But this form of procedure is open to objections of various kinds. If the price paid turns out to have been too high, the directors are subject to criticism from those whom they still represent, while those they have benefited are no longer interested in them or in the company. If to avoid this danger, they buy only when the price is exceedingly low, they cannot avoid the appearance of having taken unfair advantage of the necessities of their stockholders. Furthermore, such undisclosed market operations may afford opportunities for questionable profit by directors and insiders.

The Bendix Aviation Company recently passed its dividend and concurrently announced its intention of purchasing a large block of shares in the open market. Other companies rich in cash have followed the same policy, though generally without even this saving grace of revealing their plan to buy in stock. Such a procedure contains possibilities of grave injustice to the shareholders. When there is an accumulated surplus and excess cash on hand, the directors' first duty is to use the free cash to maintain a reasonable dividend.

The prime reason for accumulating the surplus in good years was to make possible the continuance of dividends in bad years. Hence the absence of earnings is in itself no justification for stopping all payments to shareholders. To withhold the owners' money from them by suspending dividends, and then to use this same money to buy back their stock at the abnormally low price thus created, comes perilously close to sharp practice.

Such considerations should make it clear why the writer does not regard open-market purchases as the best method of returning corporate cash to stockholders. Retirement of stock pro rata involves no conflict of interest between those selling out and those staying in; and it provides no opportunity for errors in judgment of unfair tactics on the part of the management.

Examination of the partial list of companies selling in the current market for less than their net current assets, as well as reference to the table [Table 1] offered in our first article last issue (see p. 124), will disclose many instances in which the cash holdings are clearly excessive. If stockholders will bring sufficiently strong pressure upon their managements, they can secure the return of a good part of such surplus cash, with great benefit to their own position, to stock market sentiment, and to the general banking situation.

In order to obtain these desirable results, stockholders must first be aware that surplus cash exists; and therefore they must direct at least a fleeting glance to their company's balance sheet. In recent years financial writers have been unanimous in pointing out how unimportant are asset values as compared with earning power; but no one seems to have realized that both the ignoring of assets and the emphasis on earnings can be—and have been—carried too far, with results of the most disastrous kind.

The whole New Era and blue chip madness is derived from this exclusive preoccupation with the earnings trend. A mere $1 increase in profits, from $4 to $5 per share, raised the value of a stock from $40 to $75, on the joyous assumption that an upward trend had been established which justified a multiple of 15 instead of 10. The basis of calculating values thus became arbitrary and mainly psychological, with the result that everyone felt free to gamble unrestrainedly under the respectable title of "investment."

It was this enticement of investors into rampant speculation which made possible the unexampled duration and extent of the 1928–29 advance, which also made the ensuing collapse correspondingly disastrous, and which—as later appeared—carried the business structure down into ruin with the stock market.

A peculiar offshoot of the obsession with earnings is the new practice of writing fixed assets down to $1, in order to eliminate depreciation charges and thus report larger profits. The theory is that by destroying asset values we can increase earning power and therefore enhance the market value. Since no one pays any attention to assets, why carry any assets on the books? This is another example of Alice in Wonderland financial logic.

It is in amusing contrast with the much berated stock watering practice of a generation ago. In those days fixed assets were arbitrarily written up, in order to enlarge the book values, and thus facilitate a fictitious market price. In place of watering of assets, we now have watering of earnings. The procedures are directly opposite, but the object and the underlying deception are exactly the same.

Because of the superstitious reverence now accorded the earnings statement by both investors and speculators, wide variations in market prices can be occasioned by purely arbitrary differences in accounting methods. The opportunities for downright crookedness are legion, nor are they ignored.

One company, listed on the New York Stock Exchange, recently turned an operating loss into a profit by the simple expedient of marking up its goodwill and adding the difference to earnings, without bothering to mention this little detail. The management apparently relied, and not unreasonably, on the fact that stockholders would not examine the balance sheets closely enough to detect their charming artifice.

The disregard of assets has also introduced some new wrinkles into reorganizations and mergers. Creditors are no longer permitted to receive the cash directly available to pay off their claims; stockholders are forced into consolidations which give other securities a prior claim on cash which formerly was theirs.

The Fisk Rubber Co., for example, showed around $400 in cash on hand for each $1,000 of overdue debt, and nearly $900 in net quick assets, excluding the extensive factories, etc. Yet the proposed reorganization plan offers these creditors no cash at all, but only stock in a new company.

Similarly, while Prairie Pipe Line stockholders were taking comfort from the fact that there had lately appeared to be $12 per share in cash equivalent behind their stock, they suddenly found themselves owners of shares in another company which had no cash at all directly applicable to their holdings, this new stock, moreover, having a total market value equal to less than half the cash equivalent alone which they formerly owned.

In the writer's view, all these strange happenings flow from the failure of the stockholder to realize that he occupies the same fundamental position and enjoys the same legal rights as the part-owner in a private business. The panoply and pyrotechnics of Wall Street have obscured this simple fact. If it only could be brought home to the millions of investors the country over, a long step would be taken in the direction of sounder corporate practices and a sane attitude toward stock values.

12

Should Rich but Losing Corporations Be Liquidated?

The unprecedented spectacle confronts us of more than one industrial company in three selling for less than its net current assets, with a large number quoted at less than their unencumbered cash. For this situation we have pointed out, in our previous articles, three possible causes: (a) Ignorance of the facts; (b) Compulsion to sell and inability to buy; and (c) Unwillingness to buy from fear that the present liquid assets will be dissipated.

In the preceding articles we discussed the first two causes and their numerous implications. But neither the ignorance nor the financial straits of the public could fully account for the current market levels.

If *gold dollars without any strings attached* could actually be purchased for 50 cents, plenty of publicity and plenty of buying power would quickly be marshaled to take advantage of the bargain. Corporate gold dollars are now available in quantity at 50 cents and less—but they *do* have strings attached. Although they belong to the stockholder, he doesn't control them. He may have to sit back and watch them dwindle and disappear as operating losses take their toll. For that reason the public refuses to accept even the cash holdings of corporations at their face value.

This article is part three of a three-part series titled Is American Business Worth More Dead Than Alive? Reprinted by permission of Forbes Media LLC © 1932. Reprinted from *Forbes* (July 1, 1932).

In fact, the hardheaded reader may well ask impatiently: "Why all this talk about liquidating values, *when companies are not going to liquidate?* As far as the stockholders are concerned, their interest in the corporation's cash account is just as theoretical as their interest in the plant account. *If* the business were wound up, the stockholders would get the cash; *if* the enterprise were profitable, the plants would be worth their book value. *"If* we had some cash, etc., etc."

This criticism has force, but there is an answer to it. The stockholders don't have it in their power to make business profitable but they do have it in their power to liquidate. At bottom it is not a theoretical question at all; the issue is both very practical and very pressing.

It is also a highly controversial issue. It includes an undoubted conflict of *judgment* between corporate managements and the stock market, and a probable conflict of *interest* between corporate managements and their stockholders.

In its simplest terms the question comes down to this: Are these managements wrong or is the market wrong? Are these low prices merely the product of unreasoning fear, or do they convey a stern warning to liquidate while there is yet time?

Today stockholders are leaving the answer to this problem, as to all other corporate problems, in the hands of their management. But when the latter's judgment is violently challenged by the verdict of the open market, it seems childish to let the management decide whether itself or the market is right. This is especially true when the issue involves a strong conflict of interest between the officials who draw salaries from the business and the owners whose capital is at stake. If you owned a grocery store that was doing badly, you wouldn't leave it to the paid manager to decide whether to keep it going or to shut up shop.

The innate helplessness of the public in the face of this critical problem is aggravated by its acceptance of two pernicious doctrines in the field of corporate administration. The first is that directors have no responsibility for, or interest in, the market price of their securities. The second is that outside stockholders know nothing about the business, and hence their views deserve no consideration unless sponsored by the management.

By virtue of dictum number one, directors succeed in evading all issues based upon the market price of their stock. Principle number two is invoked to excellent advantage in order to squelch any stockholder (not in control) who has the temerity to suggest that those in charge may not be proceeding wisely or in the best interest of their employers. The two together afford managements perfect protection against the necessity of justifying to their stockholders the continuance of the business when the weight of sound opinion points to better results for the owners through liquidation.

The accepted notion that directors have no concern with the market price of their stock is as fallacious as it is hypocritical. Needless to say, managements are not responsible for market fluctuations, but they should take cognizance of excessively high or unduly low price levels for the shares. They have a duty to protect their stockholders against avoidable depreciation in market value—as far as is reasonably in their power—equal to the duty to protect them against avoidable losses of earnings or assets.

If this duty were admitted and insisted upon, the present absurd relationship between quoted prices and liquidating values would never have come into existence. Directors and stockholders both would recognize that the true value of their stock should under no circumstances be less than the realizable value of the business, which amount in turn would ordinarily be not less than the net quick assets.

They would recognize further that *if the business is not worth its realizable value as a going concern it should be wound up.* Finally, directors would acknowledge their responsibility to conserve the realizable value of the business against shrinkage and to prevent, as far as is reasonably possible, the establishment of a price level continuously and substantially below the realizable value.

Hence, instead of viewing with philosophic indifference the collapse of their stock to abysmally low levels, directors would take these declines as a challenge to constructive action. In the first place, they would make every effort to maintain a dividend at least commensurate with the minimum real value of the stock. For this purpose they would draw freely on accumulated surplus, provided the company's financial position remained unimpaired. Secondly, they would not hesitate to direct the stockholders' attention to the existence of minimum liquidating values in excess of the market, and to assert their confidence in the reality of these values. In the third place, wherever possible, they would aid the stockholders by returning to them surplus cash capital through retirement or share pro rata at a fair price, as advocated in our previous article.

Finally, they would study carefully the company's situation and outlook, to make sure that the realizable value of the shares is not likely to suffer a substantial shrinkage. If they find there is danger of serious future loss, they would give earnest and fair-minded consideration to the question whether the stockholders' interests might not best be served by sale or liquidation.

However forcibly the stock market may be asserting the desirability of liquidation, there are no signs that managements are giving serious consideration to the issue. In fact, the infrequency of voluntary dissolution by companies with diversified ownership may well be a subject of wonder, or of cynicism. In the case of privately owned enterprises, withdrawing from business is an everyday occurrence. But with companies whose stock is widely held, it is the rarest of corporate developments.

Liquidation *after* insolvency is, of course, more frequent, but the idea of shutting up shop *before* the sheriff steps in seems repugnant to the canons of Wall Street. One thing can be said for our corporate managements—they are not quitters. Like Josh Billings, who in patriotic zeal stood ready to sacrifice all his wife's relations on the altar of his country, officials are willing to sacrifice their stockholders' last dollar to keep the business going.

But is it not true that the paid officials are subject to the decisions of the board of directors, who represent the stockholders, and whose duty it is to champion the owners' interests—if necessary, against the interests of the operating management? In theory this cannot be gain-said, but it doesn't work out in practice.

The reasons will appear from a study of any typical directorate. Here we find: (a) The paid officials themselves, who are interested in their jobs first and the stockholders second; (b) Investment bankers whose first interest is in underwriting profits; (c) Commercial bankers, whose first interest is in making and protecting loans; (d) Individuals who do business of various kinds with the company; and finally—and almost always in a scant minority—(e) Directors who are interested only in the welfare of the stockholders.

Even the latter are usually bound by ties of friendship to the officers (that is how they came to be nominated), so that the whole atmosphere of a board meeting is not conducive to any assertion of stockholders' rights against the desires of the operating management. Directors are not dishonest, but they are human. The writer, being himself a member of several boards, knows something of this subject from personal experience.

The conclusion stands out that liquidation is peculiarly an issue for the stockholders. Not only must it be decided by their independent judgment and preference, but in most cases the initiative and pressure to effect liquidation must emanate from stockholders not on the board of directors. In this connection we believe that the recognition of the following principle would be exceedingly helpful:

The fact that a company's shares sell persistently below their liquidating value should fairly raise the question whether liquidation is advisable.

Please note we do not suggest that the low price proves the desirability of liquidation. It merely justifies any stockholder in raising the issue, and entitles his views to respectful attention.

It means that stockholders should consider the issue with an open mind, and decide it on the basis of the facts presented and in accordance with their best individual judgment. No doubt in many of these cases—perhaps the majority—a fair-minded study would show liquidation to be unjustified. The going concern value under normal conditions would be found so large as compared with the sum realizable in liquidation, as to warrant seeing the depression through, despite current operating losses.

However, it is conceivable that under present difficult conditions the owners of a great many businesses might conclude that they would fare better by winding them up rather than continuing them. What would be the significance of such a movement to the economic situation as a whole? Would it mean further deflation, further unemployment, further reduction of purchasing power? Would stockholders be harming themselves? Superficially it might seem so, but powerful arguments can be advanced to the opposite effect.

The operation of unsoundly situated enterprises may be called a detriment, instead of an advantage, to the nation. We suffer not only from overcapacity, but still more from the disruptive competition of companies which have no chance to survive, but continue to exist none the less, to the loss of their stockholders and the unsettlement of their industry.

Without making any profits for themselves, they destroy the profit possibilities of other enterprises. Their removal might permit a better adjustment of supply to demand, and a larger output with consequent lower costs to the stronger companies which remain. An endeavor is now being made to accomplish this result in the cotton goods industry.

From the standpoint of employment, the demand for the product is not reduced by closing down unprofitable units. Hence, production is transferred elsewhere and employment in the aggregate may not be diminished. That great individual hardship would be involved cannot be denied, nor should it be minimized, but in any case the conditions of employment in a fundamentally unsound enterprise must be precarious in the extreme. Admitting that the employees must be given sympathetic consideration, it is only just to point out that our economic principles do not include the destruction of stockholders' capital for the sole purpose of providing employment.

We have not yet found any way to prevent depression from throttling us in the midst of our superabundance. But unquestionably there are ways to relieve the plight of the stockholders who today own so much and can realize so little. A fresh viewpoint on these matters might work wonders for the sadly demoralized army of American stockholders.

PART 3

Broadening the Profession

Benjamin Graham always felt that the analyst has a responsibility to study not just securities but the state of the world. Knowing everything about a tree but nothing about the forest made no sense to him.

Among the questions he considers in this section are: What kind of relationship with corporate managements is appropriate? How might taxation be improved? Is it practical or wise for "corporate democracy" to operate along the same principles as political democracy? What is the likely effect of wartime inflation on stock prices? How should legislators and government officials manage the problems of unemployment, the trade deficit, and the weakening value of the U.S. dollar?

Graham was no slouch when he ventured outside his usual fields of expertise. He wrote two books on international economics, *Storage and Stability* and *World Commodities and World Currency*, arguing that pegging currency values to a diversified basket of commodities could help manage inflation and minimize fluctuations in exchange rates.[1] Even the great John Maynard Keynes endorsed Graham's viewpoint, taking the time to write a personal note informing Graham that "you and I are ardent crusaders on the same side."[2] In 1943, Friedrich von Hayek praised Graham's plan as "important . . . very simple and eminently practical."[3] Decades later, Jan Tinbergen, who shared the first Nobel Prize in Economics in 1969, again cited Graham's proposal favorably.[4] It is striking that Graham, whose formal training in economics was limited to four weeks of an introductory class during his sophomore year of college, was lauded by such eminent macroeconomists for work outside his specialty.[5]

In "A Questionnaire on Stockholder-Management Relationship," Graham reports on the results of a survey he collected from 573 members of the New York Society of Security Analysts in 1947. Graham crafted his questions carefully to determine how analysts defined competence in corporate management and what steps they regarded as appropriate to take when management falls short. In effect, the article constitutes a manifesto for action, a capitalist call to arms: By the analysts' own responses, it is clear that they believe that there is such a thing as poor management, that bad managers should not be passively permitted to run companies into the ground, and that the analysts themselves have an affirmative duty to intervene by acting in concert to depose incompetent managers.

Yet, as Graham pointed out with increasing annoyance over the years, investors love to complain about bad corporate management but hate to do anything about it. It's one thing to get hundreds of analysts and investors to agree that action is often appropriate; it's another thing entirely to get even a single one of them to take any action.

In 1949, in *The Intelligent Investor,* Graham wrote in words of deliberate ferocity:

Nothing in finance is more fatuous and harmful, in our opinion, than the firmly established attitude of common stock investors and their Wall Street advisers regarding questions of corporate management. That attitude is summed up in the phrase, "If you don't like the management, sell your stock." . . . [I]nvestors as a whole have done nothing to improve managements that require correction. . . . The stockholders are a complete washout. As a class they show neither intelligence nor alertness. They vote in sheeplike fashion for whatever the management recommends and no matter how poor the management's record of accomplishment may be. . . . Years of experience has taught us that the only way to inspire the average American stockholder to take *independently* intelligent action would be by exploding a firecracker under him.[6]

The findings of Graham's survey of analysts in 1947 are probably not much different from what a comparable questionnaire would turn up today. The specific results are worth noting:

- 97% of the participants believed that determining the competence of management is part of the analyst's job.
- 50% thought that half of all companies have unsatisfactory management.
- 61% favored cumulative voting for directors.
- 72% believed that at least a "substantial minority" of directors should be independent, with 51% of all analysts favoring a majority.
- 94% felt that a poor earnings record "calls for inquiry by shareholders."
- 57% believed that the directors should set dividends at a level that reflects the intrinsic value of the stock.
- 83% agreed that management has a duty to inform shareholders of "any offer to purchase a substantial number of shares at more than current market price."

One term warrants explanation here. Under "cumulative voting," shareholders can divide their proxy votes however they choose. The owner of 10,000 shares, for example, could cast all 10,000 votes for (or against) a single director, or divide them up among the directors at will. Common in the United States in Graham's day, cumulative voting has been gutted in recent decades by state legislators. On occasion, cumulative voting has been abused by greenmailers and others who used large share blocks to secure special treatment for their own interests, and it has led to disruptive divisions in the boardroom. But it also is a highly effective way for intelligent investors to exercise their legitimate right to influence the companies they own. Graham was strongly in favor of it—especially as a means of bringing independent outsiders onto an entrenched board with the express purpose of monitoring the competence and fairness of management. Today, Graham might wonder why more investors have not considered pushing for a restoration of at least some cumulative-voting rights to state law.[7]

In "Controlling versus Outside Stockholders," Graham explores the puzzle of why, in a political democracy, corporate democracy does not exist. Graham lists the conditions that must be met before "the mass" of investors can "choose leaders and pass upon major policies" at companies the same way they do at the voting booth:

- First, no individual or united group owns the majority of the stock.
- Second, supporters of management do not have working control (or more than 20% of the shares).
- Third, "the outside stockholder is able and willing to form independent judgments about specific corporate questions."

Theoretically, nothing more is required. But, warns Graham, "to translate theoretical power into effective democratic action will require a great advance in stockholder education." Analysts should take a leading role in helping investors understand that dividend policy is at the heart of the struggle between controlling and outside owners. Controlling shareholders have a vested interest in keeping dividends low to avoid high current income tax on their large holdings. Furthermore, to minimize gift and estate taxes, they are often quite happy to let the market value of the shares languish at low levels; a depressed share price also can enable them to increase their own holdings or to take the company private on the cheap. Thus, controlling and outside stockholders may have diametrically opposed interests. Graham provides a startling example of two companies with similar book value but drastically different market prices; investors clearly favored the dividend-paying firm, even though the two were otherwise similar.[8]

Cash is power, and dividends take cash out of the control of insiders and distribute it to outside investors. So dividends are one of the only effective means of leveling the playing field. Graham makes the striking argument that the definition of fiduciary duty should be extended to protect minority shareholders from "serious loss due to an essentially arbitrary or selfish dividend policy." In the meantime, companies should make their dividend policies transparent—explaining, in advance, what proportion of earnings investors can expect to receive as dividends under normal circumstances.

The need for vigilance does not expire as soon as you buy a stock; it expires only after you sell. As Graham wrote in 1951:

> Sound investment in common stocks requires sound attitudes and actions by stockholders. . . . [I]f the stockholder is to regard himself as a continuing part-owner of the business in which he has placed his money, he must be ready at times to act like a true owner and to make the decisions associated with ownership. If he wants his interests fully protected he must be willing to do something on his own to protect them.[9]

Graham never stopped believing that the intelligent investor must also be an intelligent owner. But sadly, Graham did stop believing that he could ever succeed in persuading investors to exercise their rights. As the years passed, Graham gave up on the effort to talk analysts and investors into monitoring the policies, actions, and compensation of managers at the companies they owned.

In 1949, Graham devoted more than an eighth of the first edition of *The Intelligent Investor* to a discussion of shareholders' rights and responsibilities. By the last revision in his lifetime, in 1972, Graham had stripped that message down to a perfunctory eight-page explanation of dividends. After decades of urging investors to assert their legitimate rights, only to have his urgings fall on deaf ears, Graham finally threw in the towel.

We can only hope that a new generation of analysts and investors will step up and follow Graham's suggestions that corporate managements everywhere should be held to simple and consistent metrics of performance and compensation. We can also hope that, whenever management does fall short, shareholders will choose not to vote with their feet but to think with their heads.

In "Which Way to Relief from the Double Tax on Corporate Profits?" Graham tackles a problem that is still with us well over a half-century later: how to eliminate the burdensome double tax on corporate dividends. He wrote at a time of higher corporate income tax rates and much higher individual tax rates than today, but little else has changed. Graham was concerned that companies would move to replace equity with debt in their capital structure—since, as investment bankers like to say, the tax-deductibility of interest expense makes "bonds cheaper than equity" to the issuer. He expected companies to use more "income bonds" (very long-term debt whose interest payments varied with the net earnings of the issuer) as a means of minimizing their tax burden. Income bonds never seem to have had the renaissance Graham expected.[10] But the unequal tax treatment of stocks and bonds continues to distort the behavior of issuers and investors alike—for example, causing companies to pile on debt to repurchase shares rather than pay a dividend. Graham offers several solutions, none of which have been fully implemented. In a world where fiscal pressures may force tax rates higher—but where capital will also tend to flow to the markets with the least punitive tax rules—analysts may find it worthwhile to study how interest and dividends are taxed in different domiciles.

In "The War Economy and Stock Values," Graham fires a broadside against the doomsayers of every era, including our own. Then, as now, the world was in the grip of turmoil and terror. The Korean War, on a faraway peninsula, was the least of America's worries; the Cold War between the United States and the Soviet Union stood a real chance of exterminating the human race. As Graham put it, "the United States faces the new and harrowing danger of large-scale physical destruction and civilian casualties of inestimable magnitude." That same year, he also wrote that:

> [T]he possibility of a third world war weighs heavily on all our minds. . . .
> The effect of such a war upon ourselves and our institutions is incalculable.
> But in the field of security analysis we need consider only its bearing on
> the choice between various securities and between securities and (paper)
> money. . . . [S]ince war and inflation are inseparable, paper money and
> securities payable in specific amounts of paper money would seem to offer
> less financial or basic protection than soundly chosen common stocks,
> representing ownership of tangible, productive property.[11]

Thus, concludes Graham, the market's rise since the beginning of the Korean War is rational. Instead of panicking, as they have so often done at the beginning of other wars, investors are sensibly incorporating assumptions of higher future inflation into their expectations of stock values. (He notes elsewhere that neither World War I nor World War II had "an exceptional impact on stock prices."[12]) Graham also observes that in the long run, rising inflation and a falling dollar appear to correlate with higher stock prices, although stocks are not a perfect hedge against inflation. Thus, he concludes, investors were right to bid stocks up in the face of war; he turned out to be right, as the 1950s unfolded as one of the most bullish decades in stock market history.

In "Some Structural Relationships Bearing upon Full Employment" and "Our Balance of Payments: The 'Conspiracy of Silence,'" Graham tackles two issues of macroeconomic policy from the point of view of the security analyst.

In the first, Graham finds that, in the long run, productivity has grown even faster than consumption. Thus, concludes Graham, the problem is not that the U.S. economy cannot provide enough jobs; the problem is that too many Americans are working even harder than they need to. The solution, he suggests, would be to shorten the work week, freeing up room for more workers.[13] The thirty-five-hour work week, tried in France for a few years, did little to reduce unemployment there, but Graham's analysis applies specifically to higher-growth economies near the peak of capacity utilization. His idea may still have potential for reducing unemployment in rapidly expanding countries.

In the second, Graham argues that politicians and commentators misunderstood the causes in the deterioration of the U.S. balance of payments—which had led to a fall in the value of the dollar. He contends that it arose not from basic trade imbalances or excessive U.S. expenditures abroad but rather from a rapid rise in the rate of foreign investments made by U.S. companies and citizens. In other words, the United States was not overconsuming or overimporting from abroad; it was overinvesting. Graham points out that investments made overseas should be regarded as assets, not liabilities. He also warns that raising interest rates in the United States might not succeed in attracting "long-term capital" from abroad and that further devaluing the U.S. dollar might not solve the balance-of-payments deficit either. Almost a half-century later, as budget deficits loom and the dollar is on the defensive again, Graham's arguments warrant rereading.

NOTES

1. Benjamin Graham, *Storage and Stability: A Modern Ever-Normal Granary* (New York: McGraw-Hill, 1937); Benjamin Graham, *World Commodities and World Currencies* (New York: McGraw-Hill, 1944).

2. Janet Lowe, *Benjamin Graham on Value Investing* (New York: Penguin, 1996), p. 116.

3. F. A. Hayek, "A Commodity Reserve Currency," *The Economic Journal,* vol. 53, no. 210/211 (June–Sept. 1943), pp. 176–184; quote from p. 179.

4. Benjamin Graham, *The Memoirs of the Dean of Wall Street* (New York: McGraw-Hill, 1996), p. 335.

5. Ibid., pp. 104–105, 293. For a detailed discussion of Graham's views on commodities and currencies, see Perry Mehrling, "The Monetary Economics of Benjamin Graham: A Bridge between Goods and Money?" *Journal of the History of Economic Thought* (2010, forthcoming).

6. Benjamin Graham, *The Intelligent Investor* (New York: Harper & Row, 1949), pp. 19–20, 217, 240. Italics in original.

7. We are grateful to Prof. Tamar Frankel of Boston University School of Law for providing this background. See also Jeffrey N. Gordon, "Institutions as Relational Investors: A New Look at Cumulative Voting," *Columbia Law Review*, vol. 94, no. 1 (Jan. 1994), pp. 124–192, and Benjamin Graham and David L. Dodd, *Security Analysis* (New York: McGraw-Hill, 1951), p. 619.

8. Graham's example comes from Norvin R. Greene, "How Much Responsibility Does Management Have for the Price Level of Its Company's Stock?" *Financial Analysts Journal*, vol. 8, no. 5 (Nov. 1952), pp. 42–43.

9. Graham and Dodd, *Security Analysis* (1951), p. 620.

10. Some high-yield corporate bonds and tranches of mortgage-backed securities offer payment streams that vary with fluctuations in the underlying mortgage cash flows, but the issuers were not motivated mainly by tax considerations.

11. Graham and Dodd, *Security Analysis* (1951), p. viii.

12. Ibid., p. 12.

13. Elsewhere, Graham proposed what he called the "flexible work-year," a program to reduce the number of hours worked per year by the average worker. He spent about 20 years refining these ideas, which he summarized in *Benjamin Graham on the Flexible Work-Year: An Answer to Unemployment* (Santa Barbara, Calif.: Center for the Study of Democratic Institutions, 1964).

13

A Questionnaire on Stockholder-Management Relationship

In June 1947 the writer of this report sent a questionnaire to the members of the New York Society of Security Analysts, comprising seven questions on stockholder-management relationships. A total of 573 replies was received. It is our intention to include the results of this questionnaire in a comprehensive revision of our textbook, *Security Analysis*, on which the coauthors are now engaged. The members of NYSSA may be interested in the following discussion of the various questions and of their answers thereto.

QUESTION 1: Do you believe that the competence of management is a practical consideration in the selection of securities?

REPLIES: Yes   558
            No   14
            No answer   1

DISCUSSION: The keyword in the question is "practical." Everyone will agree that the competence of the management has a most important effect on the success of any stock investment. But can that competence be appraised by a security analyst in

Reprinted from *The Analysts Journal*, vol. 3, no. 4 (Fourth Quarter 1947): 57–62 with permission.

such wise as to enter into his selection of common stocks? The analysts themselves have answered overwhelmingly in the affirmative. Clearly, they do try to form some idea of management competence in their practical work of analyzing securities.

QUESTION 2: Of 100 listed companies taken at random, about what percentage do you think would have a fully satisfactory management?

The replies covered a wide range and are summarized as follows:

Percent "Fully Satisfactory"	Replies
0–25%	142
26–50%	143
51–75%	140
76–100%	61
	486
No estimate	87

The midpoint of the estimates is under 50%.

DISCUSSION: Most of the analysts were willing to express some idea, admittedly rough, of the prevalence of good or poor management. We used the phrase "fully satisfactory" without explanation. In our view the management would be "fully satisfactory" if no concrete criticism could be offered against it. Those not entirely satisfactory might deserve to be retained, but presumably their methods could be improved on. The replies show a very wide variation in the view of our members as to the prevalence of "fully satisfactory" managements. Regardless of just how the phrase might be construed, the median figure of under 50% would seem to signify that in the minds of security analysts there is wide room and perhaps need for changes in managerial methods or personnel.

If the analysts are right on this point, then it would seem that stockholders, as the owning groups, should interest themselves actively in the question of managerial competence. Where it seems to be lacking, they should take whatever steps are reasonably appropriate to improve the situation. In the opinion of the writer, if as low as 10% of the corporate managements are unsatisfactory, it would mean that the issue is of real significance in the investment field.

QUESTION 3: Do you favor cumulative voting for directors?

REPLIES: Yes   349
          No   169
          No answer   55

DISCUSSION: Cumulative voting is one means by which a fairly large minority group of stockholders can exercise some part of the managerial function by securing representation on the board of directors. Nearly half the states have made cumulative voting mandatory;[1] in most others it may be provided for by inclusion in the charter or by-laws. If the majority view of our members on this point is sound, stockholders would be well advised to introduce cumulative voting in their respective corporations. This can be accomplished by voting a resolution to that effect at an annual meeting.

The incumbent management is likely to oppose such a resolution, as in some way threatening its position, and to make the issue one of general confidence in its integrity and ability. The typical stockholder almost automatically backs the management in matters of this kind. Thus the proponents of cumulative voting or any similar corporate reform will be fighting against heavy initial odds. They can be overcome, however, by a persistent campaign of education, which must lean heavily on the support of security analysts and other financial authorities.

QUESTION 4: Do you believe that a majority (or a substantial minority) of the directors of the typical corporation should be independent of the operating management—in particular, that they should not be recipients of salaries or other substantial income from the corporation?

REPLIES:	A majority	291
	A substantial minority	120
	Neither	80
	No answer	82

DISCUSSION: Critics of our corporate machinery often contend that the typical board of directors, although in theory the selector and appraiser of the operating management, does not in fact exercise independent judgment in this field. This is clearly the case where the officials themselves constitute a majority of the board, or where the majority is made up of themselves and other directors closely associated with them by ties of friendship or function.

Our question implied a fairly radical solution of this problem, by making the majority or a substantial minority of the board independent of the operating management. Since three replies were possible, there was a wider distribution of answers to this question than to the others. Over half voted in favor of a majority of independent directors, and more than four-fifths of those expressing an opinion preferred either a majority or a substantial minority.

In the writer's opinion, the prevailing view here is eminently sound. It would be appropriate for stockholders to move to change the setup of many corporations so as to provide a majority—or at least a substantial minority—of independent stockholder-directors. We do not imply that when the officers dominate the board the result is always unsatisfactory to the shareholders. On the contrary, a number of our most successful corporations have had such an arrangement. But certainly these companies would not have been hurt by the presence of several representative outside stockholders. And many relatively unsuccessful corporations might have greatly benefited by the injection of new and independent thinking into their boards.

On this point we should like to quote from a letter sent us in answer to our questionnaire by a member holding a high position in one of our leading banks:

> It is my opinion that the primary job of a director is to see that there is good management. If a majority of a board are members of the management, that makes it self-perpetuating, and it is impossible to get rid of a management that is bad. I think it is extremely important that a majority of a board should be independent of the operating management. However, they should have salaries in an amount that would make it possible to attract the right kind of men to those boards and to compensate them adequately for the risks they take as directors. It is becoming more common every day to pay directors salaries up to $5,000 and in some cases as high as $10,000.

The suggestion that a fair-sized annual salary be paid to independent directors was made in several of the replies. Such compensation would ordinarily not be so substantial as to make the directors the equivalent of additional operating personnel.

QUESTION 5: If a company's average earnings fail to show a reasonable return on the stockholders' equity, and if they are substantially lower than in the industry as a whole, do you believe that this fact calls for inquiry by shareholders?

REPLIES: Yes   539
           No   18
           No answer   8

DISCUSSION: This question shifts the emphasis from the make-up of the management to measuring its results. If poor management is to be improved on, it must first be identified as poor. The test given in the question affords *prima facie* evidence of the need for improvement. We do not suggest that if the results are bad the managers should be changed—as usually happens in baseball—but only that the owners then proceed to look carefully into the question.

The overwhelming vote in favor of an inquiry by shareholders, in such cases, might seem a bit surprising when we reflect that such action is almost unheard of in practice. In our view this vote is perhaps the most significant in the questionnaire, because it highlights the wide gulf between what should happen and what does happen in stockholder-management relationships.

Machinery for setting up such an inquiry by shareholders is readily available. As in the case of cumulative voting, all that is needed is an appropriate resolution at an annual meeting. The resolution should call for a study of the methods and general efficiency of the management to be made by established experts in the field, who should report directly to a committee of independent stockholders named in the resolution.

The problem, of course, is to push through such a resolution, when justified, even against the management's opposition. If the security analysts would support stockholder efforts of this kind in practice—as they apparently favor them in theory—it would not be long before this technique is widely adopted as a means of improving the position of the ownership interest.

QUESTION 6: Do you believe that it is the duty of the directors to pay such dividends, within the average earnings of the business, as will be reasonably commensurate with the intrinsic value of the shares, as they determine such value?

REPLIES: Yes   329
            No   162
            No answer   74

DISCUSSION: One source of complaint by stockholders is inadequate dividends. The management invariably justifies a niggardly dividend on the ground that the company and the shareholders will benefit from keeping the earnings in the business. The question implies as a simple criterion of proper dividend action that, where earnings are large enough, the stockholders should receive a dividend commensurate with the value of their investment. Under present conditions an appropriate rate would be not less than 4% on such value. Since the latter term is subject to much argument, our question implies that the directors form their own idea of the value of the enterprise and then do their best to keep the dividend policy reasonably in line with that value.

A number of replies remarked that dividend policy must take into account the company's financial position and needs as well as its average earnings. This is undoubtedly true. A weak financial position clearly calls for conservatism in dividends. But a real controversy generally arises when the management has expansion in mind. The stockholders might well contend that such expansion would be better financed through the sale of additional stock rather than by withholding dividends, since the latter choice often condemns their shares to both an unduly low income and an unduly low market price. Which policy should be followed to finance expansion will depend on the particular case. But it would be of advantage to stockholders if directors were guided by the premise that they should pay a reasonable dividend on the reasonable value of the stock, unless compelled to act otherwise by conditions which left them no sound alternative.[2]

QUESTION 7: Do you believe that it is the duty of the management to transmit to stockholders any offer to purchase a substantial number of shares at more than current market price?

REPLIES:		
	Yes	477
	No	67
	No answer	21

DISCUSSION: One way of improving unsatisfactory management is through acquisition of control by new interests. They are sometimes willing to pay well above the market for such control, especially since the market might be quite depressed because of the shortcomings of the incumbent management. Our members take what seems the obvious view that every stockholder is entitled to decide for himself whether or not to accept such an offer for his shares. Yet managements have been able to find legal sanctions for refusing to make such offers available to the owners of the business. As in other matters covered by this questionnaire, the difference here between the opinion of the security analysts and what actually happens indicates clearly that stockholders should wake up.

NOTES

1. In 1941 these were Arizona, Arkansas, California, Idaho, Illinois, Kansas, Kentucky, Michigan, Mississippi, Missouri, Montana, Nebraska, North Dakota, Pennsylvania, South Carolina,

South Dakota, Washington, West Virginia, Wyoming. Minnesota, Ohio, and North Carolina have mandatory cumulative voting under certain conditions.

2. Compare the following from the *Wall Street Journal* of August 7, 1947, in discussing stockholder relations: "Company officers privately tell Exchange representatives that the best stockholder relations are steady dividends *at a satisfactory rate.*" (Italics ours)

14

Which Way to Relief from the Double Tax on Corporate Profits?

A tax reform bill is on the way, and it is universally expected to provide some relief from the double dividend tax. Apparently no one supports the principle of the "double bite"; its only excuse is the need for revenue. To eliminate the second tax entirely would cost the Treasury at least $3½ billion. In today's budget picture so large an annual sum can be neither forgone nor replaced by other levies. Investors must limit their initial hopes, therefore, to partial relief amounting perhaps to one-fifth of the total involved. The prediction most generally made is that taxpayers will be allowed a credit against their tax bill of 5% to 10% of dividends received. This type of relief has already been granted by Canada. Others expect a flat exemption of a small amount of dividend income—say 10% or $200, whichever is less.

Much more effort has gone into condemning the double tax as unfair and destructive than into thinking about the most practicable and desirable forms of relief. It should be borne in mind at the outset that there are two basically different approaches to the problem. The first would tax the corporation only; the second would tax the stockholder only and exempt the corporation to the extent that profits are distributed. Both of these approaches have a background in our tax history, and have analogies in our present tax law. Each also has its own advantages, particularly

Reprinted from *The Analysts Journal*, vol. 10, no. 1 (February 1954): 15–17 with permission.

in the direction of remedying unsound viewpoints and practices that have been generated by the heavy rates of tax.

In this article we shall consider some specific implications of the present system of double taxation, in relation to business and investment policies. We shall not discuss the generally discouraging effect on business enterprise of the heavy combined burden. This is a familiar subject of complaint. Contrariwise, the point should be noted that no substantial contraction in overall business activity can *so far* be identified and blamed on the tax rates. This fact may be explained in part by the large nonmonetary or noncalculating component in American business, especially large-scale business—a theme not adequately explored by our economists and sociologists. More important, probably, is the factor of inertia or delayed reaction. Businessmen and investors do not now act as tax logic would have them act, because it takes a long time for an external consideration like tax rates to change ingrained attitudes and habits of business and life.

This will account also for the rather surprising failure of businessmen and investors to adopt specific policies—in the fields of organization form, capital structures, dividend attitudes and procedures, and so on—designed to minimize the tax impact as far as feasible. But, unless the burden is lightened in the future, it is safe to predict that these adaptations will be made at an increasing rate of speed. If our economy should ever come to be really controlled by tax factors—if all the implications of our tax laws and regulations should be fully reflected in our business and investment activities—the United States would find itself in a pretty pickle.

Reactions to the Corporate Income Tax

The corporate-tax portion of the double impost should logically produce two major counter-reactions or tendencies. The first should be the replacement of the corporate form, wherever practicable, by the partnership form—especially the limited partnership form. The second should be the introduction of the largest possible component of interest-bearing securities in the capital structure—preferably, income bonds—in order to enjoy the interest deduction from taxable profit.

There are limitations on the availability of both of these methods of defeating the corporate tax. It is inconceivable, of course, that our large corporations could ever be transformed into any form of partnership. But, when it is recalled that there are some 500,000 incorporated businesses in the United States, covering every possible gradation of size and ownership structure, it becomes apparent that there is room for far-reaching changes in the organizational forms of business. The recent imposition of an excess-profits tax—for the fourth time in about a generation, and in the last three instances applied only to corporations— has given an extra dimension to the gulf between corporate and partnership tax rates.

Years ago incorporation was adopted widely to *reduce* the tax impact on private business. With reinvestment of profits, thus avoiding the dividend tax, and with the corporate levy at the rate of 15% or less, arithmetic clearly favored a corporation over a wealthy partnership. Today, assuming no dividends at all but ultimate realization of profits through a capital-gains sale, the typical corporate proprietor faces a tax of about 63%. In most cases the effective tax burden is even higher.

It is fundamentally unsound to have the corporate and noncorporate forms of business affected by completely different tax systems. We shall comment on this point again later.

Bond interest is tax-deductible by a corporation; preferred and common dividends are not. Thus, if all present dividends could be paid in the form of bond interest, double taxation would be ended. For, by our assumption, whatever was paid out would be free of corporate tax, and whatever was retained would be free of individual tax. There are two ways in which this result could conceivably be attained. The first is by changing the law to put dividend payments on the same tax basis as interest payments; the second is by changing corporate capital structures so that all but a nominal amount of present capital is transformed into debt—presumably income bonds of long maturity.

The way in which traditional or "institutional" thinking prevents prompt adjustment of policy to new conditions is well illustrated by the failure of corporations to make use of the income-bond device for its tax-saving value. (The generally bad repute of income bonds is a strong factor here, of course, but a few issues put out by really strong companies would go far to break down this barrier.) The Treasury and the courts will not permit the income-bond stratagem to be carried beyond certain limits—not as yet clearly defined—but the decisions on record clearly give far more leeway here than corporations are willing to accept.

Our prediction would be that the weight of double taxation will eventually overcome the traditional objections to income bonds—or other debt with "escape clauses" for the issuer—and that, once the new procedure is firmly established, it will spread more and more rapidly. This will serve to create a tax gulf between companies with and those without full-scale debt structures. Such a development could hardly be welcomed. For much too much of apparent earning power and investment value would then depend on the choices made concerning capital structure. Furthermore, the contribution of different companies to tax revenues would vary widely and undeservedly.

This analysis suggests that one of the best ways to grant relief from double taxation would be to allow as large a portion as possible of dividend payments to be deducted from taxable income. If we assume that the Treasury's loss is to be limited at the outset to, say, $500 million, the initial deduction or credit could be no more than about 10% of the distributions. But just as with other possible forms of relief, this percentage could be increased when and as Congress decides that further reform is feasible.

The end result envisaged by such a policy would be the (approximate) equalization of tax rates for corporations and other business enterprises. For, if all dividends were eventually deductible by the company, and if the regular corporation rate were about equal to the composite individual tax rate on dividends, then the total tax take would be the same, regardless of the amount disbursed—and this take would be the same as from an equivalent amount of partnership or proprietorship income. Readers with long memories will recall that this was the avowed objective and pattern of the original Administration draft of the tax bill of 1936—which was later transformed into the undistributed profits tax provision, on which so much obloquy has been heaped. What started out as potential relief ended as penalty, because the old corporate tax was retained and the new tax added on. If this time the tax relief provisions start out modestly, they would be in no danger of distortion into an additional burden.

Current and recent tax provisions include two precedents for treating dividend payments as tax-deductible by the corporation. One was the deductibility accorded by the Revenue Act of 1942 to certain preferred-stock dividend payments made by public utility companies. (This was limited to the so-called normal tax.) The other relates to regulated investment companies (mutual funds, etc.) under section 362 of the Revenue Code. Corporations coming under and complying with these special provisions incur no tax on profits paid out to stockholders.

An overlooked aspect of our present tax system is that it makes the government a 50% partner with corporations in their net profits, but not a part owner of their net assets. Suppose a company can earn just enough *before taxes*—say 10%—to support the realizable value of its capital. After the 50% take these earnings are cut in two, and the value of the business as a going concern apparently becomes only half of what it would be if it sold out or shut up shop. The higher the rate of tax, the greater the percentages of businesses that are worth more asset-wise than earning-wise. An allowance or deduction for a moderate dividend on invested capital *before* dividing with the Treasury would go far to mitigate this unsound factor in the present economy.

Relief to the Stockholder

If we turn now to the stockholder's tax position, the most obvious way of easing his burden is by exempting his dividend income from the second tax. For the greater part of our income-tax history—from 1913 through 1935—such exemption was in fact accorded with respect to normal tax but not surtax. The theory was that the corporate tax about corresponded to the normal tax on individuals, so that the credit saved him from two normal taxes. This simple reasoning is no longer applicable in our present complicated system, where the corporate levy itself contains both a normal tax and a surtax, and where the corporate rate is much higher than the individual rate for some stockholders and much lower for others. Nevertheless, it would still be feasible to grant welcome relief by again exempting dividends from the lowest bracket of personal tax—now set at 20%.

There is a special economic distortion created by the present dividend tax, and that is the growing tendency of high-income investors to favor capital gains over ordinary dividend income. Since the maximum tax rate on long-term gains is now 25%, its advantage for high-bracket people is tremendous. This disparity in rates has great capacity for mischief. It can undermine sound distinctions between investment and speculation, create schizophrenic thinking on dividend policies, and set the interests of investors in direct conflict with those of small stockholders. If the burden of double taxation is to be lightened at all, there would be a special advantage in doing so in such a way as to bridge the tax gulf between capital gains and dividends.

A neat method of accomplishing just this would be to treat all domestic dividends as the equivalent of long-term capital gains. There is a precedent for this in our present tax law, which already provides, in section 362, for "capital-gain dividends." These are distributions made by regulated investment companies out of their own capital gains, and they are taxed at *capital-gain rates* to the receiving stockholders. If this reform were adopted 100%, it would probably reduce the present tax on dividends by about two-thirds, an inadmissible concession to begin with. But any desired measure of relief can easily be accorded by designating some portion of dividend income to be treated as capital gains, the remainder to continue to be taxed as at present. Similarly, if special relief is wanted for the small investor, this could be achieved by giving, say, the first $400 of dividend income the same tax status as capital gains.

The Two Approaches Compared

If we assume a retreat from double taxation, is it better to reduce the burden on the corporation or on its stockholders? Considerations of equity and broad economic strategy would favor equalizing the tax position of corporate and noncorporate business, except for a moderate franchise tax on companies, in return for their various immunities. Probably the most advantageous method of procedure would be to allow a credit to corporations for dividends paid, similar, on the one hand, to the present interest-paid credit or, on the other hand, to the excess-profits tax credit. We have pointed out important collateral benefits from this approach.

From the standpoint of common-stock valuation, relief given to corporate earnings will probably have a more beneficial effect than relief given to dividend recipients. The reason is that the effect of the former can be computed directly in terms of higher earnings per share, whereas a lower tax on dividend income has different results for different stockholders. But any reduction in the combined tax rate must operate to make common stocks more attractive and thus more valuable.

Tax relief to the shareholder is not so logical as equivalent relief to the corporation, but it is likely to have more of a personal or voter appeal. This probably explains why expectations always run in this direction. Even here a strong case could be made for reducing the burden by equalizing the rates on dividends and on capital gains, instead of merely granting a limited exemption of dividends from the regular tax.

15

Controlling versus Outside Stockholders

The practical working of corporate democracy is intimately bound up with the question of corporate control. If the average or outside stockholder of a given company has no real power to influence the choice of its directors, then the basic concept of democracy or "power of the people" is there inapplicable. The mass of stockholders may demand information, they may assert the right to discuss and criticize at annual meetings, but they cannot govern or control a single corporate decision—except sometimes, in a negative sense, those requiring a two-thirds or three-quarters approval.

Financial men distinguish between three kinds of corporate control—"absolute," where an individual or cohesive group owns a majority of the stock; "working," where as little as 20% of the shares, so concentrated, may actually "run the company"; and "open-market," where the holdings of the "insiders" are so small that an outside group can acquire control by steady purchase. Interesting enough, the latter category does not envisage actual exercise of control by the outside or public stockholders acting en masse and independently of management. The latter is theoretically possible, and has actually been known to occur. But such definitive exercises of corporate democracy are exceedingly rare. In most cases of the kind, there is a nucleus of outsiders who

© *Virginia Law Weekly*. Reprinted from *Virginia Law Weekly*, vol. V, no. 21 (April 16, 1953): 1, 3–4 with permission.

start by controlling more stock than the management, and the struggle is really between two important groups to win the requisite additional amount of public support.

Thus we are very far from having a corporate democracy in any sense analogous to our political democracy, in which the full power to choose leaders and pass upon major policies resides in and is wielded by the mass of the citizens. Such a condition can arise in corporate affairs only when *both* (a) there is no absolute or strong working control, in the hands of insiders, and (b) the outside stockholder is able and willing to form independent judgments about specific corporate questions. To translate theoretical power into effective democratic action will require a great advance in stockholder education. This writer believes, further, that the initiative and direction in this area will have to come from the numerous agencies that have special qualifications to form expert and impartial opinions on corporate issues— e.g., investment fund managements, investment counsel, Stock Exchange houses, security-analysts groups.

Something of a paradox emerges out of this rather pessimistic view of the present state of corporate democracy. It is possible that the outside stockholder may derive more positive protection out of the *trusteeship obligation* of majority interests toward the *minority*, than through exercising his potential right to form a controlling majority of his own by joining with his fellow outsiders. The fiduciary obligations of the majority are a matter of legal principle, subject to widening judicial interpretation. If the minority is mistreated—as mistreatment has been and will be defined—then a *single* stockholder may obtain court relief for all the minority. But if the public holders constitute a numerical majority, the courts may well require that abuses be cured via a stockholder vote overruling and possibly replacing the management. This is exasperatingly difficult to obtain, even when the issues appear crystal clear.

This paradox is actually operative in two important sectors of the corporate front—Chapter X reorganizations and break-ups or recapitalizations under the Public Utility Holding Company Act of 1935. Here the ideal of corporate democracy is sharply circumscribed by the realistic concept that public security holders cannot be trusted to vote in their own interest without the guidance and superior control of the S.E.C. and the courts. No matter how large a majority may favor a plan or deal, it may still be turned down if found unfair or unfeasible by the regulatory bodies. As a consequence, a single determined security holder, with right on his side, may prevail against overwhelming numerical odds. This possibility, in turn, makes majority groups more attentive than otherwise they might be to the views of minority holders.

In ordinary corporate affairs, however, a dissatisfied individual holder, or minority group, has no legal forum for a complaint, unless it relates to certain specific and limited types of overreaching by those in control. As this layman understands the case, there is redress against the following: (1) Unfair business transactions between the company and controlling persons, including payment of clearly excessive compensation. (2) The diversion of "corporate opportunity" from the company to a controlling person. (3) By statutory provision (Sec. 16b, etc., of the Securities Exchange Act of 1934), the making of short-term profits in the purchase and sale of the company's securities. Relief under the first two categories is clearly appropriate; that under the third is open to objection, I think, as implying wrongdoing in transactions that may be entirely innocent.

However, it is our thesis that there are far more important areas of conflict of interest between controlling and outside stockholders, which have so far escaped legal recognition and which therefore permit overreaching of the less powerful by the more powerful group. These areas relate to competence of management, to control of assets, and to dividend policy. Of these, the most obvious is dividend policy, and I shall devote most of my attention to this question.

The outside stockholder is harmed by an inadequate dividend when the company's position would permit payment at an adequate rate. He suffers both in income and in the market value of his holdings. Since these are the only two places in which he can obtain concrete benefit from his investment, the damage done him by an unduly low dividend is comprehensive. It may be made up later, of course, by a more liberal dividend policy; but since low dividends almost invariably induce a substantial number of holders to sell out at an unfairly low price, much of the harm done must be termed irreparable.

The position of a controlling stockholder, as regards dividends, is completely different. He has the right to view the concern as one would his private business. In the typical case dividends are not needed to meet his living expenses, and they do involve a high-bracket tax. The inclination, therefore, is often strongly toward a "conservative" dividend policy, which means that almost any excuse is welcomed for keeping the dividend down. Such excuses are always easy to find; in fact, one may be readily manufactured at any convenient time by a simple decision to expand the scope of the business, thus increasing the need for retaining earnings.

Controlling stockholders may not be as much concerned as outside holders by the unduly low market price that follows in the wake of an unduly low dividend. For the most part, the former's investment is permanent and unmortgaged. Low market prices make for lower gift and estate taxes; they may also create opportunities to acquire additional shares on a bargain basis. If those in control desire to "cash in," they usually arrange a merger or sell out at a realistic price related to earning power and assets, and thus far above the market levels prevailing for some time past. If necessary for sale or other purposes, the dividend may always be increased to a suitable figure.

To what extent do we actually find a policy of inadequate dividends carried out apparently in the interests of controlling stockholders and contrary to that of the outside or public owner? The occurrence would seem to vary about inversely with the size of the enterprise. Most of the really large companies endeavor to be entirely fair in their disbursement rate; they are conscious of an obligation to protect the position of all stockholders; where the payout is rather low—as it has been in many cases since 1946—the reasoning behind the policy is tenable if not always convincing.

Most of the abuses in the field of dividend policy have occurred among the smaller corporations, especially in cases where there is concentrated control in a single family. A typical case is Company D, now listed on the New York Stock Exchange. In 1946, shares were sold to the public, apparently for the first time, and priced at 23. The book value was 22½, the last year's earnings (adjusted) $2.41, the currently declared dividend at the rate of $1.00 annually. In 1948 the earnings were over $3 per share (before deducting an inventory reserve, never used), and the year-end book value had increased to $29.67. However, early in that year the dividend was omitted and the price dropped to 11. At that time, the company had no debt or preferred stock, and the net current assets alone were over $19 per share.

Another kind of example was provided in a recent article by Norvin Greene, appearing in the November 1952 issue of *The Analysts Journal.* Here compared companies X and Y, in the same business, of almost the same size, and sharing similar operating results and financial position. Yet Company X sold at 24¾ (against book value of $16.60), while Company Y sold at 15¾ (against book value of $18.60). The difference was clearly due to the "investor relations," including notably the respective dividend policies. Company X had paid $2.15 in 1951 while Company Y paid only $1.40. Other differences—in the place of listing, frequency of reports, data given in reports—also favored Company X.

No doubt scores of instances could be given of lesser-sized companies which have sold shares to the public at very full prices, and have later pursued dividend policies which are completely inadequate in relation to the price paid by the outside stockholders, and which inevitably entailed a drastic shrinkage of market value of their investment. Some of these unfortunate happenings may be justified by adverse business developments; but in many more cases, the average earnings were sufficient to pay an adequate dividend, and the low rate was defended in terms of the need for larger capital. Is it too much to say that in the latter instances, the business was being run in a way to confer benefits on the controlling stockholders and to inflict injury on those outsiders who in good faith had contributed capital to the enterprise?

It is interesting to speculate on the possibility that some day the doctrine of the fiduciary obligation of controlling persons toward minority stockholders may be expanded to protect the latter against serious loss due to an essentially arbitrary or selfish dividend policy. Perhaps conscientious underwriting houses—recognizing how vulnerable is the price of newer common-stock issues to unfavorable developments of all sorts—will in due time require managements to express their intention of maintaining a reasonably adequate dividend, unless unsatisfactory business conditions make such a dividend clearly inadvisable. A representation of this kind would make controlling interests think twice before they jeopardized the dividend rate by expansion or by other avoidable decisions. It would also bring into clearer focus the right of minority holders to legal relief if they suffered from dividend policies which at the same time helped rather than hurt the insiders.

One of the anomalies of the dividend problem is that it results in large part from failure on the part of the entire financial community to think through the proper role of dividends in investment policy under present conditions of high tax rates and high reinvestment needs because of expansion and inflation. Most of the underlying conflict of interest between insiders and outsiders in the matter of dividends could be neatly resolved by resort to a carefully formulated and clearly expressed policy of periodic stock dividends representing the retained portion of current earnings. But new thinking to meet new underlying conditions comes very slowly to Wall Street.

The second broad area in which insiders may benefit while outside stockholders are penalized is that of control of assets. The right to hold and administer corporate assets is a normal perquisite of control; that it confers certain advantages—e.g., the right to place insurance, etc.—may hardly be gain-said, but these are not objectionable per se if the business is a sound one, properly run. But there have been numerous instances in which the structure of the business itself is demonstrably of value only to those in control, and the outside stockholder loses through its continuance. Holding companies belong in this general category. The classic example, I think, is that of Mission Corporation— because the inherent unfairness of the set-up to minority owners was forcibly expressed by its own president at a time when he was opposing a highly unusual merger deal proposed by the con- trolling stockholder. The details of this case—on which finis has not yet been written—will repay careful examination by students of the question of control.

Probably the most controversial idea of all would be that outside stockholders are entitled to relief from poor management by the controlling people. It is generally held that a minority holder accepts the management of the majority for better or for worse; only in the rare instances of a clear-cut wastage of assets by an equivalent of gross negligence can he hope for some legal protection. (The pending move for a receiver to take over the R-K-O Pictures Corp. is an example—necessarily somewhat spectacular—of such a situation.) It is conceivable, however, that in due time minority stockholders as a class will establish in the courts their right to at least *reasonably good* management—on the ground that the perpetuation of its own inferior management by the majority represents the placing of its own selfish interest ahead of that of the public owners, and as such constitutes an abuse of fiduciary obligation. Such a reform in legal interpretation will come slowly, if at all. It will require recognition that there are some relatively simple and dependable prima facie indications that a given management is unsatisfactory and requires improvement.

The matters we have been discussing may appear to fall outside of the broad theme of corporate democracy, because they deal with rather the opposite concept of protection of minority interests. But in this domain, as in many others, an alert and an energetic few may show the way to the many who are unperceptive and sluggish. Standards and criteria of fair treatment, which minority stockholders may establish through invoking the trusteeship obligation of those in control, should without too much difficulty be accepted as guides to intelligent action by public stockholders constituting a true majority and exercising this majority control through their votes.

16

The War Economy
and Stock Values

When the Korean crisis burst upon us last June, Wall Street analysts rightfully began to forecast a near-war or full-war economy, complete with price controls, at least some rationing, and a heavy excess profits tax. Granting that the volume of business would be tremendous, they still were inclined to anticipate a serious reduction in corporate net after taxes. This prospect, combined with the war situation itself, led to widespread predictions of lower stock prices.

Stock Market Has Gone Up

The stock market, proceeding with its usual disregard of the majority views of experts, has gone up instead of down in the past six months. By this behavior it has displayed two characteristics hitherto rather foreign to the security exchanges. The first has been the absence of panicky or deeply pessimistic reactions to international developments of the most disquieting sort. We cannot ignore the fact that the United States faces the new and harrowing danger of large-scale physical destruction and civilian casualties of inestimable magnitude. This possibility would justify—by past traditions it would almost demand—a severe and prolonged case of jitters among both speculators and

Reprinted from *The Analysts Journal*, vol. 7, no. 1 (First Quarter 1951): 34–35 with permission.

investors. Secondly, the market seems to have been subordinating medium-term to really long-term considerations. For it is fair to assume that the recent rise in stock prices has reflected essentially the public's conviction that a war economy is an inflationary economy, and that, *in the long run, inflation means higher average prices for common stocks.*

Gives Rise to Two Questions

This interpretation of the recent course of the market gives rise to two questions: First, is the long-term bullish view of stock values a valid one? Second, even if it is, how did it happen that stocks have been acting in a response to this view, instead of giving way first to short-term pessimism and even to panic? In this short article I shall try to find answers to these two questions.

Historically the broad pattern of war—with which this generation is now all too familiar—is that of inflation followed by deflation. The inflation may be "contained" by rigid controls during the period of hostilities, as it was during World War II and is likely to be during the present imbroglio. But, at the war's end, controls are relaxed, and then the pressures generated by deficit financing are likely to vent themselves in an explosive rise of general prices. War weakens and cheapens the dollar—especially if it is a paper dollar.

Is it not reasonable to expect that stock prices as a whole must rise, sooner or later, to reflect this cheapening of the dollar? The course of the stock market from 1900 to date shows a fairly close *overall* correspondence between the rise in stocks and in general prices, although there have been significant divergencies for fairly long periods. Business has been able to adjust itself not too badly to higher costs, notably higher wage scales, and even to a progressively increasing burden of income tax. But the combination of a sharp increase in the normal tax rate plus a drastic excess profits tax now appears certain to reduce corporate earnings below the average of recent years. Thus not only is it easy to imagine the tax take rising to a level that will prevent corporate net from keeping pace with inflation but also one can even envisage a decline in earning power, despite an ostensible increase in the value of business assets. Since earnings have a far greater influence on stock prices than have asset values, such a development would apparently justify a bearish view on the long-term course of the stock market.

Weight of Probabilities

That war conditions *could* be destructive of stock values is hard to deny but the mere possibility proves nothing of significance. It is the weight of *probabilities* that we are interested in. In reflecting on this question, we would do well to start with past experience. We have been unfortunate enough to have undergone two world wars in our own lifetimes; the least we should have to show for this travail is some added knowledge and perhaps some access of wisdom. It is fashionable to insist that a third world war will be completely different in its economic impact from the first two. This is a statement that requires proof. In its absence, it is better to take our cue from what has gone before.

Earning Power Was Held Down

During World War II, the earning power of our leading companies was held down by price controls, renegotiation, and the excess profits tax. Nevertheless the Dow Jones Industrial unit averaged earnings about 20% higher than in the prewar period. Secondary or smaller companies showed, in the main, a much larger expansion of net profits. The *postwar* earnings of business as a whole proved unexpectedly large and well maintained.

Conservative analysts, who allowed for a considerable falling off of long-term profits from the 1946–50 rate, were still compelled to assume a new plateau or average for earning power at least 50% above the 1936–40 figure. Thus for the Dow Jones unit there was a tendency to estimate average peacetime profits at about $15, against $9 odd in the prewar years.

The average price of the Dow Jones unit in 1936–40 was 135; in 1946–50 it was about 180. My own calculations of its central value (made as of 1947) set it at about 215.

If this overall pattern is assumed to hold good for the looming war economy, we should then anticipate the following: (1) restricted but substantial earnings during the period of mobilization or hostilities, (2) an appreciable rise in the basic dollar earning power in the next postwar period, as against the prewar "normal," (3) irrational or at least unpredictable fluctuations in stock prices in the next few years, (4) no sound reason to believe that stock *values* would be diminished by war conditions, (5) persuasive reasons to expect that the ultimate central level of stock values would be well above our recent calculations.

Some Actual Figures

Some of the actual figures relating to the Dow Jones unit will point up our conclusions. For 1946–49, the earnings before taxes averaged about $30, leaving about $18 after taxes. At the end of 1950, they appear to have been running at a rate as high as $60 before taxes and more than $30 after taxes. The present maximum overall tax rate is 62%; in World War II, it was 72%. If we assume wartime earnings before tax of, say, $50 per unit, and an effective overall tax of 70%, then the unit would show net profits of $15—the same figure that was projected for average peacetime earnings after 1945. If a "normal multiplier"—related to the interest rate and the quality of the Dow group—were applied to these earnings, the result would about support the initial price level of 1951. Actual figures would probably be better than this projection. Though the effective tax rate may well rise above 70%, the earnings before taxes are also likely to exceed $50 for the unit.

Tax Shelter for Railroads

The excess profits tax shelter now accorded the railroads, coupled with their heavy traffic, give them possibilities of fantastically high net profits. This situation is too favorable to last, but it seems likely that the principle of tax preference will remain to their benefit, as it has for oil and mining companies through many changes in the scale of rates. The public utilities are not likely to be war beneficiaries; but they too have been given a tax shelter, and the stability of their earning power does not appear seriously threatened.

The calculations just made reflect wartime business activity rather than war-induced inflation. Judging from the past, most of that inflation will be experienced when peace is restored. No one has enough foresight to project the economic conditions that will confront us then, but I believe enough in logic to predict that stock values will stand up better than the value of the paper dollar.

The Price Value, Asset Values, and Earning Power

The pessimistically minded can easily conjure up a picture of high wages and crushing taxes, which together will hold down corporate profits to a figure "lower than any assignable quantity," in spite of an extremely inflated general price level. It should be pointed out that such a result would be incompatible with the American system—which, in spite of growing governmental controls and other obstacles, has remained essentially one of free *investment choices*. The core or keystone of that system is the voluntary investment annually of huge sums in additional capital goods. Large-scale commitments of this kind will be made continuously *only* if the existing capital investment by and large is showing an adequate profit. This profit, in turn, must be measured to some degree against the *replacement value* of the existing plant. In other words, an inflated price level, which raises the replacement cost of capital goods, must reflect itself also in a corresponding increase in the dollar profits produced by past investment.

Relation of Asset Values and Earnings

This relationship between asset values and earning power is neither precise nor uniform. In fact, the variations in earnings on invested capital are so extraordinary as to suggest that the idea of *any* relationship is a fallacious one. But, when the economy is viewed broadly, we can see that large-scale new investment presupposes adequate earnings on the *composite* or the *typical* old investment. In fact, we may suggest the rule that, as the quantity of annual new investment increases, the relationship between the earnings on old capital and the earnings on new capital tends to become closer and more logical.

Encouragement of New Investment

The emphasis by government on maintaining full employment makes the encouragement of new investment a primary element of state policy. This in turn sets practical limits to governmental interference with the making of a "fair rate" of profit after taxes. Here we may have in part the explanation of the paradox that, while American business was complaining in recent years about the hostile attitude of Washington, it was registering the largest recorded rate of earnings on invested capital, computed at original cost.

Conclusion

Our conclusion is that the public is instinctively right in its present emphasis on the inflationary aspects of the developing war economy, and its consequent bidding up of stock prices just when the rule book called for near-panic selling. It is interesting to conjecture why investors and speculators are acting logically in the present crisis, whereas under similar conditions in the past they have been dominated by the more obvious psychology of fear. Let us venture the suggestion that what we are witnessing is the maturing of inflation consciousness, which—by an awkward but not too surprising coincidence—is about contemporaneous with the maturity of the first Series E Savings Bonds. There can be such a thing as a panic to buy as well as a panic to sell. The stock market since last June is far from resembling a "buyers' panic"; but the definite signs all around us of uneasiness concerning the value of the paper dollar, and of investments tied to the dollar, suggest that a definitely new guiding force is entering into the psychology of the investing public.

The spectacular and ill-fated New Era stock market of the 1920s began about 1924 with an analogous and quite soundly documented realization of the long-term superiority of stocks over bonds. Other conditions, however, were as different from today's as one could imagine. Perhaps that is a good reason for repeating the French maxim that was made to order for Wall Street: "The more it changes, the more it's the same thing."

17

Some Structural Relationships Bearing upon Full Employment

The full-employment commitment, which was greeted skeptically by many of us in 1946, seems now on the way to becoming an accepted premise of politics and economics. Both major parties acknowledge government's responsibility for preventing continued mass unemployment.

Our earlier concern as to how this engagement can be fulfilled is no longer so manifest. The excellent employment record of the past thirteen years—and particularly the resistance shown by our economy to the depressive influences of 1954—has given American business a new confidence in its ability to keep forging ahead without nasty setbacks of the old-fashioned kind.

This optimistic thesis might be restated by some in different terms, but with the same consequences, namely: Either business will expand indefinitely at the accelerating rate required to maintain full employment, or else the Administration (of either party) will intervene as massively as is necessary to rescue us from any tailspin. This view would hold, in other words, that active business and nearly full employment are guaranteed; the only question is whether we shall have them with or without further inflation. It is probable that the bull market of 1953–55 has been reflecting the gradual permeation of investors' minds by this revolutionary conception of the future.

Reprinted from *The Analysts Journal*, vol. 11, no. 2 (May 1955): 13–16 with permission.

Before a security analyst or other economic student decides to accept or reject this crucial hypothesis, he might do well to ponder over some long-term economic relationships, which have had a significant bearing on the question of full employment in the past. We have now available reasonably dependable aggregate figures, covering the four basic factors that together determine changes in the number of unemployed: (1) productivity, (2) per-capita product (or consumption), (3) hours of work, (4) labor force. These four elements are mathematically joined in the following equation:

Unemployment = labor force − gross national product (consumption) − [GNP per man-hour (productivity) × average annual hours per worker]

In this article I propose to discuss some rather striking arithmetical relationships, which have existed among the four enumerated factors in the past, and then to compare the record with a recent authoritative projection to the year 1965. The source of this projection and of most of our statistical material is a recent study by the staff of the (Congressional) Joint Committee on the Economic Report, entitled "Potential Economic Growth of the United States during the Next Decade" (October 1954).

For our purpose, it has been convenient to examine the percentage changes in the four factors over four approximately equal intervals between 1900 and 1953, namely: 1913 versus 1900, 1927 versus 1913, 1940–41 average versus 1927, and 1953 versus 1940–41. None of the years taken marked a depression period, as measured by the general business index of the Cleveland Trust Company. However, 1953 would stand out as a year of business boom, whereas the other reference years show activity moderately above or below normal, as follows:

1900	+ 3%
1913	+ 4½
1927	+ 3
1940–41	– 1½
1953	+15½

It follows from our previously stated formula that the maintenance of full employment depends on the interaction of three basic arithmetical relationships:

1. *The Productivity-Product Ratio.* This is the ratio of the *rate of increase* in productivity (GNP per man-hour) on the one hand and in consumption or living standard (GNP per capita) on the other. It produces intermediate result I, which is the change in man-hours required (worked) per unit of population.

2. *The Change in Hours of Work.* This is a composite quotient, found by dividing total man-hours worked by the number of employed. Combined with result I, it produces intermediate result II, which is the change in workers needed (employed) per unit of population.

3. *The Change in the Labor Force.* The significant figure here is the labor force in relation to population. Combined with result II, it produces final result III, which is the change in unemployment per unit of population.

Our Table 1 sets forth the basic data used in the study and some resultant figures of importance. In Table 2, the relationships previously discussed are developed as percentage changes for each of the four intervals selected. In Table 3, approximate average percentages are worked out, and these are compared in turn with the projected changes for the twelve years 1953–65 as estimated in the staff report.

Table 1

Basic Economic Data Used

	1900	1913	1927	Average 1940–41	1953	Projection 1965*
Population, millions	76.1	97.2	119.0	132.8	159.6	190.0
Adjusted population, millions**	63.8	82.7	102.1	117.5	138.1	163.5
Gross natl. product in 1953 dollars, billions	75.6	113.1	160.5	220.1	364.9	535.0
Avg. work week, hours	58.0	51.4	48.1	42.9	40.6	37.1
Working force, millions	29.1	38.7	46.9	56.9	67.0	79.0
Employment, millions	27.7	37.6	45.0	50.0	65.5	76.0
Unemployment, millions	1.4	1.1	1.9	6.9	1.5	3.0
Total man-hours worked, billions	83.5	100.4	112.6	111.5	138.2	146.6
Productivity, GNP per man-hour, 1953 dollars	0.905	1.126	1.461	1.974	2.640	3.649
Per Capita Adjusted						
GNP, 1953 dollars	1,185	1,367	1,570	1,873	2,643	3,272
Man-hours worked	1,308	1,214	1,103	949	1,001	897
Labor force	0.456	0.468	0.460	0.484	0.485	0.483
Employment	0.434	0.454	0.442	0.426	0.474	0.465
Unemployment	0.021	0.14	0.18	0.058	0.011	0.018

Joint Committee Staff Report, October 1954.
** *Children under fourteen counted as one-half.*

Table 2

Percentage Changes between Period Dates*

	1913 vs. 1900	1927 vs. 1913	1940–41 Avg. vs. 1927	1953 vs. 1940–41 Avg.
Productivity, GNP per man-hour	+19.6% h	+22.9% h	+26.0% h	+25.0% h
Product or consumption, GNP per capita adjusted	+13.4	+12.9	+16.2	+29.1
Man-hours worked**	–7.2	–9.3	–14.0	+5.2
Work week	–11.5	–6.3	–10.8	–5.4
Employment**	+4.6	–2.9	–3.6	+10.1
Labor force**	+2.8	–1.7	+4.9	+0.2
Unemployment**	–38	+28	+69	–81

* *Percentage increases are calculated against higher figure. See text.*
** *Per capita adjusted.*

Table 3

Projected Changes 1953–65 versus Average Changes in the Past

	Approx. Avg. Change per Past Period in 1900–53*	Projected Change, 1965 vs. 1953
Productivity	+22% h	+27.5% h
Product or consumption**	+16½	+17.9
Man-hours worked**	−6	−10.4
Work week	−8	−8.6
Employment**	+2	−1.9
Labor force**	+1½	−0.5
Unemployment**	—	+3.0

* *Adjusted to twelve years.*
** *Per capita adjusted.*

The reader should be warned that our calculations have two unusual characteristics, which we believe will make them more meaningful. Our per-capita figures are based on "adjusted population," which counts children under fourteen as half-persons. The purpose of this device is to allow in our comparisons for the significant decline in the proportion of such children, for example, from 32.3% of total population in 1900 to 23.1% in 1940.

Second, our percentage changes are related to the "higher figure"—which means, for example, that an advance from 100 to 200 is a rise of 50 "% h," just as a decline from 200 to 100 is a fall of 50%. This technique has interesting advantages, particularly in successive comparisons.

When we examine the percentage changes shown in the various periods we are impressed by certain interesting structural relationships, as follows:

1. Productivity has advanced throughout the fifty-three-year period at an accelerating rate. Since increased

productivity by itself—i.e., if not offset by other factors—reduces the need for workers, this aspect of the employment picture has tended to present increasing difficulties.

2. Per-capita GNP, or consumption, has also increased in each period, at a fairly constant rate. Although the big upsurge in 1940–53 is most encouraging, it is exceptional in its magnitude. A good deal of it is due to the rise in the level of business, from slightly below normal in 1940–41 to a record boom activity in 1953.

3. The figures important to employment are not productivity changes or consumption changes, considered separately, but their *comparative* rates of growth— what I have called the productivity-product ratio. In three periods out of the four, productivity increased faster than product (or consumption), yielding a "productivity excess." In a similar study, published in 1947, covering a greater variety of periods, I found a "productivity excess in all intervals between years of approximately similar business activity.[1]

Where there is a productivity excess, the necessary result is to reduce man-hours worked per population unit. Between 1900 and 1953, this figure fell from 1,308 hours to 1,001 hours, per-capita adjusted. If the work week had not been shortened, the consequence would have been a decline of 23% in per-capita employment, producing some 16 million more unemployed in 1953.

4. The important offset to the productivity excess has, of course, been shorter hours. The work week has declined in every period, but at a somewhat irregular rate. There is no indication that hours of work have

been consciously adjusted downward in an amount calculated to maintain the level of employment in good times, but the actual results have not been too far from such an objective.

The important question here is whether the productivity excess is a structural characteristic of our American economy. If there is a built-in tendency for productivity to increase faster than consumption—and the half-century figures point strongly to that conclusion—then the gradual reduction of the work week (or, better, the work year) becomes mathematically necessary to prevent a growth in unemployment.

5. Changes in labor force relative to population appear to be independent of other factors, and they have an independent effect on unemployment. Over the past fifty-three years, the number of workers has increased at a slightly greater rate than the population, that is, from 407 to 420 per 1,000 unadjusted, and from 456 to 485 per 1,000 adjusted. This difference alone, if not offset by other factors, would have increased 1953 unemployment by several millions.

There is something perverse about this expansion in our labor force. One might have expected that the tremendous advance in scale of living would have reflected itself in some decline in the working portion of our population. (Actually the influx of women into jobs has more than offset both the elimination of child labor and the trend toward earlier retirement.) The embarrassing aspect of the change in labor force is that it was concentrated almost entirely in the 1927–40 period, when it greatly aggravated the unemployment situation produced by the productivity excess.

6. Finally we must recognize that unemployment—the final and key figure—represents at bottom a *marginal* relationship among the four determining factors of *(a)* increasing productivity, *(b)* increasing consumption, *(c)* falling hours of work, and *(d)* variations in the labor force. The productivity increase, taken by itself, could create a serious unemployment problem in only two years; the average productivity excess would create such a problem in six years; a perverse change in the labor force could presumably do so in twelve years.

From the theoretical standpoint, at least, this is a major objection to the full-employment commitment. It could conceivably require strenuous governmental intervention in the economy when a relatively slight imbalance appears between the major factors determining employment and unemployment.

This fact is pointed up by the developments between 1952 and 1954. (The data are not given in our tables.) In these two years, real product per capita remained about unchanged, but average unemployment nearly doubled, rising from 1,673,000 to 3,200,000. The controlling elements were a rise of 4.4% in productivity, offset in part by declines of 1% each in hours of work and relative working force.

Implications for the Future

The projections into 1965, made by the staff of the Joint Committee on the Economic Report, have an interesting bearing on the previous analysis—and possibly vice-versa. Their study concluded that the economy could reach a satisfactory balance ten years hence, on the basis of a gross national product of $535 billion—47% greater than in 1953—with no change in the price level.

But to achieve this balance, in accordance with the model presented in their study, three structural requirements will have to be met. To begin with, the staff points out, the amount of disposable income *saved* will have to be reduced from a recent 8 to 6%, in order to create the necessary demand for consumer goods. Second, nonmilitary expenditures by all sections of government will have to expand much more rapidly than GNP itself. Finally, there must be a substantial further shortening of the work week; although not saying so explicitly, the discussion indicates that the alternative to such shorter hours is likely to be an inadmissible level of unemployment.

In brief, the conditions require that people work less and save less, and that civil government spend more, than at the 1953 rate. Topsy-turvy as this may sound, it is an authentic reflection of our twentieth century economy of abundance, which in turn is founded on our ever-increasing productivity.

We have worked out the percentage changes between 1953 and 1965, implied in the staff's projection, for the factors governing the level of unemployment. The figures appear in Table 3.

It will be noted that productivity is estimated to increase at a somewhat faster rate than in 1940–41 to 1953. However, the advance in consumption (per-capita GNP) is projected at a much lower rate than in 1940–41 to 1953. It is set, in fact, at about 10% more than the annual rate for the entire period 1900–53. The result is a substantial productivity excess (10.4%), and a corresponding fall in the man-hours required per capita.

The decline in the work week is anticipated (or stipulated) to be almost exactly at the average rate for the half-century. The composite result of the three factors is a decline of just under 2% in per-capita employment, one-quarter of which is offset by a minor shrinkage in relative labor force. The final calculation shows an increase in unemployment from 11 to 18 per 1,000 population, adjusted.

This is, of course, a very encouraging projection. (But the staff warns us that it presents rather a picture of how maximum economic growth *may* be achieved than predictions of actual developments.) It is certainly not Utopian, for it appears to be quite closely in line with the secular growth of our economy, as analyzed in our four-period comparisons.

But, even if the estimates impress us as reasonable, two caveats should be borne in mind by those studying the figures as a possible guide to investment and business decisions. The first is that these satisfactory twelve-year advances are not in themselves incompatible with a substantial interim setback. In each of the three periods during 1900–41 we had business depressions, although the economy showed rather consistent growth between all the terminal years.

The prevention of a *cyclical* downturn, with resultant high unemployment, is a separate problem. Will the economy be able to resist depressive forces in the future as well as it did in 1953–54? I doubt whether our analysis, or that of the Joint Committee's staff, sheds any definitive light on this important question.

The second caveat brings us back to the marginal nature of the unemployment total. It would take a comparatively small adverse change in the first three of our controlling factors to change the final figure of unemployment from a fairly satisfactory to a problem-making figure. For example, if the work week should fall 2 hours instead of 3½, the arithmetical result would be to double the unemployment figure—i.e., to 6 million. Nor is it impossible that the fourth factor—labor force—may add substantially to difficulties created by the other elements.

The American economy has been doing remarkably well in recent years. But it would be premature to conclude that it is now both depression-proof and unemployment-proof. Nor are the two characteristics necessarily the same.

All data for 1913 and later years are taken from the Joint Committee's Report. Man-hours employed have been raised to allow for general government employees, excluded in their figures. The 1900 data came from various sources, selected to accord most reasonably with the Joint Committee's series.

Use of the "Percent of High" Convention

Percentage increases are calculated in this article against the higher or terminal figure. I have long believed that this convention is better suited to the work of economists and security analysts than the standard method of calculating percentage gains against the starting figure. I am emboldened to employ it here because of its use in a study published by the Department of Economic Affairs of the United Nations entitled "Instability in the Export Markets of Underdeveloped Countries" (1952). As pointed out in Appendix B of that paper, the "percent of high" or "% h" convention (my designations) has several advantages over the standard method, namely:

1. By the "% h" method the series 100, 80, 100 shows a fall of 20%, followed by a rise of 20%, instead of the conventional (and troublesome) 20% fall and 25% rise.
2. A single rise is always under 100% h, corresponding to the maximum single decline (where positive numbers only are used).
3. In two series such as 10, 5, 8, 10 and 5, 10, 8, 5 the average absolute fluctuations are the same under the "% h" method, whereas they differ markedly under the standard method.

Note that "percent of high" is recommended only for comparing changes between successive values. It is not applicable to calculating percentage of profit mortality and the like.

NOTES

1. See Benjamin Graham, "National Productivity: Its Relationship to Unemployment in Prosperity," *American Economic Review*, vol. 37 (May 1947), pp. 384–396.

18

Our Balance of Payments:
The "Conspiracy of Silence"

The problem, in relation to our balance of payments, is a highly paradoxical one. On the one hand there has been a real threat in the international position of the dollar; on the other, this threat arose from reasons which are in no sense basic and which differ completely from the standard causes of foreign-exchange difficulties.

In this paper I shall refer to more recent developments, and inquire further into a question which I have found most intriguing: Why have the innumerable commentators on the problem—from President Kennedy at one end of the spectrum to U. S. Steel's Robert Tyson at the other—failed to mention (except in completely inadequate fashion) the underlying cause of our "dollar crisis"? It is this virtually unanimous ignoring of the most important fact in the case that has invited the phrase "conspiracy of silence" used in our title.

This paper will be written in an uncompromising style and will be highly critical of other people's statements. It will surely hurt the feelings of some and will strike many as intemperate and even arrogant. My excuse (for what it is worth) is that the strength of the dollar, a primary interest of the United States, may well depend on a proper understanding of a much misunderstood situation. To bring that about, a forthright utterance may be essential.

Reprinted from *The Analysts Journal*, vol. 18, no. 6 (November–December 1962): 9–14 with permission.

Rise and "Disappearance" of the Dollar Crisis

Our balance-of-payments problem began in 1958. In 1951–57 we had experienced an overall adverse balance averaging about $1 billion a year. This was regarded as a favorable development for international stability, since it permitted other nations to acquire gold and dollars to build up their sorely needed monetary reserves. But in the next three years our adverse balance averaged $3.7 billion, and in 1961 it was about $2.5 billion. This four-year loss of some $13½ billion in international "liquidity" transformed our net position from a credit balance of $6.7 billion to a debit balance of about the same amount (Table 1). It became evident that we could not long continue a liquidity drain at this rate and maintain the international value of the dollar. Hence the "dollar crisis," and the widespread view that it would soon have to be devalued in terms of gold.

Table 1

U. S. Liquid Position and U. S. Equity Position 1949–61 (in billions)

	Dec. 1949	Dec. 1957	Dec. 1961*
Gold	$24.6	$22.8	$16.9
Less Due Foreigners on Short-term	7.0	16.1	23.8
Primary Liquidity	17.6	6.7	def. 6.9
Add:			
U. S. Private Investment			
Short-term (gross)	1.3	3.2	6.0
Long-term (net)	8.4	20.8	30.2
U. S. (Private) Equity	27.3	30.7	29.3
Add:			
U. S. Government Advances	11.0	17.3	17.0
Total Equity	38.3	48.2	17.0

Partly estimated from balance-of-payments figures.

Our government steadfastly denied any such necessity or intention. It stated its expectation that various steps would place our foreign accounts in balance by the end of 1963. Figures for the second quarter of this year showed improvement—the adverse balance falling to an annual rate under \$1 billion; and the anticipated deficit for 1962 was placed at about \$1½ billion.

At the September convention of the World Bank and the IMF in Washington, central bankers from many countries "hailed the end of the dollar crisis" and "dismissed devaluation" as no longer a threat. In fact, they began to express worry at what would happen to their own trade balances and international liquidity when our own deficits had ceased. (Whether our balance-of-payments problem is indeed under full control is a separate question, to be dealt with later.)

An observer might well suspect that the threat to the dollar could not have been a fundamental one if it could be dispelled by a change in the figures of a single quarter together with some reassuring official statements. This brings us to our thesis: The loss of liquidity by the United States since 1957 can be traced directly and exclusively *to the increase in the annual rate of our net foreign investments.* A development of this kind is not basic to a country's foreign-exchange position; it has never compelled a devaluation in the past, and need never be permitted to bring on an unwanted devaluation in the future.

The true situation was summed up epigramatically by a delegate to the recent world bankers' convention as follows: "The United States has not been living beyond its international means, but it has been investing beyond its international means."

The correctness of this diagnosis will be demonstrated by the comparative data which follow. We shall then deal with certain contentions that seek to absolve our foreign-investment rate from responsibility for the dollar crisis. Later we shall ask why the facts in the matter have been all but universally ignored. Finally we shall indicate how in our opinion the origin of our difficulty itself suggests the best way of dealing with it.

Our Balance of Payments in Longer Perspective

In Table 2 we summarize our foreign accounts for the long period 1929–61 in a revised form intended to bring out the true significance of the figures, and in particular the extraordinary change in our foreign-investment operations in recent years as against all previous periods. The accounts are combined here into only three basic groups:

A. All private transactions, net, except private capital accounts.
B. All government transactions, net, including capital accounts.
C. Private capital accounts, net (excluding foreign *short-term* capital) plus "unrecorded transactions (errors and omissions)."

Group A includes imports and exports, various services, transferred income from foreign investments, and our private remittances abroad. It excludes government services and "military transactions," which the official classification lists among "exports and imports of goods and services." We add these items—important since 1940—to other government receipts and payments in Group B.

The "unrecorded transactions" are included with our capital accounts, in Group C, since it is generally understood that most of these items represent transfers of capital into or out of this country which move "outside channels normally covered by our reporting network." Foreign short-term capital movements are excluded from Group C, because they are treated as a balancing item similar to gold movements. (Our own private and

Table 2

Our Balance of Payments in Long-Term Perspective (Annual averages in millions)

Period	Group A All Private Accounts (Excl. Capital)	Group B All Gov't Accounts (Incl. Capital)	A + B Current Balance (Equity Change)	Group C Private Investment (Net)*	A + B + C Final Balance (Change in Liquidity)
	cr	dr			
1929–41	$ 650	$ 100	cr $ 550	cr $ 570	cr $1,120
1942–45	—	—	dr 1,530	dr 170	dr 1,700
1946–49	7,942	5,928	cr 2,020	dr 100	cr 1,920
1950–57	4,537	4,877	dr 340	dr 940	dr 1,200
1958–61	5,016	5,326	dr 310	dr 3,130	dr 3,440

* Excl. foreign short-term investment here.

Aggregate Balances for Two Periods

	21 Years 1929–49	12 Years 1950–61
Current Balance (Change in Equity)	cr $ 9,100	dr $ 4,000**
Our Foreign Investments (net)	cr 6,300*	dr 20,000
Final "Balance" (Change in Liquidity)	cr $15,400	dr $24,000

* Disinvestment—i.e., excess of foreign investment here.
** Our equity in unremitted earnings would exceed this debit balance.

governmental short-term balances abroad are not considered offsets against the foreign balances here, mainly because our government cannot use them at will to meet demands on our gold.)

It is instructive to divide our foreign account developments since 1929 into five periods: (1) Prewar—1929–41; (2) World War II—1941–45; (3) Postwar—1946–49; (4) Korea-Suez—1950–57; and (5) Dollar crisis—1958–61. Our true "balance of trade" in each period is found by combining Groups A and B, and excluding our net private capital transactions. This balance may be considered as our "net profit or loss" in dealing with the rest of the world, or as our "balance on current account," or as our "net change in foreign equity."

Here we see varying results between 1929 and 1949, followed by a very moderate average adverse balance in the past twelve years. Actually, the adverse balance disappears when our unremitted gains on investments are taken into account. Thus, our overall "equity" position has increased somewhat since 1949 and since 1957, without counting any part of our government advances, some of which are being currently collected.

The important point to note is that the small "current loss" was slightly lower in the dollar-crisis years than in the "contented period" of 1950–57. Not only that, in 1961—at the very height of the dollar scare—we were reporting one of the largest favorable *current* balances in our history (exceeded only in 1946–47), even after deducting over $5 billion net of government expenditures abroad.

The chief figures to observe in Table 2 are those of our net foreign investments (Group C). From 1929 through 1949 we actually had a net *dis*investment—excess of foreign purchases here over ours abroad—aggregating over $7 billion.

For the 1950–57 period our net private investments averaged somewhat under $1 billion.

We started that period in an extremely liquid position, with too much of the world's gold, and it was logical for us to exchange excess liquidity (earning no return) for profitable foreign long-term investments. But later our behavior resembled that of investor-speculators in our own bull market.

As our liquidity decreased—i.e., our capacity for making foreign investments without monetary strain—we stepped up enormously the *annual rate* of such investments. Excluding offsets by other investors here, our capital transfers rose from $600 million in 1949 to $1.3 billion in 1955 and then to $4.6 billion in 1961. (Unrecorded transactions of $600 million are included in the latter figure). We have indeed been investing beyond our international means.

Challenges to Our Thesis

My emphasis on the rise in the rate of foreign investment as the basic cause of the dollar crisis has been challenged on various accounts. Consideration of these objections should help clarify the picture. The first argument is that there is no valid reason for singling out the investment item for blame, since our adverse balance is the resultant of many factors—including, on the debit side, notably our huge outlays for foreign aid and military expense abroad. One aspect of this general viewpoint was stated by one who certainly should know the subject, Walter Lederer, Chief of the Balance of Payments Division of the United States Department of Commerce. He says: "However, as long as the offsetting relationship between capital movements and changes in other transactions continues, both have to be considered in an evaluation of the balance of payments, and one cannot view some types of transactions as more 'basic' than the others."

The implication here seems to be that each year's foreign investments may have generated offsetting credit items of corresponding magnitude, and thus this category may not be usefully analyzed by itself as a causal factor in our difficulties.

But what are facts and figures? Let us look first at Table 3, which compares the results for 1961 with those for 1949. In 1949 we had a small adverse balance on current account, but our investments abroad were then *less* than foreigners' here (treating unrecorded transactions as investments). Hence we ended 1949 with a slight increase in liquidity. In 1961 we had almost a $1½ billion favorable balance on current account, but net investments abroad of nearly $4 billion changed this figure into a very embarrassing final adverse balance of some $2½ billion.

Table 3

What Is Responsible for the Change in Liquidity Balance between 1949 and 1961?

(in millions)

	(Merchandise Balance Only)	Group A All Private Excl. Capital	Group B All Government	A + B Current Balance	Group C Private Investment, Net	A + B + C Final Balance
1949	($5,424)	cr $6,140	dr $6,270	dr $ 130	cr $ 341	cr $ 211
1961	(5,340)	cr 6,815	dr 5,327	cr 1,488	dr 3,949	dr 2,461
Change	(dr 84)	cr 675	cr 943	cr 1,618	dr 4,290	dr 2,677

Should the blame for this spectacular *change* be spread about indiscriminately between our trade accounts, our government expenditures, and our foreign investments? Does the primary cause of the trouble defy identification? How can we ascribe the deficit to lagging exports—to "being priced out of the market," as so many have done—when our favorable merchandise balance in 1961 ($5.3 billion) was about equal to that of 1949, in spite of the trade advantages we enjoyed in the postwar years of European reconstruction?

Furthermore, our combined credit balance for goods and services (nongovernmental) was actually $675 million *better* than in 1949. Yes, say some, but the real culprit is obviously our government's program of foreign aid and military support. Are these experts aware that we spent $940 million *less* for these purposes in 1961 than in 1949? By what logic can one blame an element that shows *improvement* for a great deterioration in the overall picture? Since foreign investments are the only group that shows a significant adverse change, and since this change is of extraordinary magnitude, its role as architect of our embarrassment should be obvious to anyone who looks at the figures.

Objections Cited

But, again say the objectors, these investments generate large offsetting credits, and so they do our liquidity no overall damage. Chief of these is our income therefrom. In 1961 this income received from abroad totaled $3,645 million and was not much less than the $3,951 million we added to our investments (excluding here the unrecorded transfers). It is widely held that the closeness of these items of income and outgo prove that our annual foreign investments have been responsible for only a small part of our recent balance-of-payments deficits.

Plausible as this contention may sound, it is entirely fallacious. It fails to consider that nearly all the income from investments received in, say, 1960 and 1961 would still have been received even if we had not added a single dollar to our $45 billion of capital abroad at the end of 1959.

A reasonably accurate calculation on this point, covering 1958–61, appears in Table 4. It shows that the $14 billion of private capital sent out of this country in the last four years produced at most about $1.2 billion of *additional* remitted

---

Table 4

Effect of 1958–61 Foreign Investment on Our Income from Abroad (in millions)

Investment income as at Dec. 1957	$2,900
Expectable income 1958–61 without new investments (Four times the Dec. 1957 rate)	11,600
Actual investment income 1958–61	12,815
Gain in income as a result of 1958–61 investments	1,215
Our capital outflow 1958–61 (about)*	14,700
Net loss in liquidity: 1958–61 capital outflow less gain in income	13,500

* Includes unrecorded transactions aggregating about $1,200 million net.

income—an offset of less than 10% against our outlay. The entire "deficit" of 1960 and 1961—the period of maximum dollar crisis—would probably have been obviated had we reduced our gross capital outflow to, say, $1 billion each year instead of about $4.5 billion. (The current loss of investment income from this reduction would have been quite minor.)

Defenders of our huge capital commitments argue further, in this context, that they produce other important balancing credits in the form of additional exports of capital goods, which presumably would not have been made had we not increased our foreign plant accounts. Hence there is no way of determining the overall effect of these outflows on our final balance of payments.

In the narrow sense of complete accuracy this is of course true. But we have some data which throw light on the approximate magnitude of the claimed offsets. (These appear in an elaborate study of "U. S. Business Investments in Foreign Countries," published in 1960 by the United States Department of Commerce.) The figures indicate that our foreign interests in 1957 bought about $1 billion of capital goods from the United States, as against a total of $4.9 billion they spent that year on plant account. Our total outflow for foreign investments in 1957 was $3.2 billion, of which $2 billion was for these "direct investment enterprises."

There is an indication from these figures that our foreign investments in any year may generate about 30% in offsetting capital exports. On the other hand, our direct investment enterprises exported over $3.7 billion of goods to this country in 1957, a figure which apparently well exceeded their total purchases of goods from us. (The "incomplete total" of the latter, as compiled by the study, was $2.6 billion.) The text of the study emphasizes the dollar-saving advantages to the countries in which our investments are made. The implication is quite clear that, apart from remittances of income (already discussed), we lose rather than gain in the net effects of such investments on our balance of payments.

The Conspiracy of Silence

The data presented in our four tables should show clearly that the greatly enlarged rate of our investments abroad has the primary responsibility for the recent dollar crisis. Has any of my readers seen this aspect of the problem recognized, or the problem discussed in any detail, in the numerous pronouncements of the subject from nearly every authoritative source? I have not—before last September, at least. Let me now deal with the way the subject has been handled and the possible reason therefor.

There has been no recognition of the essential difference between the loss of liquidity from an unfavorable trade balance and one occasioned by investments. The January 1962 discussion by the Council of Economic Advisers combines both groups of transactions into what they term the "basic accounts."

Could the plant investment made by a business be "basic" in the same sense as its profit or loss from operations? By contrast the official Canadian analyses carefully distinguish between what they call the "Current Account Balance" and the "Net Capital Movement." A comparison between the highly unfavorable current balance of Canada since 1955 and the approximately break-even results of the United States in that period would have brought home the fact that Canada was to experience a true foreign-exchange crisis, while ours could be only a superficial or artificial one.

President Kennedy, in his February 1961 Special Message on the Balance of Payments, stated: "The surplus of our exports over imports, while substantial, has not been large enough to cover our expenditures for military establishments abroad, for capital invested abroad by private American business, and for government economic assistance and loan programs."

Note that our foreign investments are *sandwiched between* military expenditures and government aid—as if they were all of essentially the same character. This burying of capital items

in the middle of expense items became the general treatment—
and a most misleading one.

In his May 1962 speech to the U. S. Chamber of Commerce
the President further stated: "It costs the United States $3 billion
a year to maintain our troops and our defense establishment and
security commitments abroad. If the balance of trade is not sufficiently in our favor to finance this burden, we have two alternatives: one, to lose gold, as we have been doing; and two, to
begin to withdraw our security commitments." Here our foreign
investments are not even mentioned. The fact is that our *balance
of trade*—with investments excluded—has been sufficiently in
our favor to finance virtually all our government outlays abroad.

The President, in ignoring the role of enlarged investment,
may be plausibly ascribed to his strong desires in two directions:
first to prevent wage and price increases here; and second, to
persuade our prosperous allies to assume a larger share of our
overseas burdens. For one purpose it is useful to assert that our
exports must be substantially increased; for the other, to imply
that the dollar's position is really precarious and in need of aid
from our allies.

Finance Chairman Tyson of U. S. Steel, last March, put the
case in stronger language—and in my view, with even greater
inaccuracy. Said he: "There is only one real solution of the
problem of unfavorable balances of payment: it is the development or restoration of greater ability to compete in international markets." The purpose of that statement is clear from the
next sentence: "That means, in turn, I think, that Americans
must find the fortitude to bring to an end the era of flat wage
inflation."

Most of us would agree that wage inflation should be
halted. But some of us would disapprove basing that demand
on an alleged impairment of our ability to compete in foreign
markets—when the trade figures had just shown for both 1960

and 1961 two of our largest favorable merchandise balances in peacetime history, considerably exceeding the 1950–57 average.

The Silence Continues

The Wall Street Journal, always pursuing its own *bete noire*, summarized the situation thus in an editorial last July: "Though a lot of confusion has developed about the payments deficit, the essential facts are perfectly plain. U. S. business enjoys a large export surplus; it is primarily the Government's policies at home and abroad that have created the deficit." *BusinessWeek*, more judicious in tone but hardly more respectful of the facts, expressed a similar view at the same time in this fashion: "The plain—if disagreeable—fact is that the U. S. has committed itself to a considerably larger program of overseas military operations and foreign aid than it can finance within the present structure of international trade." Neither publication as much as mentions our stepped-up rate of investment, without which there would have been no dollar crisis. (Presumably, had we been investing $8 billion instead of $4 billion a year, and running a $7 billion final deficit, our government policies and commitments would still be responsible for all of it.)

These inaccurate characterizations have influenced other periodicals to even more exaggerated comments. Typical, perhaps, would be one from my own newspaper, one of the country's largest: "International bankruptcy is the theoretical disaster facing the U. S. if the bad news about the puzzling imbalance of payments problem continues. . . . We owe more in world markets than other countries owe us. Our liabilities exceed our assets. . . . U. S. liabilities include imports, military expenditures overseas, investments in foreign enterprises, and foreign aid."

Note here the listing of foreign investments in the midst of our "liabilities," with the concomitant suggestion that we are on the verge of international bankruptcy. No wonder people have expected a cut in the gold value of the dollar, and some have transferred huge sums to Switzerland and elsewhere.

It took the British Chancellor of the Exchequer to set the situation in almost its proper perspective last September, by stating: "The nature of this deficit is a very special one. On current commercial transactions the U. S. has a massive surplus and the problem has arisen because of the enormous amounts spent abroad on aid, defense, and investment. It could be said that the problem is less one of a balance of payments than a balance of generosity." These words imply that our huge foreign investments are part of our "generosity" which is scarcely true; but they *resemble* generous deeds in that their continuance is purely voluntary.

I have been chiefly concerned by the failure of our leading economists to take the trouble to look the facts in the face and to pay adequate attention to the key role of foreign investment in bringing about our dollar crisis. Relevant quotations are too numerous to be feasible. Suffice to say that an authoritative volume, issued last year containing thirteen essays on the subject by as many leading economists, devotes so little and so unilluminating discussion to the investment component to put the entire picture completely out of proper focus.

I am at a loss to explain what I consider a failure of professional competence. One explanation—which undoubtedly will seem plausible to many readers—is that my own diagnosis is completely incorrect. In self defense may I ask only that they go back over my data and my arguments, and consider them carefully before deciding who is right and who is wrong in this matter of transcendent importance.

Future Dangers and Possible Remedies

Even though our problem may have arisen from a "balance of generosity," plus overseas investment, it did pose a real threat to the international position of the dollar. The improvement shown in the first half of 1962 does not in itself carry assurance that it will continue to the point needed to put the dollar out of danger. (I should place that point at an annual loss of liquidity of not more than, say, $1 billion.)

Our foreign trade balance, so satisfactory for many months, may take a turn for the worse, and our military expenditures may have to be greatly increased. These appear more than outside possibilities in the atmosphere of real international crisis in which these words were written (October 28, 1962).

Assume that our liquidity loss is not sufficiently stemmed in the months to come, and assume that our foreign investments persist at their recent embarrassing rates; what steps can and should be taken to deal with the situation? It is obvious that we cannot rapidly step up our merchandise exports sufficiently, by means of the plant modernization expected to follow the recent granting of tax incentives. The reliance on this procedure for a *quick* solution, constantly expressed by highly-placed officials, had overtones of absurdity.

A deep cut in our overseas expenditures by the government is not out of the question, but involves a basic change of policy at a time when world events seem strongly against it. A rise in interest rates to attract or retain *short-term* capital from abroad is already under way; but this cannot change our overall liquidity position—it only prevents conversion of our short-term liabilities into gold withdrawals.

Whether much *long-term* capital could be brought in by higher interest rates appears uncertain; in any event there is strong opposition to moving up radically our entire domestic interest-rate structure for this or any other purpose. Let us discuss three other possibilities.

The first is devaluation of the dollar. Whether that would really solve the problem is a matter of controversy. But how could we possibly justify such an "act of bankruptcy" if it is brought on by our persistence in investing huge sums abroad? Has any nation, corporation, or individual ever gone bankrupt for such a fantastically inadequate reason?

The second possibility is obvious and logical. Let us cut our coat to our cloth—in other words, let us cut down our annual *new* foreign investments, net, to the amounts available for this purpose from all our other transactions. This would correspond to the normal behavior of an individual, who invests each year his surplus earnings above living expenses, taxes, and contributions.

The most appealing place to start such a policy would be in the area of foreign bond and stock flotations in this country. These have always been large, and appear to be larger than ever in 1962—reaching a rate of $1 billion or more.

Secretary Dillon has already indicated that, should the necessity arise, some steps to restrict that outflow of dollars will be taken. On the other hand, the compulsory reduction of our private investment abroad is opposed to our objectives of financial freedom. All of us would be reluctant to see such controls imposed—even though there is ample precedent therefor in the fiscal history of Great Britain.

To my mind the least objectionable way of dealing with the problem would be by means of *long-term* borrowings abroad made by our corporations and/or the U. S. government. Our difficulty grows essentially out of our incurring short-term liabilities to foreigners to finance long-term investments made in their countries. The evident solution would be to finance long-term foreign investments, to the extent required, by long-term foreign borrowings. These do not reduce our liquidity balance, for the year, or in total, as do short-term debts.

Such a program would entail the payment of appreciably higher interest rates than on borrowings floated in the U. S. But if our new investments are sufficiently profitable we can afford to pay these larger borrowing costs against them. If they are not, we should not make them.

It is claimed that such borrowing is "impossible" because foreign capital markets are not well-enough organized. However, investors in the prosperous European countries are lending large sums to their own enterprises; some of our corporations have already borrowed abroad; securities payable at the lenders' option either in their own currency or in U. S. dollars would be especially attractive.

The question surely is not "Can we borrow abroad on long term?" but rather "How much will it cost us?" To balance this extra cost against the position of the dollar as the world's key currency, it is well to consider the relative magnitudes involved. One billion dollars worth of foreign borrowing at an extra interest cost of 1½% would involve an annual expense of $15 million. Place this amount in the context of our annual foreign accounts exceeding $30 billion on each side, and our Gross National Product of some $550 billion. If future threats to the dollar could be dispelled by expenditures in annual units of $15 million, the price paid would be a small one.

PART 4

The Voice of the Profession

Benjamin Graham stepped down from active money management in 1956, with a multidecade track record of brilliant performance behind him. But he did not retire. Graham incessantly thought, wrote, and spoke about the future of the profession he had founded. Proud of how far financial analysis had come, he also felt the urgent need for the field to continue growing—and he worried about the multitude of ways in which Wall Street can go wrong. As always, he wrapped a warning around each bit of praise.

The articles in this section capture Graham delivering the spoken word, either in speeches or in interviews. This is Graham unfiltered: eloquent, literate, passionate about ideas, indignant at the mistreatment of investors, and incapable of anything short of complete intellectual honesty. In "Benjamin Graham: Thoughts on Security Analysis," we see Graham at his most relaxed, as he answers questions by telephone from students in a business class at Northeast Missouri State University.

He also displays his rapier-sharp wit. It's hard to think of any quip ever uttered that sums up the financial community more devastatingly than this offhand remark from Graham: "They used to say about the Bourbons that they forgot nothing and they learned nothing, and [what] I'll say about the Wall Street people, typically, is that they learn nothing, and they forget everything."[1]

While Graham believed that individuals can and should be trained to do better, he did not believe that human nature can be changed. Any one of us can learn and remember. But the markets as a whole are essentially doomed to learn nothing and forget everything. Therefore, analysts must always be prepared to stand alone as markets swarm around them toward emotional extremes.

The question of how analysts could add value in a market teeming with trained experts was foremost on Graham's mind in the final years of his life. He was keenly aware of the paradox that, having inspired thousands of people to become Chartered Financial Analysts, he was effectively responsible for making the market even harder to beat than ever. "I am no longer an advocate of elaborate techniques of security analysis in order to find superior value opportunities," he said to Charley Ellis in "A Conversation with Benjamin Graham." Only six months before he died, Graham told Hartman Butler in "An Hour with Mr. Graham," "I have a considerable amount of doubt on the question of how successful analysts can be overall when applying these selectivity approaches [that is, trying to pick specific securities that will outperform]."

If the massive spread of security analysis has made security selection more difficult than ever, then what other legitimate functions should the analyst serve?

In "The Future of Financial Analysis," Graham changes his long-standing term for investment professionals from "security analysts" to "financial analysts." He wants us to recognize that it is the analyst's "obligation" to study investments and investors alike—not just how securities behave but how the human beings who own them behave. Graham praises Level III of the newly implemented CFA examination for requiring formal knowledge in managing investments and advising clients. Returning to the medical comparison he introduced decades earlier when he first proposed the idea of a CFA charter, Graham urges analysts to seek the "financial health" of each client (or "patient") just as a doctor must act.[2]

He foresaw a time when all investment recommendations would carry the signed approval of a CFA charterholder, much the way financial reports in the United States must now be certified by senior management under the Sarbanes–Oxley rules. That vision of Graham's has still not been realized, but such a "Good Housekeeping" seal of approval might do a considerable amount of good.

Graham believes that the collective work of trained analysts has achieved "reasonably defensible relative prices"—making the market as a whole more efficient and less prone to extremes of overvaluation or undervaluation "at most times and for most stocks." But Graham also points out that the attempt by so many intelligent and highly trained analysts to outperform inevitably makes it harder for any of them to do so. "Neither the financial analysts as a whole nor the investment funds as a whole can expect to 'beat the market,'" he warns, "because in a significant sense they (or you) are the market." (There were already at least 8,000 analysts by 1963.)

Because of this fierce competitive pressure, says Graham, analysts can add only minimal value by determining which stocks offer maximum value. Instead, analysts should seek to draw a bright line between investment and speculation. Only after thorough research, meticulously establishing safety of principal and an adequate return, can an analyst conclude that a security is an investment at all. Graham refers here to his letter to the editor of the *Wall Street Journal*, which is worth quoting:

> By what definition of "investment" can one give the name "investors" to small people who make bets on the stock market by selling odd lots short?
>
> If these people are investors how should one define "speculation" and "speculators"?
>
> Isn't it possible that the current failure to distinguish between investment and speculation may do grave harm not only to individuals but to the whole financial community—as it did in the late 1920s?[3]

Graham advocates that analysts, in studying a security, should decompose its price into two components. One looks backward, the other forward. The first is what Graham calls "minimum true value," based on a company's historical earnings and assets; the second, "present value," appraises expectations for the future and takes speculative risk into account. It is here, in getting the weights of these two approaches right, that Graham believes analysts can earn their keep. And he points out that different analysts will—and should—arrive at different weights as they decompose value into its investment and speculative components.

If Graham had his wish, every research report would decompose the current market price of a security into the analyst's estimate of both its fundamental value and the contribution of speculation to the market price. (The speculative component, of course, can be either a positive or a negative number, depending on market sentiment.) In short, Graham wants analysts to tell their clients explicitly how risky each recommendation is.

Graham points out that separating price into its constituent parts of true value and speculative premium could help in constructing efficient portfolios "for the computers to work their magic upon." Although he has a different definition of risk in mind than Harry Markowitz did in 1952, Graham seems to be proposing a blend of active, fundamental analysis and passive portfolio management.

Graham repeats his perennial call for analysts to take a more active role in improving "unsatisfactory results" at the companies they follow. Then he offers a startling thought experiment: He asks us to imagine that the U.S. government, whose authority to tax corporate profits makes it an implicit stakeholder, starts telling companies "to make more money or else." This "brainstorm or nightmare," as Graham wryly called it, has resurfaced today as governments around the world consider how to handle their stakes in financial companies and automakers. While it is troubling to imagine government officials setting targets for the profitability of corporations, it is also troubling to note that too many private investors still neglect their own duty to monitor the companies they own.

In "The Future of Common Stocks," Graham begins by harking back to his arrival on Wall Street in 1914, when J. P. Morgan was fresh in investors' minds. In late 1912, a few months before Morgan died, the great financier had delivered his famous testimony to the Pujo Committee in Congress. Asked incessantly what the stock market would do, Morgan had long since developed a stock answer: "It will fluctuate."[4] Graham now improves on Morgan's dictum. He points out that the market will not only fluctuate, but it will fluctuate too far, leading to euphoria at the top and misery at the bottom.

Like any stock or bond, the stock market as a whole is sometimes cheap and sometimes expensive, depending on its current price and the mood of investors. As Graham points out, Edgar Lawrence Smith's book *Common Stocks as Long-Term Investments* came out when stocks were cheap. Investors found its arguments so persuasive that they eventually bid up stock prices to astronomical levels. At that point, the sensible assumptions in the book no longer made any sense at all because stocks had nowhere to go but down. And once the market crashed, driving stock prices to bargain levels, no one believed the book anymore—even though its arguments had just become valid again.

In the same vein, Graham cites the 1948 survey of investors by the U.S. Federal Reserve, which found that only 4% thought that common stock offered a "satisfactory" return, while 26% regarded it as "not safe" or a "gamble." The potential high returns on stocks, noted the Fed, "were considered only a minor advantage as compared to the disadvantages occasioned by lack of familiarity and lack of safety."[5]

"The public's attitudes in matters of finance," concludes Graham, "are completely untrustworthy as guides to investment policy." By "the public," did he mean individual investors alone—or amateurs and professionals alike?

The Dow was around 850 when Graham gave this speech in June 1974—a year and a half into a severe bear market that would take the index down below 600 by that December. At the time, pundits were already questioning whether stocks still made sense over long horizons—especially given raging inflation and interest rates, the energy crisis, "the ecology-pollution mess," "the movement towards less consumption and zero growth," and the justifiable anger of investors over Wall Street's "scandalous behavior."[6] Was buy-and-hold dead?

Graham's response: Of course not. Just as it made no sense to argue that stocks are worth buying no matter how high their price, it is "absurd to conclude . . . that . . . common stocks will be undesirable investments no matter how low their price level may fall." Later, he warns that "in the meantime stock prices may languish. But I should think the true investor would be pleased, rather than discouraged, at the prospect of investing his new savings on very satisfactory terms."

Institutional investors, according to Graham, have exacerbated the gap between price and value rather than narrowing it. Through excessive trading and the blind pursuit of momentum, they have made the market less efficient. In effect, while the proliferation of financial analysis has made prices more accurate, the pooling of giant sums of capital has created agency pressures that have undermined market efficiency.[7]

Graham alludes to the "two-tiered market," in which the Nifty Fifty stocks—including Walt Disney, MGIC Investment, and Polaroid—traded at 50 to 90 times their past earnings while the rest of the market languished.[8] "What," asks Graham angrily, "did our financial institutions do to hold down this insane speculative binge?" His answer: Nothing. In fact, momentum-chasing institutions threw financial analysis to the winds.

A similar phenomenon occurred a quarter of a century later, when institutional investors helped drive Internet and telecommunications stocks to triple-digit price-to-earnings ratios.

Graham says that the responsible financial analyst who wants to keep a clean conscience has only one choice at such a time: "to do the near impossible—namely, to turn his back on them and let them alone." This, he adds in a later understatement, requires "firmness of character."

Graham had publicly advocated indexing as early as 1955 and appears to have been in favor of it even earlier.[9] Here, he proposes that institutions could simply index their portfolios, putting financial analysis to good use by deviating from the benchmark "only on a persuasive showing that the issues substituted had distinctly more intrinsic value per dollar of price than the ones to be dropped." Graham adds that such a strategy "might well improve the actual performance."

Graham did not believe in simple answers to complicated questions. As markets roll on from euphoria to misery and back again, as analysts go about their daily work of seeking to calculate value, it is worth bearing

Graham's suggestions in mind. The job of the investor does not stop at the moment of purchase. The role of the analyst is not limited to analyzing financial statements and future trends. Like Graham, analysts and investors must forever seek to break new ground, to find the highest use for their skills, to question whether the conventional wisdom is wise, and to stand firm against any forces that might compromise the value and integrity of their work.

NOTES

1. The Bourbons were one of the dynastic families of France; the Bourbon kings Louis XV and XVI ruled in debauchery and dissipation, culminating in the overthrow of the monarchy in the French revolution.

2. In the "Rockville Center case" cited by Graham, Ronald Binday, a research analyst at the brokerage firm of Heft, Kahn & Infante in Rockville Center, N.Y., took at face value the assertions by investment bankers at his firm that a company he was following had a significant backlog of orders. They asked him not to double-check the information with the company itself, and he agreed, stating in a research note to clients that the purported backlog should increase profits by at least $2 per share. The SEC examiner concluded that Binday had demonstrated "a complete lack of understanding of, or concern with, the nature of information to be given prospective investors." The SEC revoked the firm's registration. See www.sec.gov/litigation/aljdec/1961/id19610518is.pdf, www.sec.gov/news/digest/1963/dig021263.pdf, and www.sec.gov/about/annual_report/1963.pdf, p. 61.

3. Benjamin Graham, "Rhetorical Questions," letter to the editor, *The Wall Street Journal* (July 12, 1962), p. 14.

4. Jean Strouse, *Morgan: American Financier* (New York: Random House, 1999), p. 11.

5. See the Fed's 1948 Survey of Consumer Finances (http://fraser.stlouisfed.org/publications/frb/issue/3834/download/56290/frb_071948.pdf), p. 777.

6. In 1974, inflation exceeded 12%, while the federal funds rate hit 13.5% a few weeks after Graham spoke. Between 1973 and 1975, the OPEC oil embargo roughly doubled oil prices. Pollution was so severe that the Cuyahoga River in Cleveland had caught fire in 1969. In 1972, the Club of Rome published its famous report, "The Limits of Growth," warning that overpopulation and overconsumption would lead to global economic collapse.

7. Recent research suggests that Graham's view may still hold. See, e.g., Jonathan Lewellen, "Institutional Investors and the Limits of Arbitrage" (http://mba.tuck.dartmouth.edu/pages/faculty/jon.lewellen/publications/Institutions.pdf) and Dimitri Vayanos and Paul Woolley, "An Institutional Theory of Momentum and Reversal" (www.lse.ac.uk/collections/paulWoolleyCentre/pdf/momentumshort.pdf).

8. See the classic article by Carol J. Loomis, "How the Terrible Two-Tier Market Came to Wall Street," *Fortune* (July, 1973), pp. 82–88, 186–190; reprinted in Charles D. Ellis and James R. Vertin, *Classics II: Another Investor's Anthology* (Homewood, Ill.: Dow Jones Irwin, 1991), pp. 156–164.

9. "Interview with Benjamin Graham, Expert on Investments: How to Handle Your Money," *U.S. News & World Report* (June 3, 1955), p. 47.

19

The Future of
Financial Analysis

Judged by its record in the past twenty-five years, a career as a Financial Analyst should have nothing to fear from the future.

For thinking back, it was a quarter of a century ago that The New York Society had only eighty-two members, and today it totals 2,945 members—some of whom are assigned to financial tasks in South America, Europe, and the Far East.

Moreover, there are now twenty-nine constituent societies which comprise *The Financial Analysts Federation*. And if we measured our expansion in dollar terms by annual dues collected, we might well claim to be one of the leading "growth industries" of the country.

Our growth in numbers has been accompanied by a corresponding advance in our financial influence. Would it be an exaggeration to say that the greater part of security transactions today are based to some degree on work done by Financial Analysts—ranging from perhaps the tangential influence of a brokerage house circular to full direction of portfolio changes?

With this growth of numbers and influence there should have come a somewhat corresponding increase in responsibility. But until recently there had been few visible signs of

Reprinted from the *Financial Analysts Journal*, vol. 19, no. 3 (May/June 1963): 65–70 with permission. This article was adapted from the remarks of Dr. Benjamin Graham on the occasion of the twenty-fifth anniversary of The New York Society of Security Analysts.

such a development. Now, with the foundation in 1959 of *The Institute of Chartered Financial Analysts*, and with arrangements completed to award the CFA designation, we may celebrate a *major* milestone in our progress toward a true professional status, accompanied by *truly* professional obligations to the public.

This move has been made none too soon to meet a rising demand for changes in Wall Street's ways of doing business. The recent decision of the Securities and Exchange Commission—in the "Rockville Center case"—indicates that Financial Analysts will be held to new accountability in the areas of fraud, and possibly beyond. Putting on a prophet's mantle I might foresee a perhaps distant time when all printed material that analyzes and/or recommends a security (and is distributed to the public) will have to appear over the signature and with the responsibility of a Chartered Financial Analyst.

For our profession I think the broader term "Financial Analyst" is preferable to "security analyst," because most senior analysts must now be prepared to go beyond the impersonal study of securities and to consider the requirements of the individual client. Examination III for the Chartered Financial Analysts designation covers "Investment Management," including the construction of portfolios suitable for various types of investors (and speculators). There is thus double function of the Financial Analyst, related in part to securities and in part to people. As portfolio adviser he prescribes for the financial health of his "patient" in much the same way as a doctor does for his physical or mental health.

It is my basic thesis—for the future as for the past—that an intelligent and well-trained Financial Analyst can do a useful job as portfolio adviser for many different kinds of people, and thus amply justify his existence. Also I claim he can do this by adhering to relatively simple principles of sound investment; e.g., a proper balance between bonds and stocks; proper diversification;

selection of a representative list; discouragement of speculative operations not suited for the client's financial position or temperament—and for this he does not need to be a wizard in picking winners from the stock list or in foretelling market movements.

But regardless of my minority opinion on this point, Financial Analysts will undoubtedly continue to pursue as their chief activity the attempt to pick the stocks "most likely to succeed." And even though it is now fashionable to decry the various averages as misleading or meaningless, most will still tell you— without having their arms twisted—their opinion whether these averages are going up or down. Can we expect the Financial Analysts to do a good job in these two key areas in the future?

My views on the validity of stock-market forecasting have been unfavorable for about half a century. This may entitle me to a high mark for consistency, but it hardly qualifies me as an impartial student of the subject. Let me make only a guarded prediction here. It is more than just possible that the investigations of Wall Street's practices in the future will include a really comprehensive study of the claims and accomplishments of the leading approaches to market forecasting. (I think of something resembling the articles that appeared last year in *Fortune*, but more extensive in coverage.)

If the Securities and Exchange Commission comes to grips with this intriguing problem the results might be quite interesting, along one of at least two divergent lines. The first would argue: (a) market analysis is an important part of security analysis; (b) Financial Analysts must be fully responsible for their work; hence (c) every published market prediction will have to be made over the name and with the responsibility of a Chartered Financial Analyst. The opposite possibility is merely that all such prognostications will be required to bear in large type the legend: "For entertainment purposes only. Do not take seriously."

Passing on to the work of the Financial Analyst as the selector of the most promising common stock, I see two major obstacles here to brilliant success for the average Analyst or for Analysts as a whole. The first grows out of competitive developments, the second from the large element of speculation that newer investment concepts have injected into common stocks of superior quality.

Analysts' Problems: Competition

Let us consider first the matter of competition—not from outside sources but from the very growth in numbers and the intensified training of those inside our profession. My basic point here is that neither the Financial Analysts as a whole nor the investment funds as a whole can expect to "beat the market," because in a significant sense they (or you) *are* the market. It should be clear that if *all* market operations were Analyst-advised then the average Analyst could not do better than the "outside public" because there would be no outside public. Thus, to beat the market he would have to beat himself—an impossible bootstrap operation. Hence the greater the overall influence of Financial Analysts on investment and speculative decisions the less becomes the mathematical possibility of their overall results being better than the market's.

This overlooked fact explains, I think, a phenomenon which has aroused unnecessary controversy. I refer to the much-attacked comparisons that indicated that mutual funds have not outperformed the Standard & Poor's 500 Stock Composite in the past decade. The figures themselves cannot be challenged on the grounds that the funds are more conservative or less risky than the general market, for they suffered about the same average percentage decline in 1956 and again in 1962 as did the S&P 500 Index. But it is a completely valid answer and defense that the funds perform a valuable service for innumerable people who could not or would not do as well as the general market. I, for one, have no doubt that the funds have amply justified their existence for many years past and will continue to do so.

Analysts' Problems: Speculative Element

I come now to the second obstacle in the way of successful stock selection by Financial Analysts—which is the increased injection of the speculative element in the valuation of high-grade issues. I spoke at some length on this subject at a Financial Analysts Federation dinner as far back as 1958, under the heading of "The New Speculation in Common Stocks." My basic point then was that in the old days most stocks were speculative because of weaknesses and risks associated with the particular concern or business, but in the new days the common stocks of strong companies were becoming increasingly speculative because their price levels were discounting future growth more and more liberally. That tendency continued unchecked from 1958 to May 1962.

This new type of speculative risk can best be illustrated by reference to the stock issue which sold in 1961 at the highest aggregate value for any industrial company—just about $17 billion—and which was undoubtedly the best regarded from the standpoint of financial strength and future prospects. The company of course is IBM, which for a number of years has carried the highest quality rating given by Standard & Poor's. Yet the stock of this truly marvelous enterprise dropped in price from 607 in 1961 to 300 at its low of 1962—a loss of over 50% and of more than $8 billion in market value *in less than six months*. That loss was proportionately about 1¾ times the decline suffered by the Standard & Poor's 500 Stock Index from its all-time high to its 1962 low.

This comparison brings out sharply the relatively new tendency for high quality and high risk to go together in the field of common stock. Whether we like it or not—and I for one consider it an unfortunate development—it has every appearance of being a permanent characteristic of the stock market. I am reminded here of Marcel Proust's casual reference to "love and the suffering that is inextricably connected therewith." The public's love affair with common stocks is not likely to be any more sorrow-proof. It seems to me that the larger the speculative component in the price of the typical common stock—whether derived from internal weakness or a vulnerable market multiplier—the less dependable must become the work of the Analyst in choosing one against another.

A word should be added here about technology. Most of the high-multiplier stocks have been "technological issues"—e.g., computers, photographic processes, electronics. But technological change is one of the *most speculative* elements in the valuation picture. What it gives to one company it is likely to take away, at least in part, from others, which may have been last year's technological favorites. The high multipliers can be justified only by very long-term projection of future growth and maintained earnings; but technology itself, with the rapid changes it brings about, implies the opposite of dependable long-term expectations for any of its products or processes, and even for any enterprise largely controlled by technological factors.

It is worth spending another few minutes to consider the problem of stock selection from another angle. You are all familiar with the fact that over any span of years there has been a remarkable divergence in the relative price movement of the thirty stocks in the Dow Jones Industrial Average, as well as in almost any other representative list.

Many will say that these great variations in performance indicate clearly the opportunities for exceptional profits that are open to expert Analysts who can identify the most promising issues. The contrary implication is that Analysts as a group are incapable of evaluating the future of individual companies with reasonable accuracy; for if they were, the market prices would have discounted much more closely the actual developments in the ensuing years.

In this connection it is interesting to note the comments of a Wiesenberger Manual on its tabulation. The authors state that their figures show: (1) the wisdom, if not the necessity, of diversification in modern markets; (2) how unrealistic can be the impression created by any market "average"; (3) how "selective" have become modern markets. To my overcritical eye these remarks seem to partake of the copious confusion into which we have plunged ourselves in recent years. To begin with, the greater the wisdom and necessity for diversification, the more realistic for actual investment results become these much maligned market averages.

The fact is that, despite the wide difference in the composition of the Dow Jones 30 and the Standard & Poor's 500, the year-by-year changes of these two indexes have been remarkably close, and these in turn have been approximated by the overall performance of the mutual funds. Contrariwise, the quoted reference to the selective nature of modern markets seems to support Wall Street's favorite claim that good Analysts can select the best stocks, in such manner that those they advise can prosper even when the averages decline. But basically, of course, the concept of selectivity is opposed to that of wide diversification. If Financial Analysts as a whole could really be good selectors, the diversification policies followed by the funds would be quite illogical.

What I have been saying undoubtedly sounds highly unflattering to the pretensions of security analysis in its cherished activity of common-stock selection. Is the case really as bad as I have made it? Well, there are at least two large grains of comfort to consider. But even these involve a paradox. The first is that the Analysts do in fact render an important service to the community in their study and evaluation of common stocks. But this service shows itself not in spectacular results achieved by their individual selections but rather in the fixing at most times and for most stocks of a price level which fairly represents their comparative values, as established by the known facts and reasonable estimates of the future. These comparative valuations may not be highly dependable when judged against subsequent developments; but they are probably the best that can be made by any process and as such are of real utility to those buying and selling stocks.

To bring this subtle point home, let us imagine for a moment that some ukase from Washington resulted in banishing Financial Analysts from the Wall Streets of America much as Plato would have banished all poets from his Republic. What would happen? Common stock prices would become much more irrational than they have been in recent years—a state of affairs a little difficult for some of us to imagine. Financial Analysts would still ply their outlawed trade in secret—meeting perhaps in dank cellars instead of in more plush surroundings to exchange their findings; a black market for their services would soon spring up, and they might even be paid more than their present munificent salaries, because their work would be illegal and attended by more serious risks than the familiar one of being wrong.

The fact that the combined work of Financial Analysts tends to bring about reasonably defensible relative prices is greatly to their credit, but generally escapes recognition and proper appreciation. Conversely—and here is the paradox—the Analysts have been able to claim credit for good overall results for their clients over a span of many years, but this achievement must be admitted (in private) to be not so much the result of their superior abilities as of the long bull market that began in 1949. Going back much farther, these satisfactory investment results may be ascribed to an underlying tendency of common stocks for the past eighty years to yield a return of some 7½% compounded, in dividends plus price appreciation. Most of your "advisees," if you had merely kept them from doing foolish things, should have realized an excellent annual return over the years. Nor is there reason to fear for the long-term future in this regard, if we can assume that common stocks will continue to fluctuate about some price curve that tends upward.

No Tinge to Speculation

My long-held concern about the growth of the speculative element in common-stock prices leads me to consider the subject now from quite a different angle. The great and praiseworthy campaign of Wall Street in the past decade has been directed at creating "a nation of investors." But to accomplish this, Wall Street has insisted more and more on the investment character of common stocks generally and on the pleasing concept that everyone who came into the stock market is engaged in investment operations. Speculation was in no way prohibited by the S.E.C. legislation, but it seems to have been virtually outlawed by the new semantics of Wall Street. Some of you may recall some rhetorical questions I posed in a letter to *The Wall Street Journal* last June apropos of their front-page headings: "Many Small Investors Bet on Further Drop; Step Up (oddlot) Short Sales." This was about as far as one could possibly go in distorting the proper meaning of the term "investor."

In my view the financial community has followed the wrong policy—in both its own and the public's interest—in trying to eliminate the idea of speculation from our language and thinking. If common stocks and speculation must go together—now as much as in the past, in the future as much as now—it is essential that this fact be recognized clearly, taken fully into account by Analysts and others, and made adequately clear to the public. In the past, the New York Stock Exchange very sensibly contended that there was nothing wrong in speculation if carried on by people who knew what they were doing and could afford the risks involved. Furthermore, the Exchange pointed out that speculation differs inherently from gambling, because speculative risks—such as attach to common stocks—are pre-existing and must be taken by someone, whereas the typical risks of gambling are created by roulette or horse players as they place their bets.

I haven't the slightest doubt that nine people out of ten who have margin accounts with brokers are *ipso facto* speculators. My only quarrel with this picture is that they have all been encouraged to believe that they are investors, which simply isn't true. Wall Street has no reason to be afraid of the term "speculation"; it is at least as likely to attract the public as it is to repel them. What the financial community may have to fear is the politically potent complaints of a comparatively small number of persons who have taken much greater losses than they could afford, and can with some justice place the chief blame on "account executives" who had told them they were "investing in America." Nor have the Financial Analysts been without blame here, because of their own insistence on calling nearly every purchase an investment.

Looking into the Future

The point I have just tried to make is not a digression from my main theme but ties in closely with my concept of the future role and activities of Financial Analysts. In our textbook we have held consistently to the thesis that Financial Analysts cannot deal successfully enough with basically speculative situations, and that they should try to limit their activities as far as possible to commitments they may consider justified by well-established investment criteria. Recent reflection on the matter leads me to advance some modification of that view.

Financial Analysts in general will not be able to turn their backs on the pervasive speculative elements in common stocks. It will be only at infrequent bear market levels that representative issues will be obtainable on what I should term a pure investment basis, with nothing significant paid for their speculative component. At other market levels—such as the present, for example—it will be only the exceptional common stock that can be bought on such attractive terms.

It is unrealistic to think that 8,000 or more Financial Analysts can confine their activities mainly to choosing safe bonds, to getting up more or less mechanical portfolios of leading common stocks, or even to hunting down bargain issues, of which there could not possibly be enough to go round. No, the Analyst of the future must continue his studies in depth of numerous companies; plus his endeavors to appraise management competence, technological possibilities and risks, and overall prospects; plus his comparative valuations among similar companies and against the general market level. He must then make his choices, submit his individual recommendations, and be prepared to stand or fall by his own overall record—judged, let us hope, with a reasonable degree of leniency.

But the change I suggest, in all earnestness, is that the Analyst give full and formal recognition to the speculative factors in the common stocks he deals with. This recognition might well express itself in a studied effort to present separately for each issue analyzed the investment value—as a kind of "minimum true value"—and then the additional speculative component of value. This is not the place for me to spell out how this separation of value components should be made: It is perfectly proper for different Analysts to take different approaches to this question, which may vary widely as between more or less conservative practitioners. But each of them its proponent should be prepared to defend in some intelligible and plausible manner.

May I suggest in this connection that Analysts consider the technique of developing a single-figure comparative valuation for the issue studies, based solely on the past records—including, of course the past rate of growth—and that this "past-record value" be used as a point of departure for the "present value" which will take all new and relevant factors into consideration. This present value should then have its investment and speculative components delimited as clearly as possible. (Incidentally, my "past-record value" may be termed the actual value of the stock if one could assume that the past factors would continue unchanged into the future.)

In November 1957 the *Financial Analysts Journal* published a paper of mine titled "Two Illustrative Approaches to Formula Valuations for Common Stocks" in which I developed a concrete method for determining the "past-record value" of a common stock, and worked it out for the thirty issues in The Dow Jones Industrial Average. The silence that greeted this effort was deafening and disappointing. However, this same article has been reprinted in a book just published by The Institute of Chartered Financial Analysts. The book is titled *Readings in Financial Analysis and Investment Management* (see Book Reviews in this issue of the *Journal*). I have renewed hope now that other Financial Analysts will be moved to do some work along the same lines and perhaps develop one or more "single figure" formulas that may be widely adapted.

Let me illustrate what I have in mind generally by a comparison between IBM and International Harvester (which occurs next on the NYSE list). At the end of 1961 the price of IBM was 579 against about 50 for Harvester. Both were sound and important companies, but IBM was undoubtedly the better enterprise. Did this make IBM both a more promising and a safer purchase than the other? Here was what might be called the standard type of problem for the Financial Analyst. If he tried to deal with it along the lines of my suggested procedure he might have set the investment component of IBM as low as $200—a valuation of some $6 billion for the entire concern.

The speculative component he would have valued in accordance with his own method, which in turn would reflect his temperament as much as his detailed study of future possibilities. His figure might have been higher or lower than the $380 difference between the market price and his investment value; the important point here is that he would have made clear to himself and his clients the combination of opportunity and risk that is inherent in so large a speculative component of market price or total value. Quite differently, the Analyst might well have found an investment component of say, $40 per share for Harvester—based on its average earnings, its dividend record, its asset value (about $55), and of course his conviction that the company's earning power was not likely to deteriorate in the long-term future. This would have left a speculative component of only $10, or 20% of the market quotation—from which he may or may not have concluded that the issue was attractively priced.

I am far from urging, with the ready aid of hindsight, that the much lower speculative component of Harvester proved it to be a better purchase than IBM at the end of 1961. But I do urge that the risk component—hence the actual risk—was proportionately much smaller, and that this element was worth isolating and paying close attention to in the work of financial analysis.

Putting the matter another way, let me state my conviction that the competent Financial Analyst can do a more expert and worthwhile job in the field of delimiting investment and speculative areas of value than in drawing the bald conclusion that Company A's shares are a better buy than Company B's.

This rather modest estimation of what financial analysis may reliably accomplish leads me to suggest a procedure by which the senior Analyst may combine his work as a portfolio-creator and supervisor with his penchant for selecting the most of present practice, and runs somewhat as follows: The Analyst would start with a representative group—more or less equivalent to the Dow Jones thirty stocks—which is calculated to give the buyer a future experience very close to that of the various averages. He should not reject this list out of hand as too easily put together and thus unworthy of his talents. Indeed he should treat his own "private" choices as competitive with this basic list, in the sense that each such choice would require a clear-cut demonstration of superior attractiveness (say 20% in his valuation against market price) to warrant inclusion in the portfolio as an addition or substitution.

This approach could be carried down to the level of an industry Analyst in a large organization, who studies a relatively few companies in depth. He, too, would either accept direct responsibility for the conclusion that an issue he recommends has the required 20% "margin of indicated value" (as I call it), or else present his analysis in a form to enable his superior to make such a finding.

Returning now to my outline-treatment of the future of financial analysis I should like to touch briefly on three more points. The first two may be called crusades of my own, which I have carried on for years with an outstanding lack of success, but on which I am not yet ready to concede defeat. Perhaps the future is on my side. My first demand is for comprehensive and objective record-keeping by Financial Analysts, in a form which would permit themselves and others to judge of the validity of various investment approaches in terms of their actual working out for many cases and for many years.

To my mind such compilations are essential to any true advance of our membership toward self-understanding and a professional viewpoint. The investment funds are ideally suited for the gathering and careful evaluation of this material, based on their standard forms, procedures, and record. Such evaluations of various analytical approaches could also be reported on, at proper intervals, in the *Financial Analysts Journal* and elsewhere, as a service to our profession and the public.

My second crusade has been to urge that the Analysts use their judgment and their influence in the area of managerial efficiency—not only toward avoiding the shares of poorly managed companies (which in Wall Street is often carried too far), but more positively in the support of efforts from stockholders outside the management to improve unsatisfactory results. The present method of accomplishing this is by permitting the price to decline to an intrinsically absurd level, at which point new people often acquire a controlling interest and then make the necessary changes. This is hardly the best way for existing owners to protect their investments. Whether the future will bring any improvement I hesitate to say—but I may hope so.

I did, in fact, recently get a brainstorm or nightmare on this subject that may amuse you. After all, the largest equity owner of nearly every American corporation is the U. S. government, with its present 52% share of the profits. Suppose our young President brought his famous vigor to bear on the problem of poorly managed companies, insisting that the interest of the Treasury Department required them to make more money or else. You may enjoy playing a bit with that bizarre idea.

My final point relates to the possible use of computers in various aspects of financial analysis. Lloyd S. Coughtry's article in the January–February issue of the *Financial Analysts Journal* shows how a computer may be used to project future operating results in the public utility field, which is better suited than others for such elaborate calculations. Much more controversial is the question whether computers may be of major assistance in working up portfolios or in deciding on individual purchases and sales.

Skeptical as we may be of such a prospect it would be unwise to dismiss it out of hand. I believe there is theoretical merit in the original Markowitz concept of "efficient portfolios." This seeks to find by a computer program the portfolio that offers the largest expected return compatible with a given acceptable risk, or, conversely, the least risk associated with a required or expected return. Under this approach it would be up to the Analyst to estimate the degree of risk as well as the expectable return for each issue in the large group from which the portfolio would be drawn. Perhaps the development of techniques to identify the speculative component in individual issues may aid the Financial Analyst in supplying reasonably dependable material for the computers to work their magic upon.

Be all this as it may, of one thing I am certain. Financial analysis in the future, as in the past, offers numerous different roads to success. Many will gain it by way of an intensive knowledge of one or more industries; others by specializing in technology; others by an outstanding ability to evaluate the management factor; still others by flair for the public's psychology—perhaps even specializing in fantasy; others, again, will have a good nose for bargains and be experts in special situations of all sorts. For men and women with real ability in one or more of these many directions, financial analysis (or security analysis) will continue to offer highly satisfactory rewards.

20

The Future of Common Stocks

Before I came down to Wall Street in 1914 the future of the stock market had already been forecast—once for all—in the famous dictum of J. P. Morgan the elder: "It will fluctuate." It is a safe prediction for me to make that, in future years as in the past, common stocks will advance too far and decline too far, and that investors, like speculators—and institutions, like individuals—will have their periods of enchantment and disenchantment with equities.

To support this prediction let me cite two "watershed episodes"—as I shall call them—that occurred within my own financial experience. The first goes back just fifty years, to 1924; it was the publication of E. L. Smith's little book entitled, *Common Stocks as Long-Term Investments*. His study showed that, contrary to prevalent beliefs, equities as a whole had proved much better purchases than bonds during the preceding half-century. It is generally held that these findings provided the theoretical and psychological justification for the ensuing bull market of the 1920s. The Dow Jones Industrial Average (DJIA), which stood at 90 in mid-1924, advanced to 381 by September 1929, from which high estate it collapsed—as I remember only too well—to an ignominious low of 41 in 1932.

On that date the market's level was the lowest it had registered for more than thirty years. For both General Electric and

Reprinted from the *Financial Analysts Journal*, vol. 30, no. 5 (September/October 1974): 20–30 with permission. This article was taken, with slight revisions, from a paper prepared for delivery before a group of corporate pension executives in June 1974. The last half of the article aims to answer specific questions raised in connection with the address.

for the Dow, the high point of 1929 was not to be regained for twenty-five years.

Here was a striking example of the calamity that can ensue when reasoning that is entirely sound when applied to past conditions is blindly followed long after the relevant conditions have changed. What was true of the attractiveness of equity investments when the Dow stood at 90 was doubtful when the level had advanced to 200 and was completely untrue at 300 or higher.

The second episode—historical in my thinking—occurred toward the end of the market's long recovery from the 1929 to 1932 debacle. It was the report of the Federal Reserve in 1948 on the public's attitude toward common stocks. In that year the Dow sold as low as 165 or 7 times earnings, while AAA bonds returned only 2.82%. Nevertheless, over 90% of those canvassed were opposed to buying equities—about half because they thought them too risky and half because of unfamiliarity. Of course this was just the moment before common stocks were to begin the greatest upward movement in market history—which was to carry the Dow from 165 to 1050 last year. What better illustration can one wish of the age-old truth that the public's attitudes in matters of finance are completely untrustworthy as guides to investment policy? This may easily prove as true in 1974 as it was in 1948.

I think the future of equities will be roughly the same as their past; in particular, common-stock purchases will prove satisfactory when made at appropriate price levels. It may be objected that is far too cursory and superficial a conclusion; that it fails to take into account the new factors and problems that have entered the economic picture in recent years—especially those of inflation, unprecedentedly high interest rates, the energy crisis, the ecology-pollution mess, and even the movement toward less consumption and zero growth. Perhaps I should add to my list the widespread public mistrust of Wall Street as a whole, engendered by its well-nigh scandalous behavior during recent years in the areas of ethics, financial practices of all sorts, and plain business sense.

Of course these elements—mainly unfavorable to the future values of common stocks—should be taken into account in the formulation of today's investment policies. But it is absurd to conclude from them that from now on common stocks will be undesirable investments no matter how low their price level may fall. The real question is the same as it has always been in the past, namely: Is this a desirable time or price level to make equity purchases? We should divide that question, I think, into the following: (a) Is this a desirable level to buy stocks in general, as represented by the DJIA or Standard & Poor's 500 (S&P 500)? (b) Even if the averages may not be at an attractive level, can investors expect satisfactory results by choosing individual issues that are undoubtedly worth at least what they are selling for? The distinction I have just made is clearly relevant to the present situation because of the recent advent of the "two-tiered market," resulting from the massive preference of institutions for large, high-growth companies. This in turn has brought about disparities in the P/E ratios for issues of investment character—differences as high as ten to one—that have been unexampled in all my experience, except perhaps at the height of the 1929 madness with its celebrated "blue-chip" issues.

My own answer to the double question just posed is as follows: As to the present level of the averages—say, 850 for the Dow and 93 for the S&P 500—the factor most directly affecting current security values and prices is most assuredly the high rate of interest now established for the entire spectrum of bond and note issues. One of the glaring defects of institutional attitudes has been that as recently as early 1973—when they supported the record price level of the averages—they failed to take into account that AAA bonds were then yielding 7.3% and had been above 8.5% not long before. (As it happened they were destined to surpass the 8.5% rate in 1974.) In 1964 the AAA rate averaged 4.4%. It seems logical to me that the earnings/price ratio of stocks generally should bear a relationship to bond-interest rates. If this thesis is accepted in its simplest form we must conclude: If one dollar of Dow earnings were worth $17 when bond yields were 4.4%, that one dollar is now worth only 52% of $17, or $8.80, with AAA bonds at 8.5%. This in turn would suggest a currently justified multiplier of, say, 9 for the normal current earnings of the Dow. If you place those earnings at the record 1973 figure of $86, you arrive at a current valuation of only 775 for the DJIA. You may quarrel with this figure on various grounds. One may be your expectation that bond rates will fall in the future. But that prospect is far from certain, while the present 8.5% rate is a fact. Also, if bond yields go down appreciably, then bond prices—especially of the low-coupon, large-discount issues—will advance as well as stocks. Hence such bonds could still work out better than the Dow if and when interest rates decline.

Viewing the matter from another angle, I should want the Dow or Standard & Poor's to return an earnings yield of at least four-thirds that on AAA bonds to give them competitive attractiveness with bond investments. This would mean an earnings yield of 11%, and it brings us smack back to the valuation of about 775 for the Dow that we found by comparing the early 1974 situation with that ten years before.

Furthermore, my calculations of growth rates over the past twenty-five years give an annual figure for the Dow of only 4.5%. If this rate were to continue in the future, the expectable combination of growth plus dividends would produce less than a 10% overall return, consisting of 4.5% growth plus a compounded dividend yield of, say, 5%. This second calculation would make my current 775 valuation for the Dow appear over-generous. Incidentally, a corresponding approach to the S&P 500 Index gives a somewhat less favorable result than for the Dow at current levels. The S&P 425 and 500 Indexes have both grown at about a 5% rate over the past twenty-five years. But this advantage appears to be offset by their higher P/E ratios compared with the DJIA.

Selecting Individual Common Stocks

When we come to valuing individual stocks I should like to divide them into three classes, as I find them in the NYSE list. Group I is the growth issues selling at more than 20 times their last twelve months' earnings. Group II is the relatively unpopular stocks selling for less than 7 times recent earnings—i.e., at 15% earnings yield or better. Group III has multipliers between 7 and 20.

In my count of 1,530 NYSE issues, there were 63, or 4% of the total, selling above 20 times earnings, of which 24 passed the 30 times mark. By contrast, more than 500—over a third—sold below 7 times earnings, and of these about 150—say, 10% of the total—were quoted under 5 times the last twelve months' profits.

If the earnings on which these multipliers are based can be counted on, more or less, in the future—without any special requirements as to growth—it is evident that many NYSE issues can now compete in attractiveness with bonds at 8.5%. In this large area of choice there are many that would be suitable for pension-fund investment; many indeed that may be regarded as definitely undervalued. These are especially suited for longer-term commitments as distinguished from short-term speculative purchase. Among the under 7-times-earnings list are huge concerns like Firestone (with $3 billion of sales) and intermediate-sized enterprises like Emhart, which has paid dividends for seventy-two years and recently sold under its net-current-asset value.

The Book-Value Approach

The developments that have produced these extraordinarily low multipliers for so many NYSE (and other) issues now present us with another phenomenon—namely the reestablishment of book value, or net worth, as a point of departure and possible guide to the selection of common stocks. In a large area of the present stock market we could return to a very old-fashioned but nonetheless useful criterion for equity investment—namely the value of the company as a private enterprise to a private owner, irrespective of market quotations for the shares. If the business has been prosperous, and is at least reasonably promising for the future, it should be worth its net asset value; hence an opportunity to buy an interest therein at a substantial discount from net worth could be considered attractive.

As it happens, about half the NYSE companies were selling last month at less than book value, and about one-quarter, or about 400 issues, at less than two-thirds of net worth. What is equally interesting is that about one-third of all common stocks actually sold both *above* and *below* their net worth in the past twelve months. Certainly more than half fluctuated around this figure in the last five years. For the most part, these issues selling below book are also in the low-multiplier group.

I may be so bold as to suggest that this situation makes possible a quite simple approach to equity investment that is open to almost everyone from the small investor to the quite large pension-fund manager. This is the idea of buying *selected* common stocks—those meeting additional criteria of financial strength, etc.—obtainable at two-thirds or less of book value, and holding them for sale at their net asset value—to show a nonspectacular but quite satisfactory 50% profit. We cannot predict with assurance how this apparently too simple investment program will work out in the future. But I can say that my studies covering the period 1961 to 1974 show the presence of sufficient opportunities of this kind in most years, and also excellent overall results from the assumed operations.

Since I spoke of three groupings of the NYSE list, I should now give my views of Groups I and III. Those selling at intermediate multipliers may present individual opportunities, but they have no special interest for me as a category. But the first-tier, high-growth issues present a real challenge to past experience. Obviously they would be wonderful private or market-type investments if obtainable at book value or even twice that figure. The trouble is, of course, that most of them sell at more than 5 times book value—and some more than 10 times. Last year the ratios were a good deal higher than that. At these levels, they take on a *speculative character* which is due entirely to their price level, and in no sense to any weakness of the companies themselves. (I made this point as long ago as 1958 in an address before the Financial Analysts Federation; it is reproduced as an Appendix to *The Intelligent Investor.*) The speculative risks attached to high-growth stocks have been brought home dramatically in the past eighteen months by the price declines in many of these favorites. (I need not give examples.)

However, I do want to use an instance here in connection with a brief discussion of a recently launched academic theory about the stock market, which could have great practical importance if it coincided with reality. This is the hypothesis of "the efficient market." In its extreme form it makes two declarations: (1) The price of nearly every stock at nearly all times reflects whatever is knowable about the company's affairs; hence no consistent profits can be made by seeking out and using additional information, including that held by "insiders." (2) Because the market has complete or at least adequate information about each issue, the prices it registers are therefore "correct," "reasonable," or "appropriate." This would imply that it is fruitless, or at least insufficiently rewarding, for security analysts to look for discrepancies between price and value.

I have no particular quarrel with declaration one, though assuredly there are times when a researcher may unearth significant information about a stock, not generally known and reflected in the price. But I deny emphatically that because the market has all the information it needs to establish a correct price, the prices it actually registers are in fact correct. Take as my example a fine company such as Avon Products. How can it make sense to say that its price of 140 was "correct" in 1973 and that its price of 32 was also "correct" in 1974? Could anything have happened— outside of stock-market psychology—to reduce the value of that enterprise by 77% or nearly $6 billion? The market may have had all the information it needed about Avon; what it has lacked is the right kind of judgment in evaluating its knowledge.

Descartes summed up the matter more than three centuries ago, when he wrote in his *"Discours de la Methode"*: *"Ce n'est pas assez d'avoir l'esprit bon, mais le principal est de l'appliquer bien."* In English: "It is not enough to have a good intelligence"— and I add, "enough information"—"the principal thing is to apply it well."

I can assure the reader that among the 500-odd NYSE issues selling below 7 times earnings today, there are plenty to be found for which the prices are not "correct" ones, in any meaningful sense of the term. They are clearly worth more than their current selling prices, and any security analyst worth his salt should be able to make up an attractive portfolio out of this "universe."

Inflation and Investment Policy

Let us turn now to inflation. Do the prospects of continued inflation make equity purchases undesirable at present market prices or indeed at any conceivable level? It is passing strange that this question should even suggest itself. It seems only yesterday that everyone was saying that stocks, even at high prices, were definitely preferable to bonds because equities carried an important measure of protection against future inflation.

But it should be admitted that not only recently, but for many years and perhaps decades past, equities as a whole have failed to provide the protection against inflation that was expected from them. I refer to the natural surmise that a higher general price level would produce a higher value for business assets and hence correspondingly higher profit rates in relation to original costs. This has not been borne out by the statistics. The rate of return on book equities as a whole—much understated as they must be in terms of reproduction costs—has at best held constant at around the 10 to 12 level. If anything, it has declined from the 1948 to 1953 period when the Dow was selling at only 7 times earnings.

It is true of course that the earnings on the DJIA and the S&P 425 Industrials have tripled from 1947–51 to 1969–73. But in the same period the book value of both indexes has quadrupled. Hence we may say that all the increase in postwar earnings may be ascribed to the simple building up of net worth by the reinvestment of undistributed profits, and none of it to the more than doubling of the general price level in those twenty-eight years. In other words, inflation as such has not helped common-stock earnings.

This is a good reason—and there are others—not to be enthusiastic about equities at every market level. This caution is part of my long-held investment philosophy. But what about the current situation? Should inflation prospects dissuade an investor from buying strong companies on a 15% earnings return? My answer would be "no."

What are the investor's real choices—whether as an institution or as an individual? He can elect to keep his money in short-term obligations, at a good yield, expecting that future inflation will eventually produce lower market levels for all kinds of stocks, including those with low multipliers. This choice would be justified when the investor is convinced that stocks are selling above their true value, but otherwise it is only a kind of bet on future market movements. Or he may conceivably decide on an entirely new sort of investment policy—namely, to move from stocks or bonds into things: real estate, gold, commodities, valuable pictures, and the like. Let me make three observations here.

The first is that it is impossible for any really large sums of money—say billions of dollars—to be invested in such tangibles, other than real property, without creating a huge advance in the price level, thus creating a typical speculative cycle ending in the inevitable crash. Secondly, this very type of hazard is already manifest to us in the real estate field, where numerous new ventures, financed through a combination of borrowing and quoted common-stock issues, have encountered problems of all sorts, including large stock-market losses for their investors.

My third observation is on the positive side. I think all investors should recognize the possibility—though not necessarily the probability—of future inflation at the recent 11% rate, or even higher, and should introduce what I shall call a "concrete-object factor" in their overall financial approach. By this I mean that they should not be content to have an overwhelming proportion of their wealth represented by paper money and its equivalents, such as bank deposits, bonds, and receivables of all sorts. For the shorter or longer pull—who can really tell?—it may turn out to be wiser to have at least an indirect interest—via the common-stock portfolio—in such tangibles as land, buildings, machinery, and inventories. This is relatively easy to accomplish in the execution of an ordinary common-stock investment policy. My point is only that it would be worthwhile to introduce the concept as a specific and measured criterion in analyzing one's resources. That idea is as readily applicable to pension funds as to other portfolios.

It should be obvious from my overall approach to the future of equities that I do not consider such much-publicized problems as the energy crisis, environmental pressures, foreign exchange instability, etc., as central determinations of financial policy. They enter into the value versus price equation in the same general fashion as would any such other adverse factors as (1) a tendency toward lower profit margins and (2) the higher debt burden and the higher interest rate thereon. Their weight for the future may be assessed by economists and security analysts, presumably with the same accuracy, or lack of it, as has characterized such predictive work in the past.

Institutional Dominance, Efficient Markets, and the Prospects for Security Analysis

Is there an equity bias among money managers? My answer is that there has undoubtedly been such a bias in the past decade, and that it was a powerful force in establishing price levels for the stock market generally that were out of line with bond yields. It may well have contributed to these high yields themselves, for it deprived the bond market of billions of dollars that went instead into buying shares from former holders at advancing P/E rates. Since concern is now expressed about institutional disenchantment with equities, it may well be that the bias of recent years is not only rapidly disappearing but is being reversed and that it is now the function of real old-timers like myself to caution against taking on an equally unjustified bias *against* stocks at low price levels.

What will be the effect on performance of having, say, $200 billion of institutional money in equities, plus, say 11,000 working security analysts all trying to "beat the averages"? The reader will pardon a reference here to a couplet by Heinrich Heine apropos of the appointment of forty-five German professors to some commission of inquiry 150 years ago. He wrote:

> *"Funf-und-vierzig Professoren—*
> *Vaterland, du bist verloren!"*
> (Forty-five Professors—
> Fatherland, you're ruined!)

If only forty-five professors can present such a menace, how about 11,000 analysts?

Seriously, the effect of large-scale participation by institutions in the equity market, and the work of innumerable financial analysts striving to establish proper valuation for all sorts, should be to stabilize stock-market movements, i.e., in theory at least, to dampen the unjustified fluctuation in stock prices. I must confess, however, that I have seen no such result flowing from the preponderant position of the institutions in market activity. The amplitude of price fluctuations has, if anything, been wider than before the institutions came into the market on a grand scale. What can be the reason? The only one I can give is that the institutions and their financial analysts have not shown any more prudence and vision than the general public; they seem to have succumbed to the same siren songs—expressed chiefly in the cult of "performance." They, too, have largely put aside the once vital distinction between investment and speculation. (This leads me to ask whether some day soon we shall see some legal problems for certain banking institutions growing out of their accountability for the results of *trust* investments made from 1968 to 1973 that failed to meet the strict judicial requirements of the prudent man rule.)

Let me give a concrete example of my statement that institutional investment does not appear to have contributed either stability or rationality to stock prices—American Airlines. The Standard & Poor's Monthly Stock Guide shows the holdings of this and other concerns by about 2,000 insurance companies and investment funds, though not by banks and their trust departments. In 1970, the canvassed institutions owned 4.3 million shares of American Airlines, or 22% of the total. The company reported a deficit of $1.30 per share in 1970, then earnings of 13 cents in 1971 and a magnificent 20 cents in 1972. In response, our so-called efficient stock market advanced the price from a 1970 low of 13 to a new all-time high of 49⅞ in 1972. This was 250 times that year's profits. Now what did our financial institutions do to hold down this insane speculative binge in the shares? Did they sell out their holdings somewhere along the line, to cash in a profit and rid their portfolios of a clearly overvalued issue? On the contrary. The Guide showed that during this period they actually *increased* their ownership to 6.7 million shares, or by a full 50%, held by 143 companies. And the latest figures, in 1974, show that 117 funds etc. still owned 5.7 million shares or 20% of the total. (In the meantime, the company reported a record deficit of $48 million in 1973, and the price collapsed from 50 in 1972 to 7½ in 1974.)

This story hardly suggests that the institutions have been valiant contributors to "efficient markets" and correct stock prices.

More and more institutions are likely to realize that they cannot expect better than market-average results from their equity portfolios unless they have the advantage of better-than-average financial and security analysts. Logically this should move some of the institutions toward accepting the S&P 500 results as the norm for expectable performance. In turn this might lead to using the S&P 500 or 425 lists as actual portfolios. If this proves true, clients may then find themselves questioning the standard fees most of them are paying financial institutions to handle these investments. (Incidentally, if my half-serious prophecy of a movement toward actual S&P Index portfolios is realized, we should have an ironical return to a form of investment in equities that existed here fifty years ago. The first investment funds were actual "trusts," and "fixed trusts" at that. The portfolios were set up, on a once-for-all basis, from the very beginning. Changes could be made only under compulsory conditions.)

A modification of my "fixed fund" suggestion would leave more leeway for the work of financial analysts. This modification would base equity portfolios initially on an actual or presumed imitation of the S&P Index, or—more simply—the DJIA. The operating manager or decision maker would be permitted to make substitutions in this list, but only on a persuasive showing that the issues substituted had distinctly more intrinsic value per dollar of price than the ones to be dropped. Combined with fairly heavy accountability for the results of such departures from the original list, such a program might well improve the actual performance. In any case it would give the financial analysts' profession something to do.

There has indeed been a strong intimation in this article that the DJIA and the S&P Indexes are now selling too high in relation to many issues now purchasable at low P/E ratios. If this view is correct, any competent analyst has an excellent present opportunity to earn his pay by recommending desirable substitutes for certain companies in these averages.

Please bear in mind that while I have been making a case for equity investment now—despite, or perhaps because of, institutional disillusionment with them—I am not proposing a 100% stock position for any investor. On the contrary, I think that everyone's total portfolio should always have a minimum component of 25% in bonds, along with a complementary minimum holding of 25% in equities. The remaining half of the funds may be divided between the two, either on a standard 50-50 basis (adjusted to reflect changes caused by significant price movements) or in accordance with some consistent and conservative policy of increasing the bond proportion above 50% when bonds appear more attractive than equities, and vice versa when equities appear more attractive than bonds.

Do equities win by default because there is no assumed liquidity in other alternatives? There are various answers to this query. The first is, of course, that the alternative of putting funds into short- or longer-term debt obligations does not diminish the liquidity factor. Secondly, I could argue that liquidity is itself a minor desideratum in a true investment program, and that too many value considerations have been sacrificed to an assumed need for quick marketability. But thirdly, I could not say to what extent the liquidity factor should enter into consideration of non-income-producing objects—such as paintings, commodities, etc.—as alternatives to common stocks. My hunch is that the absence of income—as against 8.5% annually on bonds—should be more important here for your investment decisions than the liquidity factor.

An Indexed Economy and a Managed Economy

What are the implications of an "indexed economy"? I have already stated views of inflation's effect on equities. I feel that an indexed economy—in the full sense of Milton Friedman's recent proposal—is too impractical and remote to warrant serious discussion here. We have it in part in cost-of-living adjustments in union contracts, including to some degree pension plans. There was once an indexed bond issue, put out by Remington-Rand Corporation at the instance of Irving Fisher (then a director), which varied the coupon payments with the cost-of-living index. Conceivably—though not probably—that idea may be revived. However, we have a growing number of debt obligations that vary the coupon rates with changes in current bond yields or bank lending rates. The floodgates seem to be opening here with the offering of $650 million of Citicorp Floating Rate Notes due in 1989.

We have all become so familiar with a more or less managed economy since the Roosevelt era beginning forty years ago, that we should be quite inured to its effect on everything including equities. Basically, the intervention of government in the economy has had two opposite effects on common-stock values. It has benefited them greatly through its virtual guarantee against the money panics and large-scale depressions of the pre-1935 decades. But it has hurt profits through the maze of restrictions and the numerous other burdens it has imposed on business operations. Up to now the net effect seems to have been favorable to equity values—or at least to their prices. This can be seen at first glance by comparing the Dow or S&P Index lines on a chart before and after 1949. In such comparisons the price declines in 1969 to 1970 and 1973 to 1974 appear like minor downturns in a massive upward sweep.

Experience suggests therefore that the various threats to equities implied in the last question are not very different from other obstacles that common stocks have faced and surmounted in the past. My prediction is that stocks will surmount them in the future.

But I cannot leave my subject without alluding to another menace to equity values not touched on in my terms of reference. This is the loss of public confidence in the financial community growing out of its own conduct in recent years. I insist that more damage has been done to stock values and to the future of equities from inside Wall Street than from outside Wall Street. Edward Gibbon and Oliver Goldsmith both wrote that, "History is little more than a register of the crimes, the follies, and the misfortunes of mankind." This phrase applies to Wall Street history in the 1968 to 1973 period, but with more emphasis to be given to its crimes and follies than to its misfortunes. I have not time even to list all the glaring categories of imprudent and inefficient business practice, of shabby and shoddy ethics perpetrated by financial houses and individuals, without the excuse of poverty or ignorance to palliate their misdemeanors. Just one incredible example: Did anyone ever hear of a whole industry almost going bankrupt because it was accepting more business than it could handle? That is what happened to our proud NYSE community in 1969, with their back-office mix ups, missing securities, etc. The abuses in the financial practices of many corporations during the same period paint the same melancholy picture.

It may take many years—and new legislation—for public confidence in Wall Street to be restored, and in the meantime stock prices may languish. But I should think the true investor would be pleased, rather than discouraged, at the prospect of investing his new savings on very satisfactory terms. To pension-fund managers, especially with large and annual increments to invest, the prospects are especially inviting. Could they have imagined five years ago that they would be able to buy AAA bonds on an 8% to 9% basis, and the shares of sound companies on a 15% or better earnings yield? The opportunities available today afford a more promising investment approach than the recent absurd idea of aiming at, say, 25% market appreciation by shifting equities among institutions at constantly higher price levels—a bootstrap operation if there ever was one.

Let me close with a quotation from Virgil, my favorite poet. It is inscribed beneath a large picture panel at the head of the grand staircase of the Department of Agriculture building in Washington. It reads:

"O fortunati nimium . . . (etc.) Agricolae!"

Virgil addressed this apostrophe to the Roman farmers of his day, but I shall direct it at the common-stock buyers of this and future years:

"O enviably fortunate Investors, if only you realized your current advantages!"

21

A Conversation with
Benjamin Graham

In the light of your sixty-odd years of experience in Wall Street what is your overall view of common stocks?

Common stocks have one important investment characteristic and one important speculative characteristic. Their investment value and average market price tend to increase irregularly but persistently over the decades, as their net worth builds up through the reinvestment of undistributed earnings—incidentally, with no clear-cut plus or minus response to inflation. However, most of the time common stocks are subject to irrational and excessive price fluctuations in both directions, as the consequence of the ingrained tendency of most people to speculate or gamble—i.e., to give way to hope, fear, and greed.

What is your view of Wall Street as a financial institution?

A highly unfavorable—even a cynical—one. The Stock Exchanges appear to me chiefly as a John Bunyan type of Vanity Fair, or a Falstaffian joke, that frequently degenerates into a madhouse—"a tale full of sound and fury, signifying nothing." The stock market resembles a huge laundry in which institutions

Reprinted from the *Financial Analysts Journal*, vol. 32, no. 5 (September/October 1976): 20–23 with permission. The *Journal* thanked Charles D. Ellis, a member of its Editorial Board, for making available this presentation, in question-and-answer format, to a recent Donaldson, Lufkin & Jenrette seminar.

take in large blocks of each other's washing—nowadays to the tune of 30 million shares a day—without true rhyme or reason. But technologically it is remarkably well-organized.

What is your view of the financial community as a whole?

Most of the stockbrokers, financial analysts, investment advisers, etc., are above average in intelligence, business honesty, and sincerity. But they lack adequate experience with all types of security markets and an overall understanding of common stocks—of what I call "the nature of the beast." They tend to take the market and themselves too seriously. They spend a large part of their time trying, valiantly and ineffectively, to do things they can't do well.

What sort of things, for example?

To forecast short- or long-term changes in the economy, and in the price level of common stocks, to select the most promising industry groups and individual issues—generally for the near-term future.

Can the average manager of institutional funds obtain better results than the Dow Jones Industrial Average or the Standard & Poor's Index over the years?

No. In effect, that would mean that the stock market experts as a whole could best themselves—a logical contradiction.

Do you think, therefore, that the average institutional client should be content with the DJIA results or the equivalent?

Yes. Not only that, but I think they should require approximately such results over, say, a moving five-year average period as a condition for paying standard management fees to advisers and the like.

What about the objection made against so-called index funds that different investors have different requirements?

At bottom that is only a convenient cliché or alibi to justify the mediocre record of the past. All investors want good results from their investments, and are entitled to them to the extent that they are actually obtainable. I see no reason why they should be content with results inferior to those of an indexed fund or pay standard fees for such inferior results.

Turning now to individual investors, do you think that they are at a disadvantage compared with the institutions, because of the latter's huge resources, superior facilities for obtaining information, etc.?

On the contrary, the typical individual investor has a great advantage over the large institutions.

Why?

Chiefly because these institutions have a relatively small field of common stocks to choose from—say 300 to 400 huge corporations—and they are constrained more or less to concentrate their research and decisions on this much overanalyzed group. By contrast, most individuals can choose at any time among some 3,000 issues listed in the Standard & Poor's Monthly Stock Guide. Following a wide variety of approaches and preferences, the individual investor should at all times be able to locate at least 1% of the total list—say, thirty issues or more—that offer attractive buying opportunities.

What general rules would you offer the individual investor for his investment policy over the years?

Let me suggest three such rules: (1) The individual investor should act consistently as an investor and not as a speculator. This means, in sum, that he should be able to justify every purchase he makes and each price he pays by impersonal, objective reasoning that satisfies him that he is getting more than his money's worth for his purchase—in other words that he has a margin of safety, in value terms, to protect his commitment. (2) The investor should have a definite selling policy for all his common-stock commitments, corresponding to his buying techniques. Typically, he should set a reasonable profit objective on each purchase—say 50% to 100%—and a maximum holding period for this objective to be realized—say, two to three years. Purchases not realizing the gain objective at the end of the holding period should be sold out at the market. (3) Finally, the investor should always have a minimum percentage of his total portfolio in common stocks and a minimum percentage in bond equivalents. I recommend at least 25% of the total at all times in each category. A good case can be made for a consistent 50-50 division here, with adjustments for changes in the market level. This means the investor would switch some of his stocks into bonds on significant rises of the market level, and vice-versa when the market declines. I would suggest, in general, an average seven- or eight-year maturity for his bond holdings.

In selecting the common-stock portfolio, do you advise careful study of and selectivity among individual issues?

In general, no. I am no longer an advocate of elaborate techniques of security analysis in order to find superior value opportunities. This was a rewarding activity, say, forty years ago, when our textbook "Graham and Dodd" was first published; but the situation has changed a good deal since then. In the old days any well-trained security analyst could do a good professional job of selecting undervalued issues through detailed studies; but in the light of the enormous amount of research now being carried on, I doubt whether in most cases such extensive efforts will generate sufficiently superior selections to justify their cost. To that very limited extent I'm on the side of the "efficient market" school of thought now generally accepted by the professors.

What general approach to portfolio formation do you advocate?

Essentially, a highly simplified one that applies a single criterion or perhaps two criteria to the price to assure that full value is present and that relies for its results on the performance of the portfolio as a whole—i.e., on the group results—rather than on the expectations for individual issues.

Can you indicate concretely how an individual investor should create and maintain his common-stock portfolio?

I can give two examples of my suggested approach to this problem. One appears severely limited in its application, but we found it almost unfailingly dependable and satisfactory in thirty-odd years of managing moderate-sized investment funds. The second represents a great deal of new thinking and research on our part in recent years. It is much wider in its application than the first one, but it combines the three virtues of sound logic, simplicity of application, and an extraordinarily good performance record, assuming—contrary to fact—that it had actually been followed as now formulated over the past fifty years—from 1925 to 1975.

Some details, please, on your two recommended approaches.

My first, more limited, technique confines itself to the purchase of common stocks at less than their working-capital value, or net-current-asset value, giving no weight to the plant and other fixed assets, and deducting all liabilities in full from the current assets. We used this approach extensively in managing investment funds, and over a thirty-odd year period we must have earned an average of some 20% per year from this source. For a while, however, after the mid-1950s, this brand of buying opportunity became very scarce because of the pervasive bull market. But it has returned in quantity since the 1973–74 decline. In January 1976 we counted over 300 such issues in the Standard & Poor's Stock Guide—about 10% of the total. I consider it a foolproof method of systematic investment—once again, not on the basis of individual results but in terms of the expectable group outcome.

Finally, what is your other approach?

This is similar to the first in its underlying philosophy. It consists of buying groups of stocks at less than their current or intrinsic value as indicated by one or more simple criteria. The criterion I prefer is 7 times the reported earnings for the past twelve months. You can use others—such as a current dividend return above 7% or book value more than 120% of price, etc. We are just finishing a performance study of these approaches over the past half-century—1925–75. They consistently show results of 15% or better per annum, or twice the record of the DJIA for this long period. I have every confidence in the threefold merit of this general method based on (a) sound logic, (b) simplicity of application, and (c) an excellent supporting record. At bottom it is a technique by which true investors can exploit the recurrent excessive optimism and excessive apprehension of the speculative public.

22

Benjamin Graham: Thoughts on Security Analysis

Benjamin Graham and Pat Ellebracht

TEACHER: Welcome to our tele-lecture series, and we certainly appreciate your spending time to talk with us.

GRAHAM: It is a new experience for me, and I hope it works out well for all of us.

TEACHER: What are the personal characteristics an individual must have if he is to be a successful long-term investor?

GRAHAM: Investment is most intelligent when it is most businesslike. I should add that it is most successful when it is most businesslike. The simple answer to the question is that one needs the characteristics of a good businessman, which would make for long-term success in business. Knowing what he is doing, having sufficient judgment to do sensible things rather than silly ones. Beyond that, I wouldn't say that any particular characteristics are required. A man who has a special flair or intuition presumably would do better than one without it, but even that is somewhat doubtful in Wall Street because one can carry one's confidence, and his flair and his intuition, too

© Museum of American Finance. Reprinted from *Financial History* magazine, no. 42 (March 1991): 8–10, 28–29 with permission. This article was based on a visit between Graham and a business school class at Northeast Missouri State University conducted by Professor Pat Ellebracht in March 1972.

far and lose out in the end. So I'll stick to my statement that one has to be an intelligent businessman.

STUDENT: What characteristics do individuals generally lack that keep them from being successful long-term investors?

GRAHAM: The primary cause of failure is that they pay too much attention to what the stock market is doing currently. They feel that what's going on now will continue indefinitely or long enough for them to benefit substantially. They want to make more money than they deserve to, and because of that, frequently lose out. They do not match their expectations to their knowledge and capabilities.

TEACHER: In your writings, you use many quotations from the classics. May we ask how have the classics influenced your view of human nature and your investment philosophy?

GRAHAM: It hasn't had any significant influence on my career. I just use the classics more out of vanity than anything else because it shows that I really know something about them. They have helped me to look at things, as Spinoza put it, from the standpoint of eternity, rather than day-to-day. I think that has been of considerable value.

STUDENT: What is your definition of an investment, and how does it differ from a speculation?

GRAHAM: That appears very early in our book on security analysis and is supposed to be very formal. It says "an investment is an operation in securities, which, upon careful analysis, promises safety of principal and an adequate return." All other operations are speculations.

TEACHER: Do you think that the investor's overall investment philosophy is influenced too much by what happened to him in one stock rather than by a more realistic approach to the market in general?

GRAHAM: I would say that there is a more universal approach to the market than the single influence. In the interview with *Forbes*, I said that people who bought IBM at an extremely low price might have been spoiled because of that successful one-time investment. They might have thought that it was quite easy to find another IBM. And so they might have wasted their investment lives looking for a second IBM. To that extent a man's viewpoint may be influenced by his own few experiences.

STUDENT: Would you please comment on the statement you made in *The Intelligent Investor*: "If you merely try to bring just a little extra knowledge or cleverness to bear on your investment program you might actually do worse than before."

GRAHAM: People seem to think that if you just know a little more than the average person about securities, you'll do better than the average person. Now the average person we'll assume, if he is not led astray, will get average results in the stock market. If you are trying to get better than average results, you're going to very likely rely on what you think is sufficient extra knowledge to do that; you don't have the sufficient extra knowledge to do better than average and very well may do worse. You are trying to be smart, but you are not going to be smart enough. This is what happens to a majority of people who are playing the market, the ones that spend a good deal of time on Wall Street, in brokerage houses, and so on, thinking that they can outsmart the other fellow or the averages themselves. One has to be very smart to be smarter than the experts who make up the stock market, that is to be smart enough to outperform the averages.

STUDENT: If you had to look at the 1970s and choose either high-grade common stocks or high-grade bonds, which would you select?

GRAHAM: This is an artificial question since my basic philosophy is not to choose one of them exclusively. If you ask me which one I would favor now, at current levels, I would certainly say the high-grade bonds since they yield twice as much as high-grade stock and more.

STUDENT: If your main interest with respect to investments was protecting yourself from inflation, how would you do it?

GRAHAM: Well, I would just make the best judgment I could as to the expected rates of inflation, and then I would make the very best decision I could to deal with this expectation. My best view over the next ten years about the rate of inflation is a rather modest 3%. I don't try to make up my mind as to the future in terms of recent experience. That is a common error that leads to bad judgment all over the place in finance. The Conference Board happened to have a 3% estimated price increase for 1972, and I have made a projection of the same amount for about the next seven years.

TEACHER: In the *Forbes* article you suggest that the stock market is likely to be subject to wide swings in the years ahead. Is the reason for this behavior the government's attempt to control the business cycle or the public's belief that fast profits can be made in the stock market, as in the late 1960s?

GRAHAM: Well, I don't believe the government's attempt to control the cycle would or should necessarily lead to wide swings. Long experience in the stock market indicates that the public always thinks it can make fast profits in one direction or another. It seems that human nature requires that stock price movements be carried too far. Too far means that there are going to be corresponding movements in the other direction. And what we'll have in the future, I assume, is pretty much of what we've had in the past, the kind of thing that you've seen in the last two years when the market declined from 995 on the Dow Jones to 630 and came back to 940, and it has been fluctuating since.

STUDENT: Do you think the bear market of 1969–70 is over?

GRAHAM: Well, technically I would say yes. You have a sufficient recovery from the 680 low on the Dow to over 900. The movement that we are in right now is not simply a minor or temporary recovery. If you want to bother with the bull and bear markets, you might as well consider that we have been having another bull market since May 1970.

STUDENT: Do you make a distinction between earning power and current earnings? How do you measure quality of earnings?

GRAHAM: Quality of earnings is not so much related to this distinction between earning power and current earnings. Historically, it is based on the two points of stability of earnings, the lack of any significant downtrend, plus the question of whether there is a pronounced and well-maintained upward movement over the years. The better the stability, the better the upward movement, the better the quality of earnings.

STUDENT: Please explain what margin of safety means with respect to common stock.

GRAHAM: That is discussed at some length in *The Intelligent Investor*. The margin of safety is the difference between the percentage rate of the earnings on the stock at the price you pay for it and the rate of interest on bonds, and that margin of safety is the difference which would absorb unsatisfactory developments. At the time the 1965 edition of *The Intelligent Investor* was written the typical stock was selling at 11 times earnings, giving about 9% return as against about 4% on bonds. In that case you had a margin of safety of over 100%. Now there is no difference between the earnings rate on stocks and the interest rate on bonds, and I say there is no margin of safety. So instead of having the effective margin of safety obtained in 1965, you have a negative margin of safety on stock, which I consider a very important negative factor in connection with buying stocks at these levels (1972).

STUDENT: In *The Intelligent Investor,* you refer to a different kind of water that has been put back in the stock market by investors and speculators themselves. Would you discuss this new kind of water?

GRAHAM: In the old days, what was known as water represented a secret mark-up of the value of the company's assets, chiefly its fixed assets, above their actual cost and above their replacement value so when a stock seemed to be worth $100 a share on the balance sheet, actually it was only worth $20 based on value behind it. Now those semi-fraudulent balance sheets have been corrected. Instead of them, the stock market itself fools with the prices the investor pays. We will put a price of $100 on a stock that has only $20 of fixed value or cost values behind it, and the difference between the stock market's valuation as against true book value corresponds to that other difference which was definitely recognized as the watered stock phenomenon. People are paying $100 for a $20 stock in the same way as in the old days a stock that was really worth only $20 was valued on the balance sheet at $100.

STUDENT: How is the new edition of *The Intelligent Investor* different from the previous edition?

GRAHAM: The basic advice and conclusions about investment procedure have not been changed to any substantial degree. The underpinning has been strengthened by my experience with inflation in the last four years, as a justification for the principles I have been pronouncing since 1949 in the first edition of *The Intelligent Investor*. These principles seem to have been set aside by an almost continuous rise in the stock market from 1939 to 1968. But the experience since 1968 seems to me to give confirmation to the reasoning expressed in the earlier editions. Naturally, I gave more attention to the question of inflation in the new edition than I did previously, because significant inflation took place since the last edition. But as you know, I do not accept it as an indication of what the future holds for us. I don't consider that 5% and 6% inflation is likely over the long term. I also pay attention to the change in interest rates, which is very significant. I think that because of the adverse change in interest rates from the standpoint of the stock buyer, the value of the Dow Jones Average is no greater now than it was five or six years ago. Any other reasons for increased value have been offset by the increase in the interest rate factor.

STUDENT: If we were successful in controlling the business cycle, would you change your investment philosophy from buying cheap and selling dear to buying and holding for an infinite period?

GRAHAM: Well, that again is a partly artificial question. I am sure we have better control over business cycles since World War II, which in itself would make for fluctuations in stock prices. But the public has offset that by its crazy idea that once business cycles are under reasonably good control, no price is too high for common stocks, so it's because of that confidence that you've had a more or less corresponding tendency toward fluctuations in the price levels of common stocks. I think there will be fluctuations in the future, but it is not an easy thing to find out just where you can expect to buy low and at what point should you sell. However, the program I propose with 25% of the portfolio in stocks and 25% in bonds, allowing the other 50% to fluctuate in accordance with the market, could be operated pretty well over the future, whether the business cycle is under better control or not. It will still be a feasible program if a man wants to give it the time and attention it needs.

STUDENT: In the *Forbes* article, you said you would buy public utility stocks because they are selling around book value. Are your gains here not going to be limited by a regulatory environment and high interest charges?

GRAHAM: Well, that is a good question, and I am glad you asked it. The gains would be limited by regulations, but there are two things on the plus side. One is that the losses should be very strictly limited, and secondly, that there is a much better promise of gain if you buy these stocks at book value than for a typical industrial stock that you would buy at book value. Utilities have very strong advantages which are not recognized in the current market. Their earnings are legally protected. Regulatory bodies must give them adequate earnings to support their investment and pick a value and particularly to encourage new investment. That has resulted in a rate structure which has resulted in stock prices about 50% above common-stock book value. You see, it would not be possible to raise substantial amounts of money through the sales of common stocks to the public unless the public had reason to believe that the value of the stocks they are buying would at least be worth the price they are paying. Under those circumstances the whole history and philosophy of regulation has virtually guaranteed a premium over book value for common stocks with the very minor danger of declining below it, and that is a very good combination. I think an investor should be well satisfied with a very good chance of having a 50% gain on his investment very quickly, with very little chance of loss.

STUDENT: Why would you select public utilities stocks over natural resource stocks, such as copper, oil, and land stocks that are selling for around book value?

GRAHAM: First, you don't find so many natural resource stocks selling about book value unless they have had some real difficulties with their earnings, the kind of thing that has not happened to the utilities. For utilities, an adverse situation is one where they earned a few cents less than the year before, instead of 2% or 3% more than they earned the year before. But for natural resource stocks, earnings are subject to all sorts of fluctuations and conditions. Suppose you take Anaconda, subject to confiscation of part of its assets, losing three-quarters of its price and about that much of its earnings in the last two years. Or look at Gulf States Land and Industrial Company. You find that they have virtually no earnings, and the price has fluctuated between 30 and 2 recently. That is completely different from a public utility investment. It hasn't got the quality of earnings which we were talking about.

STUDENT: How do you go about determining the intrinsic value of a natural resource stock?

GRAHAM: It is an exceedingly difficult thing to do. When we were putting values on companies, we had some scale of value for oil resources, like $1 a barrel for developed resources, 40 cents a barrel for probable reserves, and 10 to 20 cents a barrel for possible reserves. That can be done, but the results are not especially useful. If somebody asked me to put a value on a natural resource company, I don't think that I could do it well, and then I would not like to do it at all.

STUDENT: Do you think corporations should substitute stock dividends for cash dividends in order to more easily finance long-term growth?

GRAHAM: Yes, by all means. Dividend policy in my own opinion has been very unintelligent, especially by public utilities which pay out the typical two-thirds of their earnings in cash and then every now and then take back money for new stock, which is greater than the amount of the previous dividend that they paid out. They could have anticipated that by paying stock dividends in place of cash, and the stockholder would have been spared on income tax on those earnings. He would have built up his equity, by not having to pay taxes on the dividends he received in cash, since they were added to his equity. American Telephone and Telegraph could have saved billions of dollars for its stockholders if it had developed a stock dividend policy more or less equivalent in the final result to its cash dividend plus rights.

TEACHER: Mr. Graham, I had a question that came to mind while you were talking. We see this statement made in textbooks a lot of times, and it seems that the market disproved it in 1969–70. It is the blanket statement that stocks are an inflation hedge. How do you feel about that?

GRAHAM: Well, they are a better inflation hedge than bonds, but they certainly are not perfect. You can't assume that their earning power will increase to reflect inflation. You might say that historically, stocks have repaid their earnings on your investment capital in spite of inflation. Bonds, on the other hand, lost a considerable portion of their principal value because of inflation, so to the extent that stocks have stood still and bonds have declined over the last ten or twenty years, stocks have fared much better. The point is that the real earning power of a company is measured by the rate of earnings on its stock equity. If you double the equity, you would assume that the earnings would double. What has happened over many years is that the common stock has built up considerable stock equity, and while earnings have gone up, they have not gone up more than the equity. So that all that has happened is that they are earning a lot less, say 9.5% for Dow Jones companies where twenty years ago they were earning 12%. The change has been downward in the last twenty years in spite of inflation so to that extent you cannot say that inflation has benefited common stocks. What happened is that they pay out less than they earn and they have built up equity considerably, whether you would have expected the value to go up in relation to their earnings. The market price, on the other hand, has a rather different story. The market price has gone up a great deal simply because price earnings ratios have increased. In 1949, common stocks were selling for only 7 times earnings while now (1972) the ratio is 17 times earnings. A large part of the increase between 1949 and 1972 came about because investors are willing to pay more per dollar of earnings. Consequently the price has advanced, which is not a very meaningful development.

TEACHER: Could you tell us about some of the interesting experiences you've had and some of the companies that you remember best?

GRAHAM: Back in 1928 I went into a partnership with Bernard Baruch. We bought a company which seemed to be cheap. I think we paid $9 a share for it, and it was earning something like $1.50. I became financial vice president of the company, and they paid me $3,000 a year for that job. Well, the company had a lot of cash and a very good business selling firecrackers, but from that time on everything went wrong, including the big depression and the collapse in 1929. We were lucky to be able to get out and not lose too much money simply by holding on until 1936–37. New people came in and took the company over, its stock now $3¾ (Unexcelled Manufacturing). They began to do things that seemed impossible, such as selling bonds in Europe, and the stock went up to $63. Then the stock went down all the way to ⅜ and went up again to $68 . . . then back to $3¾, and now it is up to about $14 a share. I have always watched this company because I had a personal connection with it. I've had no investment in it for an awfully long time, but to my mind it is a pretty good paradigm for a typical corporate fluctuation over a thirty-year period.

My suggestion to you and your students is that you make studies of the vicissitudes of twenty companies, from the Standard & Poor's Stock Guide, picked in any way you want to, and see what happens to them over a thirty-year period. There is a very important lesson to be learned for anyone who wants to become a knowledgeable investor. I think it's very important to know not so much about the individual company's fluctuations but rather about general fluctuations in the past of all kinds of investments in order to have some basis for making judgments about the future. And if you say, as people have said, that the past is no longer relevant, the thing they forgot was that if the past is not relevant, what is? What do we know? If you cannot base your investment policy on the past, I think you have no basis for it at all.

STUDENT: Do you think disclosure is adequate?

GRAHAM: That is a very important question. From one point of view disclosure is excessive. If you take a new offering put out under S.E.C. rules, and the offering circular has 100 pages crammed with important and extremely unimportant disclosure, the effect of that makes me ill, because by the time anybody reads the first ten pages the issue would have been sold out. Nobody reads the prospectus in full, and the important information is buried and it takes an expert to ferret it out. Now an expert can do that, and that should be one of the jobs of a security analyst. Security analysts are so busy doing other things that they don't devote time to the hard work of disclosure such as quarterly and annual reports. I think the S.E.C. has done a good job in its requirements for quarterly, annual, and 10K reports, and the main difficulty seems to be that the analysts do not follow them up, or don't seem to pay much attention to them. The problem, all in all, is not related to disclosure. The problem is related to the question of whether the public can be protected against itself by emphasizing the absurdity of the price level for second- and third-grade stocks which have had enormous advances in price, with very little value behind them in many cases. I don't know if there is any solution. I don't know how gamblers, people who call themselves investors but who are really speculators, can be protected against the combination of greed and folly. That is my favorite three-word phrase, 'greed and folly.' The S.E.C. is just beginning some hearings to see whether the method of offering new securities could be changed somewhat. I suppose they would have to say in big red letter words, THIS STOCK IS NOT WORTH WHAT IT IS SELLING FOR. I don't know if that would make any difference either. They have the ability to sell the stock, and somebody says, "What the hell, it is going up anyway."

TEACHER: Well, Mr. Graham, we certainly appreciate your talking with us, since we think we have a very unique program.

GRAHAM: It impressed me, and that is why I took part in it. Good luck to you in the program.

23

The Decade 1965–1974: Its
Significance for Financial Analysts

The title of this seminar—"The Renaissance of Value"—implies that the concept of value had previously been in eclipse in Wall Street. This eclipse may be identified with the virtual disappearance of the once well-established distinction between investment and speculation. In the last decade everyone became an investor—including buyers of stock options and odd-lot short-sellers. In my own thinking the concept of value, along with that of margin of safety, has always lain at the heart of true investment, while price expectations have been at the center of speculation.

Let me list some of the questions relating to the value approach that confront the financial analyst now in the light of the 1965–74 experience:

1. Is the value approach a useful one in terms of
   (a) what it can accomplish on its own, and
   (b) by comparison of its results with those of other analytical methods and practices?
2. To what degree should the techniques of valuation—as presented, say, in Graham, Dodd, and Cottle,

Reprinted with permission from *The Renaissance of Value: The Proceedings of a Seminar on the Economy, Interest Rates, Portfolio Management, and Bonds vs. Common Stocks* (1974): 1–12, Charlottesville, VA: The Financial Analysts Research Foundation.

1962—be modified by more recent developments, including theoretical thinking?

3. What is the effect of institutional domination of the stock market on the valuation work of the security analyst and the decision-making procedures of the financial analyst?

4. To what extent does the sheer number of practicing analysts—some 14,000 F.A.F. members, including 3,800 CFAs and over 2,000 active CFA candidates—prevent the average or representative worker from achieving worthwhile results? This is indeed a delicate question.

The discussion that follows will not separate each of these questions from the others, but I will try to answer them as best I can.

The value approach has been founded on the premise that in many—but by no means in all—cases a dependable range of valuation can be established for a common stock by analytical techniques; that often this range differs substantially from the current price; and that such differences offer rewarding opportunities for investment operations. The phrase "rewarding opportunities" implies that the stock market itself will vindicate the value-based operation, after an interval that averages not too long for human patience—say, three years or less.

Typically, the midpoint of the value range has been found by applying an appropriate multiplier to estimated future earnings. My present view is that this is not the best technique. Instead, the earnings figure taken should be what we call "normal current earnings," and all the future prospects—favorable or unfavorable, specific or general—should enter into the multiplier. This procedural change obviates the necessity of establishing a future value and then discounting same to its present worth.

Such a procedure would carry us very far from the method first suggested in 1938 in Dr. John Burr Williams' seminal book *The Theory of Investment Value*. His technique required an estimate of the stream of dividends to be received over a very long future period, and the summation of the discounted worth of each dividend to arrive at present value. The various mathematical methods later developed for valuing growth stocks represent a sort of compromise between the Williams approach and what I now suggest. For they stop the estimated stream of dividends at a terminal year—say ten years hence—and then value the stock, usually on a conservative basis, in that terminal year. The resulting figures of dividends and terminal value would then be discounted at a uniform chosen rate to arrive at present value.

Those of you who have studied *Security Analysis* may recall that we tried to simplify the mathematical methods of several writers by suggesting a formula that employs a single variable G, representing the expected growth rate over the next seven to ten years. It read (at bottom of p. 537):

Value = current normal earnings times the sum of 8½ plus 2G.

This valuation formula—like those it purported to approximate—had the great defect of failing to allow for changes in the basic rate of interest. But the one development in the past decade that has had the greatest influence on stock values—and, somewhat belatedly, on stock prices—has been the phenomenal advance in interest rates. For the three years preceding the publication of our text, the yield on AAA bonds averaged 4.4%, and that was also the figure just ten years ago. But for the three years 1971–73 the average was 7½%, and most recently 9½%.

It would seem logical to me to make common-stock valuations vary inversely with representative current interest rates corresponding to the analyst's use of representative current earnings. Suppose we restated our 1972 formula with that objective, making it reflect the then going AAA rate of 4.4%. The expression would then read:

Value = Earnings times the sum of 37½ plus 8.8 G,
divided by the AAA rate.

Since analysts have a weakness for figures, you might like to hear two or three results based on this revised formula. For the DJIA, taking G as its historic 4½% and the AAA rate of its three-year average of 7½%, we get a multiplier of 10.2. Applying this to the 1971–73 average earnings of the Dow, its central value would be about 750. If instead of three-year average figures you took the recent bond rate of 9½% and the most recent inflation-aided annual earnings of about $93, the indicated central value would be the same 750. (The higher earnings are offset by the higher interest divisor.)

These calculations, for what they are worth, suggest that the Dow at its recent low level of 627 was undervalued by about 15%. Whether this would presage a near or delayed end of the current bear market I leave to wiser or bolder heads than mine. However, this same method when applied to individual issues would indicate that many have been more significantly underpriced in the present market. Take Firestone as an example. Its earnings have grown at a better rate in the past decade than those of the Dow; the figures for 1971–73 show a 116% increase from 1961–63 for Firestone versus 66% for the DJIA. If we assume the same future G of 4½% for Firestone as for the Dow, and hence the same multiplier of 10.2 times 1971–73 earnings, our valuation would be 24 for the tire company shares, fully 90% above their 1974 low. Incidentally, this would just about equal the current book value of Firestone—a previously minor detail in the investment picture but one to which I am inclined to ascribe major importance under today's new conditions. Firestone is, of course, only one example of the discrepancy between the current level of the Dow—which includes several first-tier institutional favorites—and that of the current run-of-the-mine good-sized company.

A multiplier based on expected growth and interest rates alone would imply that a company's financial structure and debt position do not enter into the valuation process. This might be the case if the formula were applied—as originally intended—only to high-growth companies, whose prospects are considered so good that they are assumed to face no financial problems. But if we seek to generalize our formula to apply to average-growth companies, we must recognize that many of these may be in unsatisfactory financial condition, caused in part by inflation pressures and in good part also by the overexpansion of corporate debt in the past decade. (I consider the total figures for corporate debt since 1968, published in the June 1974 issue of the *Survey of Current Business*, to be most disquieting. They show an overall increase of 74% in only five years, with more to come in 1974.)

I see no satisfactory way of reducing the multiplier to allow for a below-par debt position. My advice to analysts would be rather to avoid attempting a formal valuation of such companies. In other words, limit your appraisals to enterprises of investment quality, excluding from that category such as do not meet specific criteria of financial strength. This statement brings me back to our old position that speculative companies cannot be dealt with at all by the analyst with satisfactory overall results. By my own rather strict quantitative criteria, Firestone would pass the financial-strength test by a modest margin. Such tests might well exclude up to half of the NYSE list today from investment consideration, but there would remain enough qualifying issues to give the analysts and the investor an ample selection. It should be clear that I have faith in the valuation process as a guide to investment choices, but that I would limit this technique rather strictly to companies that meet criteria of financial soundness. Also, I should require that the buy-decisions based on this approach involve a margin-of-safety factor. This might well be a purchase price not over two-thirds of the central appraised value.

How would such a policy have worked out during the past decade? Several times the market price of Firestone fell below our formula value, but not by the one-third margin. (The indicated buying level in 1970 was 16 against its low of 17½, followed by the next year's high of 28½.) Other studies have led me to believe that a computer-type valuation job of this kind would have found a considerable number of cases where shares of sound companies could have been obtained for less than two-thirds of their formula value. On the whole one would have done quite well over this period by buying on this basis and selling at a 50% profit when obtainable. I see no reason to think that a similar policy could not be followed with satisfactory results in the future. (It should be unnecessary for me to add that these results are not guaranteed.)

There are, of course, many other approaches of the valuation type, and different analysts may favor different formulas with different parameters than the two I have been using. I have myself been intrigued by the idea of choosing stocks among those that are obtainable at not more than one-half their former high quotation, provided that they meet criteria of value independent of the price record. A technique of this sort would have worked fine, according to my studies, up to and including the post-1970 market recovery. Under more recent conditions it would merely have added a price-decline criterion to the determination of buy points based on the valuation approach. For practically all issues of the Firestone type an acquisition price at two-thirds of analysts' valuation would be at less than half of the previous market high.

Let me pass on to a factor in the valuation process that in my thinking has taken on considerable importance under present conditions. This is the book value figure, to be viewed either as a point of departure for more refined calculations or as a practically usable measure of a common stock's value. For years we have all pretty well disregarded asset values, except for financial enterprises and some special cases. But in recent markets a large number—perhaps a majority—of NYSE commons have actually fluctuated in price both above and below their asset values. Even Polaroid was recently obtainable at less than book value! This fact would seem to establish a realistic relationship in many cases between net worth and intrinsic or analysts' value. One might well speak today of "The Renaissance of Book Value."

You are all intelligent enough to appreciate that I am not now saying that Avon Products is only worth its book figure of $7.70 per share or that Chicago Milwaukee common is to be valued at the $149 per share shown on the balance sheet. In a substantial percentage of issues, the book value figures have no worthwhile connection with the investment value of the shares. But the analyst has today perhaps a thousand stocks or more to choose from in which the asset value may actually fall within his range of appraised value. In many of these cases he could then settle for the net worth as his preferred specific figure of value, and base his buy-and-sell points on this convenient measure.

This approach can put the choice of marketable common stocks on a basis corresponding to that of investment in a private, nonquoted enterprise. If the commitment would be attractive as an ordinary business venture it should be even more attractive as part of a publicly held enterprise, with the added advantages of diversification and ready marketability.

However, in my experience marketability has proved of dubious overall advantage. It has led investors astray at least as much as it has helped them. It has made them stock-market minded instead of value-minded. I have a puritanic vision of the true investor as someone who is entirely disinterested in what the stock market does except on two sorts of occasions that meet his convenience. The first occasion is when the market obligingly permits him to buy a group of common stocks at less than their indicated value; the second is when with equal courtesy it permits him to sell at not more than one-half their former high quotation those that are of no importance to him. True, he may sometimes dispose of an investment at a loss. But that should not be because the market price went down; it should be because things went badly for the company and the true value of the shares declined below the price he paid for them. (Of course the investor may also use the stock market to switch out of issues he owns into others that offer more value at ruling prices.)

(You are now hearing some of the "old-time religion." You may not be converted, but it shouldn't do you any harm.)

At this point let me consider briefly an approach with which we were closely identified when managing the Graham-Newman fund. This was the purchase of shares at less than their working-capital value. That gave such good results for us over a forty-year period of decision-making that we eventually renounced all other common-stock choices based on the usual valuation procedures, and concentrated on these "sub-asset stocks." The "renaissance of value," which we are talking about today, involves the reappearance of this kind of investment opportunity. A Value-Line publication last month listed 100 such issues in the nonfinancial category. Their compilation suggests that there must be at least twice as many sub-working-capital choices in the Standard & Poor's Monthly Stock Guide. (However, don't waste $25 in sending for an advertised list of "1000 Stocks Priced at Less Than Working Capital." Those responsible inexcusably omitted to deduct the debt and preferred stock liabilities from the working capital in arriving at the amount available for the common.)

It seems no more than ordinary sense to conclude that if one can make up, say, a thirty-stock portfolio of issues obtainable at less than working capital, and if these issues meet other value criteria including the analyst's belief that the enterprise has reasonably good long-term prospects, why not limit one's selection to such issues and forget the more standard valuation methods and choices we have previously discussed? I think the question is a logical one, but it raises various practical issues: How long will such "fire-sale stocks"—as Value Line called them—continue to be given away; what would be the consequences if a large number of decision-makers began as of tomorrow to concentrate on that group; what should the analyst do when these are no longer available?

Such questions are actually related to broader aspects of the value approach, involving the availability of attractive investment opportunities if and when most investors and their advisers followed this doctrine. I shall return to that problem later.

Some interesting questions relating to intrinsic value vs. market price are raised by the take-over bids that are now part of our daily financial fare. The most spectacular such event occurred a few weeks ago, when two large companies actively competed to buy a third, with the result that within a single month the price of ESB Inc. advanced from 17½ to over 41. We have always considered the value of the business to a private owner as a significant element in appraising a stock issue. We now have a parallel figure for security analysts to think about: the price that might be offered for a given company by a would-be acquirer. In that respect the ESB transaction and the Marcor one that followed it offer much encouragement to those who believe that the real value of most common stocks is well above their present market level.

There is another aspect of take-overs that I want to bring up here, on a somewhat personal basis, because it relates to an old and losing battle that I have long fought to make stockholders less sheeplike vis-a-vis their managements. You will recall that the first bid of INCO was termed a "hostile act" by the ESB management, who vowed to fight it tooth and nail. Several managements have recently asked stockholders to vote charter changes that would make such acquisitions more difficult to accomplish against their opposition—in other words, make it more difficult to deprive present officers of their jobs and more difficult for stockholders to obtain an attractive price for their shares. The stockholders, still sheeplike, generally approve such proposals. If this movement becomes widespread it could really harm investors' interests. I hope that financial analysts will form a sound judgment about what is involved here and do what they can to dissuade stockholders from cutting their own throats in such a foolish and reckless fashion. This might well be a subject for the FAF to discuss and take an official stand on.

There is at least a superficial similarity between the prices offered in take-overs and those formerly ruling in the market for the first-tier issues, as represented by "the favorite fifty." The large institutions have acted somewhat in the role of conglomerates extending their empires by extravagant acquisitions. The P/E ratio of Avon Products averaged 55 in 1972, and reached 65 at the high of 140. This multiplier could not have been justified by any conservative valuation formulae such as those we have been discussing. It was not made by speculators in a runaway bull market; it had the active or passive support of the institutions that have been large holders of Avon.

As I see it, institutions were persuaded to pay outlandish multipliers for shares of the Avon type by a combination of three influences: First, the huge amounts of money they have to administer, most of which they decided to place in equities. Second, the comparatively small number of issues to which their operations were confined, in part because they had to choose multi-million-share companies for their block transactions, and partly by their insistence on high-growth prospects. The third influence was the cult of performance, especially in pension-fund management. The arithmetic here is deceptively simple. If a company's earnings will increase 15% this year, and if the P/E ratio remains unchanged, then presto! the "investment" shows a 15% performance, plus the small dividend. If the P/E ratio advances—as it did for Avon in almost every year—the performance becomes that much better. These results are entirely independent of the price levels at which these issues are bought. Of course, in this fantasia the institutions were pulling themselves up by their own bootstraps—something not hard to do in Wall Street, but impossible to maintain forever.

These institutional policies raise two implications of importance for financial analysts. First, what should a conservative analyst have done in the heady area and era of high-growth, high-multiplier companies? I must say mournfully that he would have to do the near-impossible—namely, turn his back on them and let them alone. The institutions themselves had gradually transformed these investment-type *companies* into speculative *stocks*. I repeat that the ordinary analyst cannot expect long-term satisfactory results in the field of speculative issues, whether they are speculative by the company's circumstances or by the high price levels at which they habitually sell.

My second inference is a positive one for the investing public and for the analyst who may advise a noninstitutional clientele. We have heard many complaints that institutional dominance of the stock market has put the small investor at a disadvantage because he can't compete with the trust companies' huge resources, etc. The facts are quite the opposite. It may be that the institutions are better equipped than the individual to speculate in the market; I'm not competent to pass on that. But I am convinced that an individual *investor* with sound principles, and soundly advised, can do distinctly better over the long pull than a large institution. Where the trust company may have to confine its operations to 300 concerns or less, the individual has up to 3,000 issues for his investigations and choice. Most true bargains are not available in large blocks; by this very fact the institutions are well-nigh eliminated as competitors of the bargain hunter.

Assuming all this is true we must recur to the question we raised at the outset. How many financial analysts can earn a good living by locating undervalued issues and recommending them to individual investors? In all honesty I cannot say that there is room for 14,000 analysts, or a large proportion thereof, in this area of activity. But I can assert that the influx of analysts into the undervalued sphere in the past has never been so great as to cut down its profit possibilities through that kind of overcultivation and overcompetition. (The value-analyst was more likely to suffer from loneliness.) True, bargain issues have repeatedly become scarce in bull markets, but that was not because all the analysts became value-conscious, but because of the general upswing in prices. (Perhaps one could even have determined whether the market level was getting too high or too low by counting the number of issues selling below working-capital value. When such opportunities have virtually disappeared, past experience indicates that investors should have taken themselves out of the stock market and plunged up to their necks in U. S. Treasury bills.)

So far I have been talking about the virtues of the value approach as if I had never heard of such newer discoveries as "the random walk," "the efficient market," "efficient portfolios," the Beta coefficient, and others such. I have heard about them, and I want to talk first for a moment about Beta. This is a more or less useful measure of past price fluctuations of common stocks. What bothers me is that authorities now equate the Beta idea with the concept of "risk." Price variability yes; risk no. Real investment risk is measured not by the percent that a stock may decline in price in relation to the general market in a given period, but by the danger of a loss of quality and earning power through economic changes or deterioration in management. In the five editions of *The Intelligent Investor* I have used the example of A & P shares in 1936–39 to illustrate the basic difference between fluctuations in price and changes in value. By contrast, in the last decade the price decline of A & P shares from 43 to 8 paralleled pretty well a corresponding loss of trade position profitability, and intrinsic value. The idea of measuring investment risks by price fluctuations is repugnant to me, for the very reason that it confuses what the stock market says with what actually happens to the owners' stake in the business.

Let me pass now to the doctrine of the efficient market. I am particularly interested in this because of its negative implications for the work of security analysts generally. The subject is dealt with briefly in my current article in the *Financial Analysts Journal*, but it has such potential importance for this audience that I shall try another crack at it here.

Let me shorten slightly the definition of an efficient market that appears on p. 97 of *The Stock Market* by Lorie and Hamilton. "An efficient market is one in which a large number of buyers and sellers cause the prices to reflect fully what is knowable about the prospects for the companies dealt in." The key phrase for me is "reflect fully." Let us assume first that it means only that the market has and uses all knowable information about every company's prospects, and hence that there is no point for analysts to spend their time trying to obtain additional information. I dissent from that statement to the extent that it would render meaningless the current controversy and concern on the use of "material information," particularly as obtained by security analysts from managements. If in all cases the market already knows and reflects all that is knowable about each enterprise then there should be no such thing as "material inside information."

But that is not my chief quarrel with the concept of the "efficient market." There is a strong implication in the Lorie and Hamilton book that because the market reflects fully all the knowable facts it thereby establishes correct or reasonably correct prices for common stocks. Hence, only the superior security analyst can successfully select the stocks that should be bought or sold. These exceptional people—in the authors' words—"have a quicker and more profound understanding of the economic consequences to individual firms of changes in the economic environment or changes within the firm itself." They have "a rare and valuable talent." I disagree completely with this viewpoint. To establish the right price for a stock the market must have adequate information, but it by no means follows that if the market has this information it will thereupon establish the right price. The market's evaluation of the same data can vary over a wide range, dependent on bullish enthusiasm, concentrated speculative interest and similar influences, or bearish disillusionment. Knowledge is only one ingredient on arriving at a stock's proper price. The other ingredient, fully as important as information, is sound judgment. Take Avon Products, which sold at 140 early last year, or $8 billion for the company, and under 20—or a mere $1.2 billion—last month. Was the market for Avon "efficient" on both these dates, in the sense that the price reflected "fully and properly" (the latter my addition to the Lorie and Hamilton phrase) the knowable facts. Were the changes in the short period in the environment or the company's prospects sufficient to cut 85% from the true value of this highly profitable, well-managed, and strongly-financed enterprise?

Take at the other extreme the large group of stocks selling for less than their working capital. Is the market "efficient" in maintaining these "fire-sale" price levels? Surely it does not lack the essential information about companies. What it does lack is judgment, courage, and patience. In situations of this kind lie the best opportunities for financial analysts to prove their mettle.

The value approach has always been more dependable when applied to senior issues than to common stocks. Its particular purpose in bond analysis is to determine whether the enterprise has a fair value so comfortably in excess of its debt as to provide an adequate margin of safety. The standard calculation of interest coverage has much the same function. There is much work of truly professional calibre that analysts can do in the vast area of bonds and preferred stocks—and, to some degree also, in that of convertible issues. The field has become an increasingly important one, especially since all well-rounded portfolios should have their bond component.

Any security analyst worth his salt should be able to decide whether a given senior issue has enough statistically-based protection to warrant its consideration for investment. This job has been neglected at times in the past ten years—most glaringly in the case of the Penn-Central debt structure. It is an unforgivable blot on the record of our profession that the Penn-Central bonds were allowed to sell in 1968 at the same prices as good public-utility issues. An examination of that system's record in previous years—noting inter alia, its peculiar accounting and the fact that it paid virtually no income taxes—would have clearly called for moving out of the bonds, to say nothing of the stock even at prices well below its high of 86. We now have a situation in which all bonds sell at high yields, but many companies have an overextended debt position. Also, many of them do not seem to have sufficiently strong protective provision in their bond indentures to prevent them from offering new debt in exchange for their own common stock. (A striking example is the current bond for stock operation of Caesar's World.) These widespread present maneuvers seem to me to be so many daggers thrust in the soft bodies of the poor creditors. Bondholders can and should take steps, legal if necessary, to protect their interests against such forms of invasion.

Thus security analysts could well advise a host of worthwhile switching in the bond field. Even in the federal debt structure— where safety is not at issue—the multiplicity of indirect U. S. government obligations of all sorts, including some tax exempts, suggest many opportunities for investors to improve their yields. Similarly, we have seen many convertible issues selling at close to a parity price with the common; in the typical case the senior issue has offered a higher yield than the junior shares. Thus a switch from the common stock into the senior issue in these cases would be a plain matter of common sense. (Examples: Studebaker-Worthington and Engelhard Mineral preferred vs. common.)

Let me close with a few words of counsel from an eighty-year-old veteran of many a bull and many a bear market. Do those things as an analyst that you know you can do well, and only those things. If you can really beat the market by charts, by astrology, or by some rare and valuable gift of your own, then that's the row you should hoe. If you're really good at picking the stocks most likely to succeed in the next twelve months, base your work on the endeavor. If you can foretell the next important development in the economy, or in technology, or in consumers' preferences, and gauge its consequences for various equity values, then concentrate on that particular activity. But in each case you must prove to yourself by honest, no-bluffing self-examination, and by continuous testing of performance, that you have what it takes to produce worthwhile results.

If you believe—as I have always believed—that the value approach is inherently sound, workable, and profitable, then devote yourself to that principle. Stick to it, and don't be led astray by Wall Street's fashions, its illusions, and its constant chase after the fast dollar. Let me emphasize that it does not take a genius or even a superior talent to be successful as a value analyst. What it needs is, first, reasonable good intelligence; second, sound principles of operation; third, and most important, firmness of character.

But whatever path you follow as financial analysts, hold on to your moral and intellectual integrity. Wall Street in the past decade fell far short of its once praiseworthy ethical standards, to the great detriment of the public it serves and of the financial community itself. When I was in elementary school in this city, more than seventy years ago, we had to write various maxims in our copybooks. The first on the list was: "Honesty is the best policy." It is still the best policy, as our new President reminded us last month.

24

An Hour with Mr. Graham

Hartman L. Butler, Jr.

HB: Mr. Graham, I do appreciate so much being able to come and visit with you this afternoon. When Bob Milne learned that Mrs. Butler and I would be in La Jolla, he suggested that I not only visit with you but also bring along my cassette tape recorder. We have much I would like to cover. First, could we start with a topical question—Government Employees Insurance Company—with GEICO being very much in the headlines.

GRAHAM: Yes, what happened was the team came into our office and after some negotiating, we bought half the company for $720,000. It turned out later that we were worth—the whole company—over a billion dollars in the stock market. This was a very extraordinary thing. But we were forced by the S.E.C. to distribute the stock among our stockholders because, according to a technicality in the law, an investment fund was not allowed more than 10% of an insurance company. Jerry Newman and I became active in the conduct of GEICO, although we both retired a number of years ago. I am glad I am not connected with it now because of the terrific losses.

Reprinted with permission from Irving Kahn and Robert D. Milne, *Benjamin Graham: The Father of Financial Analysis* (1977): 33–41, Charlottesville, VA: The Financial Analysts Research Foundation.

HB: Do you think GEICO will survive?

GRAHAM: Yes, I think it will survive. There is no basic reason why it won't survive, but naturally I ask myself whether the company did expand much too fast without taking into account the possibilities of these big losses. It makes me shudder to think of the amounts of money they were able to lose in one year. Incredible! It is surprising how many of the large companies have managed to turn in losses of $50 million or $100 million in one year, in these last few years. Something unheard of in the old days. You have to be a genius to lose that much money.

HB: Looking back at your own life in the investment field, what are some of the key developments or key happenings, would you say? You went to Wall Street in 1914?

GRAHAM: Well, the first thing that happened was typical. As a special favor, I was paid $12 a week instead of $10 to begin. The next thing that happened was World War I broke out two months later and the stock exchange was closed. My salary was reduced to $10—that is one of the things more or less typical of any young man's beginnings. The next thing that was really important to me—outside of having made a rather continuous success for fifteen years—was the market crash of 1929.

HB: Did you see that coming at all—were you scared?

GRAHAM: No. All I knew was that prices were too high. I stayed away from the speculative favorites. I felt I had good investments. But I owed money, which was a mistake, and I had to sweat through the period 1929–32. I didn't repeat that error after that.

HB: Did anybody really see this coming—the Crash of 1929?

GRAHAM: Babson did, but he started selling five years earlier.

HB: Then in 1932, you began to come back?

GRAHAM: Well, we sweated through that period. By 1937, we had restored our financial position as it was in 1929. From then on, we went along pretty smoothly.

HB: The 1937–38 decline, were you better prepared for that?

GRAHAM: Well, that led us to make some changes in our procedures that one of our directors had suggested to us, which was sound, and we followed his advice. We gave up certain things we had been trying to do and concentrated more on others that had been more consistently successful. We went along fine. In 1948, we made our GEICO investment, and from then on, we seemed to be very brilliant people.

HB: What happened in the only other interim bear market—1940–41?

GRAHAM: Oh, that was only a typical setback period. We earned money in those years.

HB: You earned money after World War II broke out?

GRAHAM: Yes, we did. We had no real problems in running our business. That's why I kind of lost interest. We were no longer very challenged after 1950. About 1956, I decided to quit and to come out here to California to live.

I felt that I had established a way of doing business to a point where it no longer presented any basic problems to be solved. We were going along on what I thought was a satisfactory basis, and the things that presented themselves were typically repetitions of old problems which I found no special interest in solving.

About six years later, we decided to liquidate Graham-Newman Corporation—to end it primarily because the succession of management had not been satisfactorily established.

We felt we had nothing special to look forward to that interested us. We could have built up an enormous business had we wanted to, but we limited ourselves to a maximum of $15 million of capital—only a drop in the bucket these days. The question of whether we could earn the maximum percentage per year was what interested us. It was not the question of total sums, but annual rates of return that we were able to accomplish.

HB: When did you decide to write your classic text, *Security Analysis?*

GRAHAM: What happened was that in about 1925, I thought that I knew enough about Wall Street after eleven years to write a book about it. But fortunately, I had the inspiration instead to learn more on the subject before I wrote the book, so I decided I would start teaching if I could. I became a Lecturer at the Columbia School of Business for the extension courses. In 1928, we had a course in security analysis and finance— I think it was called Investments—and I had 150 students. That was the time Wall Street was really booming.

The result was it took until 1934 before I actually wrote the book with Dave Dodd. He was a student of mine in the first year. Dave was then Assistant Professor at Columbia and was anxious to learn more. Naturally, he was indispensable to me in writing the book. The First Edition appeared in 1934. Actually, it came out the same time as a play of mine which was produced on Broadway and lasted only one week.

HB: You had a play on Broadway?

GRAHAM: Yes. "Baby Pompadour" or "True to the Marines." It was produced twice under two titles. It was not successful. Fortunately, *Security Analysis* was much more successful.

HB: That was *the* book, wasn't it?

GRAHAM: They called it the "Bible of Graham and Dodd." Yes, well now I have lost most of the interest I had in the details of security analysis which I devoted myself to so strenuously for many years. I feel that they are relatively unimportant, which, in a sense, has put me opposed to developments in the whole profession. I think we can do it successfully with a few techniques and simple principles. The main point is to have the right general principles and the character to stick to them.

HB: My own experience is that you have to be a student of industries to realize the great differences in managements. I think that this is one thing an analyst can bring to the solution.

GRAHAM: Well, I would not deny that. But I have a considerable amount of doubt on the question of how successful analysts can be overall when applying these selectivity approaches. The thing that I have been emphasizing in my own work for the last few years has been the group approach. To try to buy groups of stocks that meet some simple criterion for being undervalued—regardless of the industry and with very little attention to the individual company. My recent article on three simple methods applied to common stocks was published in one of your Seminar Proceedings.

I am just finishing a fifty-year study—the application of these simple methods to groups of stocks, actually, to all the stocks in the Moody's Industrial Stock Group. I found the results were very good for fifty years. They certainly did twice as well as the Dow Jones. And so my enthusiasm has been transferred from the selective to the group approach. What I want is an earnings ratio twice as good as the bond interest ratio typically for most years. One can also apply a dividend criterion or an asset value criterion and get good results. My research indicates the best results come from simple earnings criterions.

HB: I have always thought it was too bad that we use the price/ earnings ratio rather than the earnings yield measurement. It would be so much easier to realize that a stock is selling at a 2.5% earnings yield rather than 40 times earnings.

GRAHAM: Yes. The earnings yield would be more scientific and a more logical approach.

HB: Then with roughly a 50% dividend payout, you can take half of the earnings yield to estimate a sustainable dividend yield.

GRAHAM: Yes. Basically, I want to double the interest rate in terms of earnings return. However, in most years the interest rate was less than 5% on AAA bonds. Consequently, I have set two limits. A maximum multiple of 10 even when interest rates are under 5%, and a maximum multiple of 7 times even when interest rates are above 7% as they are now. So typically my buying point would be double the current AAA interest rate with a maximum multiplier between 10 and 7. My research has been based on that.

I received in Chicago last year the Molodovsky Award.

HB: I understand that you have about completed this research.

GRAHAM: Imagine—there seems to be practically a foolproof way of getting good results out of common-stock investment with a minimum of work. It seems too good to be true. But all I can tell you after sixty years of experience, it seems to stand up under any of the tests that I would make up. I would try to get other people to criticize it.

HB: By some coincidence as you were becoming less active as a writer, a number of professors started to work on the random walk. What do you think about this?

GRAHAM: Well, I am sure they are all very hardworking and serious. It's hard for me to find a good connection between what they do and practical investment results. In fact, they say that the market is efficient in the sense that there is no particular point in getting more information than people already have. That might be true, but the idea of saying that the fact that the information is so widely spread that the resulting prices are logical prices—that is all wrong. I don't see how you can say that the prices made in Wall Street are the right prices in any intelligent definition of what right prices would be.

HB: It is too bad there have not been more contributions from practicing analysts to provide some balance to the brilliant work of the academic community.

GRAHAM: Well, when we talk about buying stocks, as I do, I am talking very practically in terms of dollars and cents, profits and losses, mainly profits. I would say that if a stock with $50 working capital sells at $32, that would be an interesting stock. If you buy thirty companies of that sort, you're bound to make money. You can't lose when you do that. There are two questions about this approach. One is, am I right in saying if you buy stocks at two-thirds of the working capital value, you have a dependable indication of group undervaluation? That's what our own business experience proved to us. The second question, are there other ways of doing this?

HB: Are there any other ways?

GRAHAM: Well, naturally, the thing that I have been talking about so much this afternoon is applying a simple criterion of the value of a security. But what everybody else is trying to do pretty much is pick out the "Xerox" companies, the "3Ms," because of their long-term futures or to decide that next year the semiconductor industry would be a good industry. These don't seem to be dependable ways to do it. There are certainly a lot of ways to keep busy.

HB: Would you have said that thirty years ago?

GRAHAM: Well, no, I would not have taken as negative an attitude thirty years ago. But my positive attitude would have been to say, rather, that you could have found sufficient examples of individual companies that were undervalued.

HB: The efficient market people have kind of muddied the waters, haven't they, in a way?

GRAHAM: Well, they would claim that if they are correct in their basic contentions about the efficient market, the thing for people to do is to try to study the behavior of stock prices and try to profit from these interpretations. To me, that is not a very encouraging conclusion because if I have noticed anything over these sixty years on Wall Street, it is that people do not succeed in forecasting what's going to happen to the stock market.

HB: That is certainly true.

GRAHAM: And all you have to do is to listen to *Wall Street Week* and you can see that none of them has any particular claim to authority or opinions as to what will happen in the stock market. They, and economists, all have opinions, and they are willing to express them if you ask them. But I don't think they insist that their opinions are correct, though.

HB: What thoughts do you have on index funds?

GRAHAM: I have very definite views on that. I have a feeling that the way in which institutional funds should be managed, at least a number of them, would be to start with the index concept—the equivalent of index results, say 100 or 150 stocks out of the Standard & Poor's 500. Then turn over to managers the privilege of making a variation, provided they would accept personal responsibility for the success of the variation that they introduced. I assume that basically the compensation ought to be measured by the results either in terms of equaling the index, say Standard & Poor's results, or to the extent by which you improve it. Now in the group discussions of this thing, the typical money managers don't accept the idea and the reason for nonacceptance is chiefly that they say—not that it isn't practical—but that it isn't sound because different investors have different requirements. They have never been able to convince me that that's true in any significant degree—that different investors have different requirements. All investments require satisfactory results, and I think satisfactory results are pretty much the same for everybody. So I think any experience of the last twenty years, let's say, would indicate that one could have done as well with Standard & Poor's than with a great deal of work, intelligence, and talk.

HB: Mr. Graham, what advice would you give to a young man or woman coming along now who wants to be a security analyst and a Chartered Financial Analyst?

GRAHAM: I would tell them to study the past record of the stock market, study their own capabilities, and find out whether they can identify an approach to investment they feel would be satisfactory in their own case. And if they have done that, pursue that without any reference to what other people do or think or say. Stick to their own methods. That's what we did with our own business. We never followed the crowd, and I think that's favorable for the young analyst. If he or she reads *The Intelligent Investor*—which I feel would be more useful than *Security Analysis* of the two books—and selects from what we say some approach which one thinks would be profitable, then I say that one should do this and stick to it. I had a nephew who started in Wall Street a number of years ago and came to me for some advice. I said to him, "Dick, I have some practical advice to give you, which is this. You can buy closed-end investment companies at 15% discounts on an average. Get your friends to put 'x' amount of dollars a month in these closed-end companies at discounts and you will start ahead of the game and you will make out all right." Well, he did do that—he had no great difficulty in starting his business on that basis. It did work out all right and then the big bull market came along and, of course, he moved over to other fields and did an enormous amount of speculative business later. But at least he started, I think, on a solid basis. And if you start on a sound basis, you are halfway along.

HB: Do you think that Wall Street or the typical analyst or portfolio managers have learned their lessons of the "Go-Go" funds, the growth cult, the one-decision stocks, the two-tier market, and all?

GRAHAM: No. They used to say about the Bourbons that they forgot nothing and they learned nothing, and [what] I'll say about the Wall Street people, typically, is that they learn nothing, and they forget everything. I have no confidence whatever in the future behavior of the Wall Street people. I think this business of greed—the excessive hopes and fears and so on—will be with us as long as there will be people. There is a famous passage in Bagehot, the English economist, in which he describes how panics come about. Typically, if people have money, it is available to be lost and they speculate with it and they lose it—that's how panics are done. I am very cynical about Wall Street.

HB: But there are independent thinkers on Wall Street and throughout the country who do well, aren't there?

GRAHAM: Yes. There are two requirements for success in Wall Street. One, you have to think correctly; and secondly, you have to think independently.

HB: Yes, correctly and independently. The sun is trying to come out now, literally, here in La Jolla. What do you see of the sunshine on Wall Street?

GRAHAM: Well, there has been plenty of sunshine since the middle of 1974 when the bottom of the market was reached. And my guess is that Wall Street hasn't changed at all. The present optimism is going to be overdone, and the next pessimism will be overdone, and you are back on the Ferris Wheel—whatever you want to call it—Seesaw, Merry-Go-Round. You will be back on that. Right now, stocks as a whole are not overvalued, in my opinion. But nobody seems concerned with what are the possibilities that 1970 and 1973–74 will be duplicated in the next five years. Apparently, nobody has given any thought to that question. But that such experiences will be duplicated in the next five years or so, you can bet your Dow Jones Average on that.

HB: This has been a most pleasant and stimulative visit. We will look forward to receiving in Charlottesville your memoirs manuscript. Thank you so much, Mr. Graham!

INDEX

ABOUT THE EDITORS

Jason Zweig writes the "Intelligent Investor" column for *The Wall Street Journal*. He has been a senior writer at *Money* magazine, an editor at *Forbes*, and guest columnist at *Time* and CNN.com. Zweig is the editor of the revised edition of Benjamin Graham's book *The Intelligent Investor* and the author of *Your Money and Your Brain* (2007). He lives in New York City.

Rodney N. Sullivan, CFA, head of publications for CFA Institute, serves as editor of the *Financial Analysts Journal* and several other leading publications. He was director of research for Trigon Healthcare, Inc. (now Anthem Healthcare, Inc.) and a senior portfolio analyst for Aris Corporation. He lives in Charlottesville, VA.

ABOUT BENJAMIN GRAHAM

Benjamin Graham was a seminal figure on Wall Street and is widely acknowledged to be the father of modern security analysis. The founder of the value school of investing and founder and former president of the Graham-Newman Corporation, an investment fund, Graham taught at Columbia University's Graduate School of Business from 1928 through 1957. He popularized the examination of price-to-earnings (P/E) ratios, debt-to-equity ratios, dividend records, book values, and earnings growth. He wrote the classic work *Security Analysis* and the popular investors' guide *The Intelligent Investor*.